YALE AGRARIAN STUDIES SERIES

James C. Scott, series editor

The Agrarian Studies Series at Yale University Press seeks to publish outstanding and original interdisciplinary work on agriculture and rural society—for any period, in any location. Works of daring that question existing paradigms and fill abstract categories with the lived experience of rural people are especially encouraged.
—James C. Scott, *Series Editor*

For a complete list of titles in the Yale Agrarian Studies Series, visit https://yalebooks.yale.edu/search-results/?series=yle10-yale-agrarian-studies-series.

SAVING A RAINFOREST AND LOSING THE WORLD

Conservation and Displacement in the Global Tropics

GREGORY M. THALER

Yale

UNIVERSITY PRESS

New Haven and London

Published with assistance from the foundation established in memory of Amasa Stone Mather of the Class of 1907, Yale College.

Copyright © 2024 by Gregory M. Thaler.
All rights reserved.
This book may not be reproduced, in whole or in part, including illustrations, in any form (beyond that copying permitted by Sections 107 and 108 of the U.S. Copyright Law and except by reviewers for the public press), without written permission from the publishers.

Yale University Press books may be purchased in quantity for educational, business, or promotional use. For information, please e-mail sales.press@yale.edu (U.S. office) or sales@yaleup.co.uk (U.K. office).

Set in Janson type by Newgen North America.
Printed in the United States of America.

Library of Congress Control Number: 2023941169
ISBN 978-0-300-27250-5 (hardcover)
ISBN 978-0-300-27248-2 (paper)

A catalogue record for this book is available from the British Library.

10 9 8 7 6 5 4 3 2 1

Contents

Preface and Acknowledgments

SOMETHING'S WRONG. SURELY YOU sense it?

Autumn feels like summer, and billionaires are launching space-ships.

I can buy Mexican avocadoes year-round, but I hardly ever see a monarch butterfly.

People everywhere are experiencing new extremes of wealth, poverty, disaster, and death.

What is to be done?

For over thirty years, a single answer has dominated global policy discourse: sustainable development. Where there is poverty, there must be development. Where there is environmental degradation, there must be sustainability. If we do more development more sustainably, our problems will be solved. That's what I was told. Did they tell you the same?

When I began studying tropical deforestation in the late 2000s, Brazil and Indonesia stood in stark contrast. The two countries together held over a third of the remaining tropical rainforests, and they were responsible for nearly two-thirds of tropical rainforest clearing annually. But deforestation in the Brazilian Amazon was plummeting while agricultural production in the region continued to grow. By apparently decoupling agriculture from deforestation, Brazil had achieved an environmental and developmental "win-win," and scientists and policymakers celebrated the country as a sustainable development success. In Indonesia, meanwhile, oil palm plantations gobbled up forests at an accelerating rate, and despite environmentalist efforts, Indonesian development remained alarmingly *un*sustainable. Why was deforestation declining in Brazil but rising in Indonesia? Thanks to an interest in languages, I speak Portuguese and Indonesian, and I decided to answer this tropical deforestation puzzle.

Some things don't make sense until you see them—until you go there and see the charred stumps studding miles of cattle pasture, or the corporate grain depots towering over the riverfront. They don't make sense until you talk to the environmentalists and bureaucrats, enthusiastic about "green" development, and then talk to small farmers whose neighbors are being forced off their land.

I don't know when exactly I first heard the words "land sparing." The term had been in use since at least 2005, describing the idea that increasing agricultural productivity could avoid agricultural expansion and spare land for nature. This land-sparing hypothesis circulated within broader sustainable development discourse, alongside concepts like "environmental Kuznets curves" and "forest transition theory." It was in the eastern Brazilian Amazon, however, sometime in 2014, that I began to recognize land sparing as much more than a scientific hypothesis. Time and again, in policy documents and interviews, I encountered the same logic: conservation and development must be compatible; forest conservation requires agricultural intensification.

What I first perceived on the Amazonian frontiers of Pará and Mato Grosso was land sparing *as policy*. While policies linking agricultural intensification and environmental conservation have a long lineage, what I saw in Brazil was the crystallization of land-sparing logic in policy and discourse at a very large scale, and at a time of heightened interest in tropical deforestation due to its role in global climate change. When I arrived in Indonesia in 2015, I found similar actors and policies promoting land sparing but meeting frustration, and I began to understand more deeply the position of land-use change within political economies of development. A growing scholarly literature discusses land sparing as a hypothesis, a model, or an empirical phenomenon—it is a very different matter to examine why and how land-sparing logic becomes institutionalized in policy and practice in some places but not others, and the concrete social and ecological effects of these political contests. What this book offers, first, is an empirical study of land sparing as policy, grounded in the experiences of tropical forest frontiers.

In scientific journals and on corporate websites, at international climate talks and in environmentalist brochures, land-sparing narratives promoted Brazil as a sustainable development success and a model for countries like Indonesia. But my experiences on the ground warned me otherwise. Brazil's land-sparing model, I knew, relied on some of the same corporations and supply chains that were driving global deforestation to new highs, even as Brazil's Amazonian deforestation declined. Wasn't everything somehow connected? How did declining deforestation in one place fit with rising deforestation in another in the transnational web linking global commodities markets with tropical forest frontiers?

In 2018, I traveled from the Brazilian Amazon to lowland Bolivia, and the answer snapped into focus. Brazil's "green development" was driving environmental and social degradation elsewhere. Brazilian land sparing did not eliminate deforestation—it displaced it, and Bolivia's lowland forests were being decimated by a wave of Brazilian extraction. This analytic of *displacement* is the second main contribution of this book. From a transnational perspective rooted in local experience, I demonstrate concrete processes of socioecological displacement, and I provide a theory to explain how displacement links productivist development with extractive destruction in the capitalist political economy. These theoretical insights are not new. Rather, I apply them in a new moment, through a new set of places and experiences, and with new evidence, to show yet again that "sustainable development" is a false solution.

I hope this book will be useful to others who are trying to work the same puzzle—trying to understand how a living world can be destroyed for profit, and why despite all the "solutions," nothing seems to get solved. To devise effective solutions, we must analyze our problems correctly. To anyone who cares about living better with the planet: I hope the tools in this book help you to better understand the problems we face, and to avoid the erroneous logics that reproduce them.

The sections of the book can be read separately, for example by those particularly interested in Indonesia (chapters 1–3), Brazil (chapters 4–7), and Bolivia (chapters 8–9), or in ecological political-economic theory (introduction), but the argument of the book is about the connections that bind these different places and theories together. Chapter 3 includes material excerpted and adapted from Gregory M. Thaler and Cut Augusta Mindry Anandi, "Shifting Cultivation, Contentious Land Change and Forest Governance: The Politics of Swidden in East Kalimantan," *The Journal of Peasant Studies* 44, no. 5 (2017): 1066–87, reprinted by permission of the publisher (Taylor & Francis Ltd., http://www.tandfonline.com). Chapter 5 (including fig. 5 and table 1) and the final section of chapter 4 are excerpted or adapted from Gregory M. Thaler, "The Land Sparing Complex: Environmental Governance, Agricultural Intensification, and State Building in the Brazilian Amazon," *Annals of the American Association of Geographers*, copyright © 2017 American Association of Geographers, reprinted by permission of Informa UK Limited, trading as Taylor & Francis Group, www.tandfonline.com, on behalf of the American Association of Geographers.

I am deeply grateful to all the people who gave their time and shared their experiences over the course of my research—in Brazil, Indonesia, Bolivia, and beyond. Their thoughtfulness, generosity, and patience sustained me. I received research funding from a U.S. National Science Foundation Graduate Research Fellowship under grant number DGE-1144153, the American Institute for Indonesian Studies under an AIFIS Research Grant, the United States–Indonesia Society under a USINDO Travel Grant, and the University of Georgia Latin American and Caribbean Studies Institute under two LACSI Ambassador Travel Awards. I am grateful to the University of Georgia Department of International Affairs for providing support for publication.

In fall 2006, I took the "Agrarian Societies" graduate seminar at Yale University as a college senior. James Scott and Michael Dove have been intellectual inspirations to me ever since. It feels fitting now to publish this book with the Agrarian Studies Series at Yale University Press, where Jean Thomson Black has been a wonderful editor. My research began at Cornell, where I am grateful to my committee: Ron Herring, Tom Pepinsky, and Wendy Wolford. Enormous thanks also go to the advisors and institutions that have hosted me: Lisa Curran and the Department of Anthropology at

Stanford University, Fabiano Toni and the Center for Sustainable Development at the University of Brasília, William Sunderlin and the Center for International Forestry Research, and Lennart Olsson and the Lund University Centre for Sustainability Studies. In Indonesia, Zach Anderson was an extraordinary fieldwork collaborator and friend. My gratitude goes also to Carol Colfer, Aaron Gavin, Jenny Goldstein, Torsten Krause, Don Leonard, Lee Mackey, Gustavo Oliveira, Kasia Paprocki, Miguel Rubiano, and Marianne Schmink. The Ecological History Group convened by Stevan Harrell and Peter Perdue in 2012 with support from the Social Science Research Council has been an incredible community of friends and scholars: Angelo Caglioti, Zachary Caple, Samuel Dolbee, David Fedman, Jenny Goldstein, Timothy Johnson, Laura Martin, Caterina Scaramelli, and the PCAS Writing Group members who gave invaluable feedback on this manuscript—Paolo Bocci, Nathan Ela, and Maria Taylor. I am grateful also to the book's reviewers, to the many colleagues who provided feedback at conferences and workshops, and to my colleagues and students at the University of Georgia and the Federal University of Pará. The remaining errors and shortcomings are my own.

Finally, tremendous thanks go to Mike and Darlene Stutts for letting me write in their home in Alabama, and to Jamie Olsen for letting me write in his yurt in Maine. My brother, Kai Thaler, has been a bulwark of friendship, intellectual and moral support, and keeping things in perspective. My parents, Karen Massey and Jeff Thaler, taught me from the beginning to value knowledge, nature, and justice. At home in Atlanta, Riley has been the consummate writing partner for this project. Stephanie Stutts has brought joy and companionship at every turn. I am so lucky and so grateful to be on this journey together.

SAVING A RAINFOREST AND
LOSING THE WORLD

Introduction

A Forest Mirage

B RAZIL NUT TREES ARE easy to identify, even for a first-time visitor to Brazil's Amazonian frontier. They grow tall and straight, with a crown of green leaves over a hundred feet in the air. They are also often the only trees in sight. Due to their valuable nuts and dwindling numbers, brazil nut trees (called *castanheiras* in Portuguese) are protected by law. When ranchers clear rainforest for new pastures, the castanheiras are left standing. They are spared the chainsaw, but their fate has been sealed: isolated castanheiras are often virtually barren. The trees, it turns out, are pollinated by large-bodied forest bees capable of lifting the petals of the castanheira flowers to access their pollen. With the destruction of their habitat, the bees disappear.[1] The castanheiras go unpollinated until they are struck by lightning, burned by fire, or poisoned with herbicide. One day their charred trunks are uprooted, along with the stumps of the long-dead forest, so the pastures can be transformed into unbroken fields of soy. The soy is exported to China or Europe for animal feed. There may be no more brazil nuts, but there are plenty of chicken nuggets.

Environmentalists have long argued that in order to save the rainforest, we need to protect it with strong regulations, like forest reserves or national park designations.[2] A more recent, though no less popular, argument holds that in order to save the rainforest, it must be made "too valuable to cut down" by creating markets for non-timber forest resources or services, such as nuts, genetic material, or carbon sequestration.[3] But returning to brazil nuts, we see that castanheiras are valuable and protected by law, yet still they fall. Protecting the castanheiras did nothing to change a political-economic system based on relentless agricultural expansion, which devours the ecosystems they need to survive. If we save the castanheiras without changing broader relations of power and profit, we in fact save nothing at all. The same is true for tropical rainforest conservation. We can declare protected areas and create markets for forest products or ecosystem services, but if we fail to change the political-economic system driving agricultural expansion, the forests we save will be like the castanheiras in the pasture.

In recent years, as global rates of tropical primary forest loss accelerated, from an average of 29,000 square kilometers per year in 2002–2009 to an average of 37,000 square kilometers per year in 2010–2019, environmental nongovernmental organizations (NGOs) and sustainability-minded researchers, policymakers, and executives have increasingly agreed that protecting conservation areas or Indigenous territories and valuing standing forests will not be enough to end rainforest destruction.[4] In the face of global demand for tropical commodities, agribusiness lobbies paint protected areas as impediments to "development," while market-based policies like carbon pricing fail to outweigh economic incentives for deforestation over large landscapes. The solution, these sustainability-minded actors assert, is to transform the political economy of tropical agriculture. Rather than increasing agricultural production by adding new land at the forest frontier, we can increase the productivity of existing agricultural land through *intensification*. By making better use of "degraded" or "marginal" lands and adopting industrial agricultural practices—such as improving crop and livestock genetics, applying chemical fertilizers and pesticides, investing in irrigation and animal nutrition, and mechanizing farm operations—agricultural production can continue to grow without deforestation. This argument is known as the *land-sparing* hypothesis, since it posits that agricultural intensification can "spare" land that otherwise would have been converted to agriculture.

Land-sparing arguments have circulated since at least the 1980s, promoted by advocates of Green Revolution agricultural modernization, such as Nobel laureate Norman Borlaug, and adopted by conservationists in the 1980s and 1990s, who sought to use agricultural intensification to alleviate deforestation pressures in the integrated conservation and development projects that were so common at the time.[5] The land-sparing hypothesis gained further prominence in the mid-2000s, when a group of conservation biologists at Cambridge University attempted to assess the environmental tradeoffs between land-sparing (high-intensity, low-biodiversity) agriculture and land-sharing (low-intensity, high-biodiversity) agriculture. The scientists came down in favor of land sparing, setting off a "land sparing versus land sharing" debate that has extended for over a decade.[6]

Land sparing is a deeply seductive proposal. It promises to transform agricultural growth, the primary driver of tropical deforestation, in a way that reconciles conservation and development. According to the land-sparing argument, there is no necessary tradeoff between industrial agriculture and forest protection. This argument appeals to powerful conservationist and developmentalist actors—NGOs and governments, corporations and funding agencies—who have come together around land sparing as a paradigm for sustainable development policy in the tropics. In Indonesia, land-sparing logic underlies "land swaps," where NGOs have partnered with the palm oil industry in an attempt to shift plantation development from forested areas to "degraded lands."[7] Half a world away in the Amazon, land-sparing logic led the Brazilian government to provide billions of dollars in "low-carbon agriculture" credit for activities like cattle pasture restoration, and spurred environmental NGOs to partner with ranchers to combat deforestation by promoting intensive ranching practices.[8] From 2004 to 2012, deforestation in the Brazilian Amazon declined over 80 percent, while agricultural production in the region increased, and advocates declared land sparing a success. This book shows that this success was a mirage: the land-sparing hypothesis is false. Land sparing saves forests locally by displacing deforestation elsewhere, trading local conservation for global destruction. How could such an influential policy model, backed by so many scientists and conservationists, be built on such an illusion?

A Deforestation Success Story?

I first began to understand land sparing through my research on tropical deforestation in the early 2010s. I was trying to explain a puzzling divergence in deforestation rates between Brazil and Indonesia. These two countries together hold roughly a third of the world's remaining tropical rainforests, and agricultural expansion is a principal deforestation driver in both countries—whether for cattle ranching and row-crop farming in the Brazilian Amazon or for oil palm plantations in Indonesia. Despite these similar problems, and similar networks of policy actors fighting deforestation in both countries, Amazonian deforestation in Brazil declined dramatically after 2004 while deforestation in Indonesia accelerated. In 2012, more primary forest was cleared in Indonesia than in the Brazilian Amazon.[9]

Why did deforestation decline in Brazil but accelerate in Indonesia? Many factors influence tropical forest clearing in a given year—from droughts to foreign exchange rates—but longer-term trends are rooted in deeper political-economic drivers. In 2013–2014, I spent a year in Brazil conducting research on the Amazonian frontier. Between sweaty offices and dusty pastures, I learned the land-sparing logic behind policies transforming Brazilian agriculture and forest governance. But why did this policy model apparently succeed in Brazil but not in Indonesia? In 2014–2015, I spent eight months conducting research in Indonesia. Between the highrises of Jakarta and the plantations of eastern Borneo, I began to perceive the deeper roots of this tropical forest divergence.

The transition from a land-use system of low-input agriculture and rapid deforestation to a system of intensive agriculture and forest conservation is not merely a technical question of increasing pasture rotations or planting more productive oil palms. Land use is a foundation of social and economic relations, and particular forms of land use are governed by particular sets of political-economic institutions. I refer to the political-economic institutions governing a specific territory as a "political-economic regime." Declining deforestation in the Brazilian Amazon was not simply the result of environmentalist sentiment and good agronomy; rather, a complex of government bureaucrats, corporate executives, farmers, ranchers, and environmental researchers and activists came together in the early 2000s to transform the political-economic regime of the Brazilian Amazon through land sparing. Where for centuries the Amazon had been an underdeveloped hinterland of colonial and neocolonial resource extraction, these actors sought to convert the region into a prosperous heartland of productivist industrial agriculture.

In Indonesia, the implications of land-sparing policy are similarly profound—a vision for transforming Indonesian Borneo (Kalimantan) and the other "Outer Islands" of the archipelago from extractive boom-and-bust peripheries into hubs of commodity-driven industrial development. I found that the complex of actors promoting land sparing in Indonesia during the 2000s was much weaker than in Brazil, however, and their efforts were stymied by the continued investment of government and corporate actors in extractive political-economic regimes.

For a researcher trained in "controlled comparison" methodologies, as I was in my political science graduate program, the puzzle appeared to be solved. Similar cases experienced divergent outcomes. I identified the variable responsible for the divergence—a categorical difference in political-economic regime (extractive in Indonesia, productivist in Brazil). In principle, therefore, a productivist political-economic regime would reduce deforestation in Indonesia, just as it did in Brazil. It would be easy to conclude that agribusiness and environmentalists worldwide should unite behind land sparing to drive productivist land-use transitions and save tropical forests.

This simple but mistaken conclusion, and the mirage of land-sparing success, is based on a fundamental methodological error. Variable-based controlled comparison, as Erica Simmons and Nicholas Rush Smith explain, relies on several key assumptions, including "that the same empirical phenomena work in the same way in different times and places; and . . . that these phenomena are independent of one another."[10] Although I tried for a time to frame my study of Brazil and Indonesia as a controlled comparison, ultimately I embraced the realization that distant frontiers are in fact intimately connected. Following common actors and processes across frontier municipalities in the Brazilian Amazon and Indonesian Borneo, I came to see forests in Brazil and Indonesia not as independent "cases" but as nodes in a global network, a perspective known as "relational comparison."[11]

Since deforestation in Brazil and Indonesia is part of a global economy and global ecology, land sparing can only succeed or fail at the global level. For land sparing to succeed, forest protection in one region must not drive forest clearing in another. My research in Indonesia showed how an extractive regime resisted land-sparing policies, while my research in Brazil showed how land-sparing policies reduced Amazonian deforestation through a regional productivist transformation. There was little to suggest that land sparing in Brazil accelerated deforestation in Indonesia, and yet there was something not quite right about the story of Brazilian success.

On Brazil's Amazon frontier, I had talked to family farmers struggling under heavy-handed environmental enforcement, without relief from agricultural lenders or technical assistance. They told of neighbors forced off the land in a new "rural exodus," their properties snapped up by wealthy ranchers. I had seen the interminable flow of tractor-trailers along the BR-163 highway, blanketing the landscape in dust and diesel exhaust as they hauled cattle and soybeans destined for southern Brazil, Europe, or China. And I knew of the rapid agricultural expansion and deforestation taking place in Brazil's Cerrado biome, the Paraguayan Chaco, and the western Amazon Basin in Bolivia, Peru, and Ecuador. Brazil and Indonesia are not the only nodes in the tropical forest network. Was Brazil's Amazonian "deforestation success story"—what one group of researchers called "one of the great conservation successes of the twenty-first century"—entirely unrelated to the rapid acceleration in environmental destruction nearby?[12] Was the closing of one frontier not somehow connected to the opening of another? And if tropical deforestation was not being reduced but simply displaced, what did that mean for all of the people and resources bound together by logics of land sparing and sustainable development?

On the Bolivian Frontier

In 2018, I returned to my research sites in the Brazilian Amazon, traveling by bus from the lower Amazon River in Pará, through the Xingu and Tapajós watersheds, to the Paraguay River in western Mato Grosso. From there, chasing a hunch, I opened a new frontier in my research, crossing into the Bolivian department of Santa Cruz and traveling by night bus to the municipality of San Ignacio de Velasco. With an area of around 49,000 square kilometers—slightly larger than Denmark—San Ignacio shades from Chiquitano dry forest in the south to humid Amazonian forest in the north. Its eastern border with Brazil is marked in part by the Río Verde, which flows north into the Río Iténez, also known as the Guaporé, on a journey of over two thousand miles to the Amazon River and Atlantic Ocean.

Up in San Ignacio de Velasco, across the Bolivian border and in the western reaches of the Amazon biome, deforestation was rising. From 2005 to 2012, as deforestation in the Brazilian Amazon declined to record lows, forest loss in San Ignacio accelerated. By one estimate, average annual deforestation in the municipality nearly tripled, from 54 square kilometers per year in 2000–2005 to 143 per year in 2005–2010, and total primary forest loss in 2005–2012 was over 1,070 square kilometers.[13] Few researchers had written about this new borderland frontier, but Brazilian farmers and investors were central to agribusiness in Santa Cruz Department since at least the 1990s, and reports indicated that Brazilian ranchers were involved in the new agricultural frontier in San Ignacio.[14] As Brazil trumpeted its Amazonian deforestation reductions, what roles were Brazil and Brazilians playing in accelerating deforestation across the Bolivian border?

Over my first visit to San Ignacio and the departmental capital of Santa Cruz de la Sierra in 2018, and another month of fieldwork in 2019, I found a region being rapidly transformed by Brazilian migration and investment. In San Ignacio in 2018, the Calzados Minas Gerais shoe store (named for the Brazilian state of Minas Gerais) was just down the street from the fashion accessory shop Estética Brasil. Outside a store selling grass seeds for cattle pasture, two women sat speaking Portuguese, while at the Brazilian-owned

Pizzaria Napolitana, the most popular restaurant in town, *moqueca baiana*—a Brazilian fish stew—was on the menu and Brazilian *sertanejo* music played over the speakers. One afternoon at the Ametauna ice cream parlor across from the cathedral, I overheard a Brazilian man from Mato Grosso do Sul discussing horses and cattle with his companions in heavily accented Spanish. When I returned a year later, the ice cream shop had added açaí bowls, a Brazilian favorite, to their menu. In just those twelve months, at least two new Brazilian restaurants had opened in the center of San Ignacio, serving Brazilian staples of hamburgers, soups, and skewered meats. Eight hours' drive to the west, in the departmental capital of Santa Cruz de la Sierra, Brazilians came for agro-industry or medical school, and Brazilian funk music dominated the dance clubs of the colonial center, more popular even than Latin America's ubiquitous reggaeton.

Some mixing of people and cultures could be expected in any border region, but a visitor to San Ignacio in the 1990s would have found few Brazilians other than timber traffickers and drug smugglers. The Brazilian presence in the late 2010s, what one Bolivian NGO director called a "cultural invasion," reflects the wave of Brazilian and transnational actors and capital that flooded into Bolivia's lowland forests at the same time as forest governance in the Brazilian Amazon tightened.[15] In 2005, just as Brazil's new Action Plan for the Prevention and Control of Deforestation in the Legal Amazon (PPCDAm) clamped down on the Amazonian soy and ranching bonanza, Bolivia legalized genetically modified soybeans, spurring the expansion of mechanized, high-input soy production. Transnational soy traders like Cargill and Bunge, who in 2006 agreed to a moratorium on soy purchases from newly deforested areas of the Brazilian Amazon, invested heavily in Santa Cruz, becoming some of the largest soy traders in the rapidly deforesting Bolivian lowlands.[16] Soy farmers in Brazil, meanwhile, who could no longer expand into forested areas, concentrated on converting cattle pasture for new croplands, driving up land values and pushing Brazilian ranchers across the border to Bolivia, where cheap land and lax environmental regulations beckoned.[17]

Brazilian farmers and ranchers and their transnational corporate partners are not the only ones profiting from Bolivian deforestation.

Petrobras, the Brazilian parastatal oil company, has invested billions of dollars in Bolivia's lowland oil and gas sector since the 1990s. Infamously, the company acquired rights to an oil and gas concession in Bolivia's Isiboro Sécure National Park and Indigenous Territory (TIPNIS) in 2007, and from 2009 to 2012, Bolivia convulsed in protests over construction of a highway through TIPNIS contracted to the Brazilian construction company OAS, with the backing of a US$332 million loan from the Brazilian Development Bank (BNDES). Critics of this environmentally and culturally destructive project tied it to Brazil's interest in a Pacific outlet for agribusiness exports, but infrastructural expansion in Bolivia also serves Brazilian interests on Bolivia's agricultural frontiers.[18] As this example suggests, Brazilian farmers and ranchers in Bolivia are bolstered by a network of Brazilian companies and Brazilian government agencies that link with other Bolivian and transnational actors to support and accelerate extractive frontiers. Even as Brazil constrained Amazonian deforestation, Brazilian capital pursued new profits in Bolivia, driving increasing deforestation in the tropical forests of the Bolivian lowlands.

Brazilians are not uniquely responsible for the loss of Bolivian forests. Brazil is only one among many countries displacing deforestation. Argentinian capital plays a growing role in the Bolivian soy sector, for example, while Chinese and European commodity imports drive deforestation across the tropics.[19] The national conception of capital—as "Brazilian" versus "U.S." or "Chinese" investment, for example—is a reification that can obscure the fundamentally transnational flows of money and resources. Tracing connections between Brazil and the Bolivian lowlands is essential, however, to dispelling the illusion of Brazil's land-sparing model. Accounts of Brazil's land-sparing success celebrate productivist development at the regional or national levels while ignoring the *displacement* of extractive degradation to new frontiers. Restrictions on forest clearing in the Brazilian Amazon did not suddenly render agro-industry "green." Rather, the "greening" and intensification of Amazonian agro-industry, just like the historical "greening" and intensification of industrial landscapes in New England or northern Europe, depends always on the supply of cheap inputs and windfall profits from ever-expanding extractive frontiers.

By adopting a transnational, relational perspective—one that views Indonesia, Brazil, and Bolivia not as discrete, independent "cases" but rather as connected nodes in a global system—this book demonstrates both the stakes of land sparing, and its fundamental limitations. Land sparing is at the core of global sustainable development policy, but its claims are based on a partial view of the system. Land sparing "solves" the problem of agricultural growth and forest protection in the Amazon, and it purports to do the same for Indonesia and elsewhere, but it ignores the global networks through which agro-industrial production is sustained: the inputs of fossil fuels, fertilizers, capital, and land; the insatiable push for consumption of meat and processed foods; and the unyielding drive for profit.

The problem runs deeper than agriculture and forest policy, calling into question the basic geographies and ecologies of modern capitalism. In the remainder of this introduction, I discuss the ecological political-economic theory behind my distinction between extractive and productivist regimes. I describe intersections of land-sparing policy with extraction and productivism in Indonesia and Brazil, and I return to Bolivia and the problem of displacement to show how scientific blind spots sustain illusions of land sparing and "green" capitalism. Drawing on fieldwork carried out over the course of six years in Indonesia, Brazil, and Bolivia, this book's central contribution is to reveal a more complete circuit of the political economy of capitalist development—the persistence of extraction, the promise of productivist modernization, and the tragic flaw of displacement—seen through the livelihoods and landscapes of tropical frontiers.

Development Ecology

Land-sparing prescriptions for efficient land-use allocation and agricultural intensification are prescriptions for regional capitalist modernization—which is often called simply "development." Since the eighteenth century, when Enlightenment ideas of progress combined with the rise of industrial capitalism, the ideology of capitalist development has asserted what Adam Smith called "the natural

Progress of Opulence," where "the greater part of the capital of every growing society is, first, directed to agriculture, afterwards to manufactures, and last of all to foreign commerce."[20] Two centuries later, this development teleology, from agriculture to manufacturing to trade and services, was repackaged by Cold War social science as "modernization theory." Much like Adam Smith, W. W. Rostow's "stages of economic growth" held that societies develop by moving from an agrarian economy, through a "take-off" stage of industrial manufacturing, to arrive finally at the "age of high mass-consumption."[21] The post–World War II international development regime has this modernization narrative at its core: the goal of all societies, and the promise of the capitalist system, is an evolutionary ascent to general prosperity through the progressive articulation of agriculture, industry, and services and trade.

But what determines which places develop when? This fundamental question lies behind most of development economics and policy, and while scholars and policymakers debate what role the state should play in economic development, there is little question that an enabling framework of governance and institutions is necessary for the growth of industry and mass consumption. Economists tend to emphasize the importance of institutions supporting markets and private enterprise, especially an efficient system of property rights, while sociologists and political scientists tend to focus on the bureaucratic organization of the "developmental state" regime.[22] In both cases, the antithesis to a developmental political economy that delivers economic growth is a regime of "extractive" economic institutions and a "predatory" state apparatus.[23] Left implicit by most of these formulations is that capitalist development is a *material* process. Because production and consumption depend on material flows of energy and resources, capitalist development is an *ecological* question as well as a political-economic one.

Through the lens of ecological political economy, we can see that "developed" core areas concentrate wealth by importing and dissipating energy and materials from peripheries through articulated circuits of industrial production and mass consumption. "Underdeveloped" peripheral areas are impoverished by the extraction of energy and materials for core areas through appropriation of the work and energy of peripheral social and ecological systems.

The role of unequal exchange in generating inequalities between core and periphery was a central insight of world systems analyses and dependency theories that emerged in the 1960s and 1970s, with roots stretching back to the classical political economists of the nineteenth century.[24] The ecological dimension of unequal exchange has subsequently formed the cornerstone of ecological world systems analysis, or what Jason W. Moore terms "world-ecology."[25] While these analyses have produced a sometimes bewildering profusion of terminology—core and periphery, production and extraction, articulation and disarticulation (referring to whether goods are produced for domestic consumption or export)—they share an understanding of capitalist development as a *dialectical*, relational process.[26] The developed, productivist, articulated core and the underdeveloped, extractive, disarticulated periphery are co-produced. Capitalist development is not something that happens at a national or regional level, as modernization perspectives would suggest. Rather, as Fernando Henrique Cardoso and Enzo Faletto affirm, capitalist development is the relation between core and periphery that "produces as it evolves, in a cyclical way, wealth and poverty, accumulation and shortage of capital, employment for some and unemployment for others"—and also ecological recovery and ecological destruction, as two sides of the same coin.[27]

My analyses draw especially on the work of Stephen Bunker, whose 1985 book *Underdeveloping the Amazon: Extraction, Unequal Exchange, and the Failure of the Modern State* provided a landmark account of ecologically unequal exchange based on a dialectic of *extraction* and *production*. Bunker observes that peripheral economies are based primarily on the extraction of energy and materials, while core economies are based primarily on "productive" processes that transform and consume those resources. These processes of extraction and production are interdependent, such that "the complex social organizational, demographic, and infrastructural forms that emerge as technological change and accumulation accelerate the flow of energy through the articulated productive systems [of the core] ultimately depend on processes that progressively decelerate the economy, disrupt the ecosystem, and simplify social organization in extractive regions."[28] Following Bunker, I focus on the relation between extraction and production as a shorthand for capitalist dialectics. Extraction refers to the appropriation and export of energy and materials, associated with ecological degradation, disarticulated economic activity, and "underdevelopment." Production refers to the importation, transformation, and consumption of energy and materials, associated with fixed capital accumulation, articulated economic activity, mass consumption, and "development." Because increased production requires increased extraction, capitalist development depends on expanded destruction—accumulating wealth means deepening plunder.

Crucially, there is a specific geography to extraction and production, and that geography is not just economic or ecological but also political. Processes of extraction or production are stabilized and regulated through policies and institutions that operate at specific territorial levels. While no territory may be wholly a zone of extraction or a zone of production (what Amy Trauger and Jennifer Fluri call "spaces of dispossession" or "zones of accumulation"), these two modes of economic activity have different institutional and governance requirements, so we can usefully analyze political-economic regimes in terms of institutions and policies that predominantly favor extraction or production within a particular territory.[29]

From this perspective, which views government and economic institutions as a unified system, I advance two ideal types of capitalist political-economic regime:

An *extractive regime* is characterized by political structures that enable appropriation of labor and resources through mechanisms such as land and resource concessions, government subsidies for extractive activities, export-oriented trade policy, and lax environmental and labor regulations that may be loosely or corruptly administered and enforced. These structures support an extractive economy characterized by windfall profits and expanding frontiers, removing value in energy and materials and thereby impoverishing or "underdeveloping" a region (though often enriching a predatory elite).

A *productivist regime* is characterized by political structures that constrain domestic frontier expansion and rely on commodified labor power and capital investments to promote resource transformation and consumption through mechanisms such as environmental and property rights protections, government subsidies for capital investment and value-added industry, and trade and foreign policies that encourage imports of cheap resources from extractive regions. These structures support a productivist economy characterized by accumulation of fixed capital and physical infrastructure, or "techno-mass," consuming energy and materials to enrich or "develop" the productivist region.[30]

Importantly, extraction is not limited to nonrenewable resources like metals or fossil fuels. Potentially renewable activities like forestry and agriculture are extractive when they overharvest resources or "mine" soil fertility for windfall profits, driving commodity booms and busts, whereas productivist forestry or agriculture regulates and invests for added value and longer-term sustainability of production.

This dialectic of extraction and production is not a hard binary. Post-structuralist scholarship has long emphasized the need to collapse or complicate simplistic core-periphery distinctions.[31] Extractive and productivist institutions and economic activities are interwoven, multilevel phenomena that have different intensities in different contexts. Yet territory matters, and governmental hierarchies regulate and stabilize extraction and production at specific territorial levels, allowing for a more structural analysis of extractive and productivist regimes.[32] Rather than reifying these regimes, however, my goal is to mobilize these concepts for dynamic political-economic analysis. Extractive and productivist regimes can overlap or nest based on their territorial extent, for example, an extractive provincial regime nested within a productivist national regime. Nor is a particular regime an autonomous property of its territory (as a modernization perspective would claim); instead, extractive and productivist regimes are co-produced through the systemic interdependence of extraction and production. In other words, an extractive regime in Indonesia cannot be understood as simply a "deficiency" of Indonesian governance but rather must be understood in relation to actions by colonial and post-colonial productivist core powers to maintain resource extraction and raw materials exports from Indonesia. Lastly, regimes are not static. Recognizing how governance structures economic activity within a territory lets us examine how changes in governance can alter a territory's economy, bringing us back at last to that foundational question—what determines which places develop when?

Land Sparing and Modernization in Brazil and Indonesia

Modernization theory argues that the goal of any society should be to transition from an extractive, underdeveloped political economy to a productivist, developed one by adopting the correct, productivist institutions and forms of governance. *Ecological* modernization theory (eco-modernism) holds that environmental problems can be resolved through this capitalist modernization process.[33] To return to the problem of land use on tropical frontiers, land sparing is a policy model that aims to realize this developmental transition. The Brazilian Amazon and Indonesian Borneo have for centuries been zones of extraction. Colonial and national governments and traders would pump the forests for timber, pelts, and latexes and resins to feed the industries and elite consumers of Rio de Janeiro and Jakarta, Lisbon and Amsterdam. The expansion of extensive cattle ranching in the Amazon and oil palm and tree fiber plantations in Kalimantan has been just another wave of extraction, as ranchers and plantation companies clear rainforest, sell off the timber, and establish agricultural operations that mine soil fertility for global commodity chains, leaving local people and ecosystems poisoned and depauperate.

Land-sparing policies call for increased investments in cattle genetics and seed stock, fertilizers and pesticides, irrigation and mechanization, to transform extractive agriculture into intensified, technified, "modern" ranches and plantations. According to the land-sparing narrative, in a productivist system, profit comes from producing in place, rather than from the windfalls of an ever-expanding frontier. By closing the frontier, the remaining rainforest can be spared. By intensifying the agricultural system, new markets and infrastructure are created for chemicals and machinery, storage and transportation, processing and value-added manufacturing, and all manner of secondary services. The economy flips from extraction to productivism, and a process of agro-industrial development and ecological modernization begins its "take-off."

The Brazilian state of Mato Grosso has been the poster child for this kind of development. Mato Grosso, whose name means "dense woods," lies in the Center-West Region of the Brazilian interior, occupying the transition zone between the Cerrado tropical savanna biome in the eastern and southern parts of the state and the Amazon biome in the north and west. Beginning in the 1970s, the state experienced rapid infrastructure development, population growth, deforestation, and agricultural expansion. In the humid forest region of north and northwest Mato Grosso, logging, mining, and extensive ranching devoured thousands of square kilometers of primary forest every year. After 2004, however, new governance initiatives—including protected area creation, tightened enforcement of federal forest legislation, and private sector pledges to eliminate deforestation for soy production—drove a rapid decline in Mato Grosso's deforestation rates. Even as deforestation slowed, agricultural production grew. Ranchers increased stocking rates, while soy farmers expanded over former cattle pastures and adopted crop rotations with corn and cotton. Dusty frontier towns like Sorriso and Lucas do Rio Verde, whose first colonists arrived in the 1970s with the construction of the BR-163 highway, grew in a matter of decades into small agro-industrial cities. Today, alongside grain silos, meat processors, and farm equipment retailers, they boast paved roads and sidewalks, modern apartment towers, and slick bars and restaurants. Local politicians celebrate this economic growth, local landowners and industrialists celebrate their increasing wealth, and sustainability researchers celebrate the apparent "decoupling" of agricultural development from deforestation.[34] The modern agro-industrial hubs of northern Mato Grosso are heralds of a new, productivist Amazonian economy and models for frontier municipalities in the state of Pará to the north.

By contrast, the Indonesian province of East Kalimantan in the late 2000s and early 2010s remained a region of rapacious extraction. The industrial logging companies that began ransacking the province's forests in the 1970s were followed by a fossil-fuel boom. The oil and gas industry grew during the 1980s, and coal mining expanded rapidly during the 1990s. Toward the end of the 1990s, industrial logging began to decline. Cheap timber exports from Kalimantan had helped fuel a construction boom in Japan and funneled millions of dollars to multinational timber companies and cronies of Indonesia's dictator, Suharto, leaving a legacy of degraded forests and livelihoods. At the turn of the twenty-first century, a new wave of extraction gained force, as East Kalimantan's logged and burned-out forestlands were increasingly converted to oil palm plantations.

In 2006, Suwarna Abdul Fatah, a retired army major general who had served as East Kalimantan provincial governor since 1998, was removed from power and ultimately convicted of improperly issuing permits for 1 million hectares of oil palm plantations that were logged but never planted, causing losses to the state of nearly $40 million.[35] Governor Suwarna's next elected successor, Awang Faroek Ishak, adopted a discourse of green development. Under Awang, East Kalimantan joined the international Governors' Climate and Forests Task Force in 2009 and declared itself a "Green Province" in 2010. The province was also a magnet for international conservation programs from the German government, World Wide Fund for Nature (WWF), and The Nature Conservancy. In an interview in early 2015 in the provincial capital of Samarinda, where a steady stream of coal barges clogs the muddy Mahakam River, a long-term advisor to Governor Awang explained to me that after East Kalimantan's timber boom and subsequent reliance on oil, gas, and mining, members of the administration realized that their extractive economic model had depleted the natural resource base and caused environmental degradation, extreme income inequality, poverty, and unemployment.[36] "We realized we were doing development wrong," a provincial planning official in Samarinda told me later that month. "Before fossil fuels are exhausted, we need to increase our renewable sectors, especially agriculture. . . . We want an economic transition from nonrenewable resources to renewable resources based on plantations, farming, and processing and manufacturing."[37] And so, under the guise of a "green" economic transition, over 1,900 square kilometers of primary forest were razed for oil palm during Awang's decade-long administration.[38]

Economic activity in East Kalimantan continued to depend on environmental degradation, and the new plantation economy continued to siphon value away from local communities. Most palm oil production is controlled by companies based in Jakarta, Singapore, or Malaysia, who own plantations or contract with smallholders and control the mills where palm fruit bunches are processed. These external companies profit from deforestation, land dispossession, and exploitative labor and exchange relations, and most of the crude palm oil they produce is exported for refining and processing outside the province.[39] Oil palm in East Kalimantan has not substantially reduced poverty, enriched local communities, or contributed to broader processes of agricultural modernization and industrial growth. Oil palm has brought not agro-industrial "development" but rather agro-industrial extraction. Despite Awang's "green development" discourse and the ministrations of environmentalist researchers and organizations, East Kalimantan failed to initiate a productivist transition, instead remaining firmly entrenched in an extractive regime.

In the early 2010s, researchers and policymakers celebrated Brazil's deforestation reductions as proof of the land-sparing model, while attributing Indonesia's rising deforestation to inadequate land-sparing policies. Brazil was achieving agro-industrial growth through intensification and forest conservation, while Indonesia's agricultural growth came through large-scale deforestation for underproductive plantations. According to sustainability scientists, Brazil was a "deforestation success story" and a model for countries such as Indonesia.[40] Just a few years later, however, the picture had changed. Amazonian deforestation spiked after 2015 under right-wing Brazilian governments, which undermined environmental policies and emboldened speculative land grabbers and ranchers. As the Temer and Bolsonaro administrations slashed budgets at Indigenous and environmental agencies and sought to open protected areas to mining and agribusiness, land thieves invaded Indigenous territories and assassinated rural activists. Brazil lost over ten thousand square kilometers of Amazonian primary forest in 2019, reaching a level of destruction not seen since 2008, while scientists and activists called for a return to the "successful" land-sparing policies of the past: creating protected areas, enforcing environmental regulations, and intensifying agricultural production.[41]

In Indonesia, meanwhile, massive wildfires in 2015 caused by a combination of land clearing and El Niño–related drought, along with international environmentalist pressure on the palm oil industry, led the government to adopt new policies aimed at curbing forest burning and increasing oil palm productivity. Indonesia's increased forest law enforcement and new environmental regulations, alongside programs aimed at improving yields in existing oil palm operations, once again sought to reconcile conservation and development through land sparing. Indonesian annual primary deforestation declined 70 percent from its 2016 peak of over 9,000 square kilometers to just over 2,700 in 2020, the lowest level of clearing since 2003.[42] Brazil was once again a deforestation hotspot, while Indonesia had become "a tentative bright spot," with researchers suggesting that "Indonesia may have turned a corner in its efforts to reduce deforestation."[43]

On twenty-first-century tropical forest frontiers, land sparing has become the universal fulcrum of conservation and development policy. The necessity of agro-industrial growth is a given in these debates. Where growth comes without deforestation, land-sparing policies are to thank; where growth comes at a cost of forest destruction, stronger land-sparing policies are needed. Growth is the unquestioned premise and land sparing the unquestioned solution. If effective land-sparing policies were applied worldwide, goes the thinking, the problem of habitat destruction for agriculture would be solved. This hegemonic status of land sparing in sustainable development policy exemplifies the broader hegemony of modernization policy discourse. If the principles of capitalist development are applied globally, modernization thinking claims, productivism and high mass consumption is attainable for everyone. If it is true that everyone can be a wealthy consumer, but environmental degradation undermines wealth, then environmental conservation and high mass consumption must be compatible. Capitalism needs land sparing to work—needs industrial growth and conservation to be compatible—or the entire ideology of "development" begins to collapse.

Displacing Destruction

How was it possible for researchers and policymakers celebrating land sparing in the Brazilian Amazon to ignore skyrocketing deforestation in the Cerrado, the Chaco, the Bolivian Chiquitania, and the western Amazon Basin? Were they not concerned that "saving" the Amazon might be destroying forests elsewhere?

This problem of displacement, also described as "leakage," "spillover," or "indirect land-use change," has not gone wholly unnoticed.[44] In the policy sphere, accounting for leakage has been a central concern for carbon offset projects, resulting in a variety of monitoring, discounting, and project design strategies to detect and minimize leakage effects. Yet as one policy researcher noted for programs for Reducing Emissions from Deforestation and Forest Degradation (REDD), "REDD leakage is impossible to eliminate completely unless all global forests and woodlands were to be REDD-enrolled simultaneously."[45]

In relation to land-use change and deforestation, academic research on displacement has mostly taken the form of statistical modeling that attempts to quantify either the amount of carbon emissions or the amount of forest loss displaced through conservation policies and commodity markets. Carbon emissions are imagined to be essentially fungible—one tonne (metric ton) of greenhouse gases emitted in Brazil has the same global effect as one tonne emitted in Europe—and geographical territories (such as municipalities, biomes, or nation-states) are naturalized as units of analysis.[46] From these studies we learn, for example, that in 2010–2014, 26–39 percent of tropical deforestation-related emissions were driven by agricultural and forestry trade, or that European Union (EU) soy imports from Brazil in 2010–2015 were responsible for 33.42 million tonnes of carbon emissions from deforestation.[47] Displacement of forest loss is analyzed through a similar set of statistical practices. For example, Patrick Meyfroidt and Eric Lambin report that while Vietnam transitioned from net deforestation to net reforestation in the early 1990s, displacement of forest extraction abroad accounted for around 39 percent of Vietnamese forest regrowth by timber volume from 1987 to 2006. Even as Meyfroidt and Lambin conclude that over 60 percent of the regrowth was "free of displacement" and "constitutes a net gain for the world's forests and carbon sink," they acknowledge that "reforestation had few benefits for the quality of Vietnam's forest," since "secondary regrowths have a low density and a poor biodiversity," and "monocultures of fast-growing exotic species make approximately half of the forest-area increase."[48] Meanwhile, imports to Vietnam were often high-value, large-diameter logs extracted illegally from primary forests abroad in Cambodia, Laos, Malaysia, Myanmar, and Indonesia.

Studies from the Brazilian Amazon have given similar statistical accounts of indirect or displaced deforestation, often focused on internal displacement between Brazilian biomes. In an estimate of indirect land-use change, one study found that as much as 32 percent of Brazil's Amazonian deforestation in 2002–2011, a total of over thirty thousand square kilometers of forest loss, was attributable to the country's soybean sector, which drives deforestation indirectly through dynamics of farm expansion and land appreciation.[49] Statistical analyses also find that policies seeking to limit Amazonian deforestation have displaced forest clearing to other biomes. Fanny Moffette and Holly Gibbs, for example, focus on Mato Grosso and find that the Amazon Soy Moratorium, where traders agreed not to purchase soy from land in the Amazon biome deforested after 2006, displaced soy production onto previously cleared land in the Cerrado biome, while agreements by slaughterhouses in 2009 to exclude cattle suppliers with illegal Amazonian deforestation were estimated to have increased deforestation in the nearby Cerrado by nearly 13 percent—over one hundred square kilometers—in 2010–2013.[50] Focusing solely on the Soy Moratorium, however, modeling by Robert Heilmayr and colleagues finds that the moratorium reduced deforestation in soy-suitable locations in the Amazon, and these reductions were not canceled out by leakage to other parts of the Amazon biome or nearby Cerrado.[51]

With these studies, the limits of statistical approaches to displacement come into view. Heilmayr's team, for example, does a tremendous amount of painstaking work to estimate the independent effect of a single policy, and even then they recognize, "These empirical models cannot rule out more distant and diffuse forms of leakage, such as accelerated deforestation in other countries. Such distant leakage . . . does not lend itself well for empirical estimation," and consequently, they note, "we are unable to make claims of the [Amazon Soy Moratorium]'s effectiveness in reducing aggregate global deforestation."[52] Similarly, with regard to REDD policies, Micah Ingalls and colleagues observe that "dominant drivers of forest change are . . . increasingly international in scope, tied to global commodity markets and investment flows, and are not easily captured or effectively addressed through nation-based carbon accounting," and although "displacement is expected to be substantial, our empirical understanding of the causal pathways of transboundary displacement remains weak."[53]

The statistical accounting framework for displacement, for all its insight on policy impacts and trade flows, has several major weaknesses. Statistical methods share with controlled comparison a variable-based perspective, using statistical correlations to estimate the causal effects of independent variables (such as the Soy Moratorium) on dependent variables (such as deforestation). The process of defining and measuring those variables involves a series of simplifications, assumptions, and abstractions that produce a model. This model is necessarily a highly simplified representation of reality, but the model is useful to the degree that it accounts for the most important variables for its phenomenon of interest.

Tropical deforestation, and the processes of frontier change that it reflects, is an inherently complex social, ecological, economic, and political phenomenon that never has a single, discrete cause. In any system, deforestation is a dynamic, multicausal phenomenon, but models that approach the complexity of real systems ("system dynamics" models) are highly sensitive to assumptions and initial conditions and do not produce efficient, parsimonious estimates of causal effects, which is often a goal for researchers attempting to quantify policy impacts for decision makers. This debacle is aggravated for studies of displacement, which must define the boundaries of two or more complex systems and account for the linkages between them. In a statistical accounting framework for displacement, researchers are relying on the premise that if they can somehow account for all the relevant connections (for example, between the Soy Moratorium, soy production, and deforestation in the Amazon and Cerrado biomes), the residual of deforestation outside the connections they have mapped is not relevant to their conclusion (for example, on the effectiveness of the Soy Moratorium). Where deforestation occurs within complex, globally connected systems with permeable borders, this partial perspective simply cannot be sustained.

A related problem for these statistical approaches to displacement is the construction of variables that can abstract local phenomena into fungible quanta for comparison. It seems easy to accept the fungibility of carbon emissions: one tonne of carbon emitted in Brazil contributes the same amount to climate change as one tonne emitted in Europe. We might balk, however, at accepting the fungibility of forests. If one hectare of forest is lost in the Amazon and one hectare of forest is gained in Europe, is there no net effect on global forestland? The "forest" variable here elides most of the values we care about when we think of protecting forests—their ecological functions, economic uses, and cultural meanings.[54] This reflection, incidentally, might also lead us to question the fungibility of carbon emissions—the nature and context of those emissions may well be a concern! The problem of fungibility in statistical approaches to displaced deforestation is amply illustrated in Meyfroidt and Lambin's study of Vietnam. If a model sees the loss of primary forest in Cambodia canceled out by the expansion of exotic, mono-cultural tree plantations in Vietnam and cheerily reports a "net gain for the world's forests," how much is that model really telling us about forests and displacement as matters of substantive concern? Studies of displacement at the global level compound these problems by combining multiple datasets (e.g., global forest loss, global trade flows), each of which contains simplifications and assumptions that in combination produce a funhouse mirror of biases and occlusions, papered over by aggregate statistical estimates or smooth global maps.[55]

The substantive importance of displacement lies in precisely the opposite direction. Tree plantations in Vietnam and primary forest in Cambodia are not fungible, economically or ecologically. Displacement is rather about particular kinds of political-economic and ecological transformation in coupled "sending" and "receiving" systems—specifically, in the case of tropical deforestation, it is about the dialectics of productivism and extraction. The Vietnamese transition from deforestation to afforestation was a transition from forest extraction (primary forest logging) to forest productivism (industrial tree plantations) engineered through the displacement of forest extraction abroad, and the continued demand for extractive, old-growth timber by Vietnamese industry drives regional ecological degradation and timber trafficking. The statistics do not satisfactorily describe this transition.

What might we learn, then, if we shift our attention to the relations and flows between coupled systems, talking with people about what is happening in their communities and observing these transformations on the ground? What can we say about *how* displacement is happening, and what displacement looks like, not in the abstract sense of hectares protected here and hectares deforested there but in the lively, material sense of socioecological change?

Qualitative research has provided tantalizing peeks at some of these connections. Conducting interviews on South American agricultural frontiers of the Chaco and Chiquitania, Yann le Polain de Waroux and colleagues note that particular companies, usually cattle ranching operations, "specialize in the colonization of forested areas, where they capture the transitory profits associated with resource frontiers," and these companies are attracted to areas with looser deforestation regulations and enforcement.[56] When windfall profits are exhausted or regulations are strengthened, in the Brazilian Amazon for example, we can imagine that these specialists in extractive deforestation do not cease to exist but rather move their operations to new frontiers. Similarly, in Brazil, Gustavo Oliveira and Susanna Hecht report:

> Indirect land-use change (ILUC) dynamics that can only be surmised in remote-sensing models become explicit through field-site inspections and interviews with agribusiness managers and soy farmers, who say that their expansion plans are not curtailed by intensification of production [near the Amazon frontier], but rather conditioned by favorable institutional settings for the "development" of "new" lands in less regulated areas like the northeastern edge of the Cerrado . . . where profits from intensified production are often reinvested.[57]

If displacement is indeed real and substantial, this kind of qualitative, contextual research is indispensable for understanding its mechanisms and significance. It is precisely this understanding of displacement that I sought in the Bolivian lowlands.

From Variables to Relations

By the time I arrived in San Ignacio, I no longer thought of Bolivia as an independent "case" to set alongside Brazil and Indonesia in a dataset—it was a node in a network through which the forests of Borneo, the Amazon, and the Chiquitania all connected. This relational approach to research, also called "incorporated comparison," traces and compares social processes to build a general understanding of a particular historical moment and set of relations. Unlike variable-based controlled comparison, the goal, Philip McMichael writes, "is not to develop invariant hypotheses via comparison of more or less uniform 'cases,' but to give substance to a historical process (a whole) through comparison of its parts."[58] Relational comparison has an explicitly spatial dimension, following key processes through different places that comprise nodes of socially produced networks.[59] As I moved back and forth between the United States, Indonesia, Brazil, and Bolivia, I began to perceive the dialectical relations between these interconnected places—relations that revealed something of the broader workings of contemporary capitalism as a whole.

Over the course of six years, from 2013 to 2019, I conducted research in frontier municipalities in Indonesia, Brazil, and Bolivia.[60] These municipalities were linked by a common actor: The Nature Conservancy, an international environmental NGO. This "follow-the-actor" research design helped to illuminate the connections between distant frontiers, providing a starting point for situating Borneo, the Amazon, and the Chiquitania in a relational network. For purposes of understanding frontier transformation, The Nature Conservancy (TNC) was a methodological tool. Although in each of the municipalities where I worked TNC was one of the actors present, this is not a book about TNC—it is a book about tropical conservation and development.[61]

My research took me from the oil palm plantations of Indonesian Borneo and the cattle ranches of the Brazilian Amazon and Bolivian lowlands to government ministries in Jakarta, Brasília, and Santa Cruz de la Sierra. Through hours in canoes and pickup trucks, over pots of rice and cups of sweet coffee, I talked with the migrant farmers, Indigenous villagers, ranchers, bureaucrats, executives, and

Fig. 1. Burned trunk in a cattle pasture in São Félix do Xingu, Pará,
Brazil, February 2014. Two living castanheiras are visible on the far left.
(Author's photo)

activists whose struggles are inscribed on the land in charred tree
trunks and forest reserves. In addition to semi-structured interviews
in Indonesian, Portuguese, Spanish, and English with over two hundred key informants, I carried out participant observation at meet-
ings and events, and collected data from news stories, policy documents, and public databases.[62] This multi-sited research approach
involved different kinds of methods and engagement in different
sites, and that strategy of "polymorphous engagement" is reflected
in this book, where different chapters adopt different perspectives
and rely on different kinds of data to give substance to the people,
places, and institutions that compose tropical conservation and development as a historical process.[63]

Much of the scientific interest in land sparing has been funneled
into the "land sparing versus land sharing" debate, which centers on
supposed tradeoffs between agricultural productivity and biodiversity.[64] My research looks beyond this technical debate to situate land

sparing—as an idea, a policy, and an empirical phenomenon—within a broader political economy of extraction, productivist intensification, and displacement. Studies of displacement, like studies of land sparing, have often mired in statistical manipulations and methodological contortions. My research goes to the ground to illuminate the relations and flows through which displacement happens. With a relational approach, the mirage of modernization-based research and policy dissolves.

Bulldozing tropical forests for ranches and plantations is one of the most tangible and immediate contributors to the ongoing destruction of Indigenous and traditional livelihoods and tropical forest ecosystems. Extraction, production, and displacement in tropical landscapes serves as an entry point for a broader understanding of the ecology of global capitalism: a political-economic system that organizes and consumes "resources" for growth and profit. This developmental cycle of extraction, productivism, and displacement appears across different resources and factors of production as a fundamental dynamic in producing what Jason Moore calls "cheap natures."[65] Capitalism profits not solely or even primarily from the "production" of value but more fundamentally from the appropriation or *extraction* of value—a continuous process of "primitive accumulation" that both guarantees profit and drives displacement and expansion. The fallacy of ecological modernization, in which "green" development drives environmental degradation, is intrinsic to the capitalist ecology. Time and again, industrial "efficiencies" do not reduce resource consumption but rather fuel growth and intensified extraction, a paradox described over 150 years ago by the English economist William Stanley Jevons. Capitalist development is an ongoing, global ecocide.

Land sparing and its modernization counterparts do not change the system—they are mechanisms of the industrial capitalist machine. Even as eco-modernists purport to save tropical forests in a particular place, they are in effect just saving a castanheira in a sea of industrial monocultures. They are saving a rainforest but losing the world.

EXTRACTION

Plundering the Periphery in Indonesian Borneo

Extractive Regimes

O N A TUESDAY IN early March 2015, a fellow researcher and I rode our motorbikes up the palm-lined driveway of the provincial Plantations Office in the East Kalimantan capital of Samarinda. The building was quiet, and we were ushered inside to speak with a provincial plantations official. We talked about plantation crops and forest conservation, and just as we were preparing to leave, the official gave us a message. "God gave us oil palm," they said with conviction, observing that the crop grows only in the tropics, and campaigns against palm oil came from countries in the Global North with no oil palms. "Oil palm was meant by God to grow in Indonesia."[1]

In the mind of this official, oil palm was development, and that development was a gift and a birthright. It seemingly mattered little that oil palm is native to West Africa, or that plantations in Indonesia were first established by Europeans during Dutch colonial rule. About one month later, as I rode a motorbike across the northeast corner of the province from Tanjung Redeb to Tanjung Batu, through miles of spiky palm seedlings planted in the ash of clear-cut forests, I could not help but reach a different conclusion: oil palm was an affliction.

Kalimantan—Indonesian Borneo—covers over 70 percent of the world's third largest island, from the Malaysian border in the

northern highlands to the peat swamps of the southern coast. Forests of towering dipterocarps, shared for thousands of years by
Dayak and Punan peoples with orangutans, hornbills, orchids, and
elephants, have for centuries supplied valuable gums, resins, latexes,
and aromatics to global markets. In 1973, around the time that the
first large-scale industrial logging concessions began operating and
the first Landsat satellite images became available, old-growth forests still covered over three-quarters of Kalimantan.[2] During the
1980s and early 1990s, more timber was exported from the island of
Borneo than from all of tropical Africa and Latin America combined,
turning old-growth forests into cheap plywood to fuel a construction boom in Japan.[3] Unsustainable logging combined with El Niño
droughts to make forests more susceptible to fire, and conflagrations in the early 1980s and late 1990s burned millions of hectares.
In less than three decades, 28 percent of Kalimantan's remaining
old-growth forests were lost.

And still, at the turn of the twenty-first century, deforestation
accelerated.[4] From an average of 992 square kilometers per year
in 2000–2005, primary deforestation in Kalimantan more than
doubled to 2,281 square kilometers per year in 2005–2010, rising
again to 2,456 square kilometers per year in 2010–2015.[5] Across
Indonesia as a whole, annual primary forest loss from 2002 to 2015
accelerated by an average of over 300 square kilometers per year,
in a mad rush to boost corporate balance sheets by turning forests
into plantations to fill the world with processed food and paper-
board. By 2012, more primary forest was being cleared in Indonesia than in the Brazilian Amazon.[6] In an anguished letter to the
Jakarta Globe in 2015, Erik Meijaard, coordinator of the Borneo
Futures Initiative and former senior scientist of TNC-Indonesia,
wrote,

> Indonesia's rates of deforestation, dewilding of forests and
> seas, and also its recent spate of fires, clearly show that noth-
> ing is under control, and that, in fact, everything in con-
> servation is utterly out of control. . . . The protected areas,
> conservation laws, and those that are supposed to enforce
> them are largely ineffective. . . . We don't need more laws,

new laws, or changed laws, if the old ones never worked because no one bothered, or felt entitled or empowered to enforce them. We need a new system. . . . Why are laws ignored. Is it corruption within the government? Financial interests within or outside the government that overrule the laws? A total disinterest among government and public in environmental conservation? Or all of them?[7]

It is not all that surprising, however, that deforestation accelerated in Indonesia at the beginning of the twenty-first century. From 2000 to 2010, global gross domestic product (GDP) increased by almost a third, and global material extraction—the physical basis for GDP growth—increased by over 40 percent.[8] This growing global economy, in other words, depended on billions of tons of cheap primary products: palm oil for processed foods and cosmetics, coal to run the factories and light the office buildings, wood pulp for paper packaging and plywood for construction. And so deforestation accelerated not just in Indonesia but almost everywhere in the tropics, from Paraguay to Angola.

This rampage of ecological destruction did not come about by accident. Among a certain set of development scholars and conservationists, a common disapproving question asks, "Why do governments in developing countries waste natural resources?" They almost invariably answer by pointing to some sort of market or policy "failure": forest products and services are not properly valued, or government structures are "malformed" and their development strategies are "shortsighted."[9] To quote a slogan that became popular in the late 2000s, however, "the system's not broken, it's fixed."[10] Blaming "developing" countries for "wasting" resources ignores not just the demand for those resources by "developed" consumers but also the intentional design of market relations and government structures by colonial powers, post-colonial elites, and transnational capitalists to plunder the natural resource wealth of the periphery to benefit the capitalist core.

This first part of the book traces historical processes and institutional configurations to show how environmental destruction happens not by accident but by design. Extraction is the appropriation and export of energy and materials from a region, and extractive regimes are sets of political-economic institutions that stabilize and regulate extractive economies at specific territorial levels. This overview gives a theoretical definition of extractive regimes. Chapters 1–3 take Indonesia as a paradigmatic zone of extraction to explore how extractive regimes work, and how they persist over time despite (or even through) numerous programs promising modernization and development. While later chapters on Brazil and Bolivia describe on-the-ground land sparing and displacement in the 2000s and 2010s, this section on Indonesia comprises a longer history of extraction as the continuous, destructive foundation for over four hundred years of capitalist "development."

Extractive Regimes

According to modernization thinking, every *developing* country can become a *developed* country, if only they could govern their "lawless" natural resource frontiers and correct their market and policy "failures." Those "pathologies" of resource degradation, however, are more often stable, institutionalized political-economic orders. Sociologist Paul Gellert writes of Indonesia, "In these islands we do not find . . . a mythical, and 'lawless' Wild West. Rather, we discover a land exploited by a government whose policies insure the accumulation of power, profit, and property by its friends—and, if the IMF has its way, by foreign investors as well—thus threatening the rights of the powerless who live in the forest and the future of the forest itself."[11]

From his research in Indonesia, Gellert developed the concept of an *extractive regime*. Building on world systems analysis and Stephen Bunker's distinction between extractive and productive economies, Gellert defines an extractive regime as a historically produced, concrete economic and political order based on natural resource extraction and export.[12] Gellert's concept is closely tied to Indonesia and other natural resource–exporting states in the post–World War II period. Taking a broader view of the political organization of material and energy flows over the history of capitalism, however, I argue that extractive regimes are fundamental building blocks of capitalist political economy. My definition expands Gellert's concept in three important ways:

First, Gellert defines an extractive regime only in relation to natural resource–based commodities. Although he recognizes that exploitation of peripheral labor is fundamental to capitalist development, Gellert does not integrate labor more fully into the extractive regime concept, nor does he distinguish labor exploitation in an extractive regime from exploitation elsewhere. My broader definition recognizes extraction in relation to both human labor and natural resources. Under an extractive regime, neither labor nor resources are articulated within local circuits of production to drive wealth accumulation domestically. Extractive institutions ensure that materials and energy flow elsewhere and enrich others.[13]

Second, Gellert's discussion is limited to post–World War II developmentalism and globalization, but there is continuity between the political structures of colonial and post-colonial extraction. I see extractive regimes as an ideal type of political-economic organization over the *longue durée* of historical capitalism. European colonialism outside the settler colonies operated quintessentially as an extractive regime, calculated to enrich a narrow domestic elite and the foreign metropole at the expense of environmental and social degradation in the colony. Across much of the world, these extractive dynamics have been reproduced and persist in the post-colonial period. Extractive regimes are the typical political-economic formations of the periphery.

Third, Gellert focuses on the extractive regime at the level of the nation-state, though he acknowledges that extraction is organized politically at different levels of the world system. I understand a regime as a mode of rule, and in the case of political-economic systems, a regime is a sociopolitical order conjoined with an economic mode of production.[14] An extractive regime stabilizes and governs an extractive economy, and a productivist regime stabilizes and governs a productivist economy. At each socially produced spatial level of the world system—the nation-state, the province, the district or municipality—there is a political-economic regime that links a sociopolitical regulatory structure with a mode of production. The interactions among different regimes across multiple levels is therefore a crucial area for analysis.

Four additional elements clarify how this theoretical framework of extractive and productivist political-economic regimes works for analyzing capitalist "development" in Indonesia and elsewhere:

1. *Regimes are hybrid.* At any political level, a regime may govern both extractive and productivist processes. Extraction and production are interdependent and fractal dimensions of the capitalist system, so no regime is ever absolutely extractive or absolutely productivist. Nonetheless, it matters whether political-economic institutions at a particular territorial level promote primarily extraction or production.

2. *Regimes are enacted.* Institutions (understood broadly as the formal and informal "ruling relations" that coordinate people's activities) must be constantly reproduced, and the extractive or productivist character of the economy is a function of behavior within these socially constructed institutions.[15] No place is predestined, in other words, to extraction or productivism due to geography or the production of a specific commodity. Extractive regimes are continually enacted through people's behaviors that reproduce extractive political-economic institutions, but it need not be thus.

3. *Regimes are sticky.* Although regimes must be continually enacted and are not inevitable, they are complex structures supported by powerful, institutionalized interests. Historically entrenched institutions are difficult to transform, especially when they are reinforced by higher-order regimes. A provincial extractive regime will be stickier when reinforced by a national extractive regime, for example.

4. *Regimes are contested.* Despite their stickiness, regimes are not static. Internal contradictions and transformative projects from above and below challenge the existing mode of production and drive institutional change. Oftentimes, regimes are reconfigured without changing the mode of production, for example when colonial extraction is replaced by neo-colonial extraction. Sometimes, regimes transform. While theoretically a shift can occur in either direction, I focus on (potential) transitions from an extractive to a productivist

regime—when a region "develops" and moves from the periphery toward the core.

The ravages of "development" are written into the societies and landscapes of Borneo. In Kalimantan, over 100,000 square kilometers of old-growth tropical forests have been lost since the 1970s.[16] Massive fires and choking haze have killed thousands of people, plants, and animals. Fish in East Kalimantan's Mahakam River delta contain over 1,300 times the tolerable level of lead and over 2,000 times the tolerable level of cadmium for human consumption, and Kalimantan's children have sharply negative expectations of their future environmental conditions.[17]

This social and ecological degradation is the product of extractive regimes that for four centuries have plundered Indonesia to funnel resources and profits to the centers of capitalist wealth and consumption. Extraction in Indonesia, in other words, is especially expansive and enduring. The following chapters use the Indonesian experience to explore how extractive regimes work, and how they persist.

CHAPTER ONE

Four Hundred Years of Extraction

THE DUTCH EAST INDIA Company (VOC) was created in 1602 to control the spice trade in the Indonesian archipelago, and over the course of the seventeenth and eighteenth centuries, despite numerous conflicts and setbacks, the Dutch expanded their economic and political control in the region. VOC efforts to secure monopolies over the nutmeg and clove trades during the seventeenth century encapsulate the ecological imperialism of the colonial enterprise. On the Banda Islands, home to the *Myristica fragrans* evergreen trees that are the source of nutmeg and mace, the VOC in 1621 massacred the Indigenous population and replaced them with a colony of white settlers cultivating nutmeg plantations with slave labor.[1]

The clove trade was more difficult to monopolize, as clove trees (*Syzygium aromaticum*) were more widely distributed across the Molucca Islands. In 1652, the VOC was at last able to leverage conflicts among local rulers to secure a contract with the king of Ternate, a Moluccan potentate, limiting clove cultivation to VOC-controlled areas, principally the island of Ambon. As historian M. C. Ricklefs observes in his classic history of Indonesia, "Ambon could by this time produce more cloves than the entire world consumption, and the VOC's aim was not to monopolise but to destroy clove cultivation elsewhere."[2] Accordingly, the VOC implemented a policy of extirpation (*extirpatie*), paying local rulers to eradicate "illegal" spice production, and organizing inspection tours through the Moluccas that would destroy even wild cloves growing outside authorized areas. One early expedition to the island of Seram in 1625 had destroyed 65,000 clove trees, "at a conservative estimate."[3] In this way, the VOC solved the problems of "smuggling" and "overproduction" affecting the profitability of its spice trade by eliminating Indigenous populations and uprooting thousands of native trees.[4]

During the seventeenth and eighteenth centuries, the Dutch focused primarily on controlling trade as opposed to occupying territory, centering their efforts around the Moluccan spice trade and exports of tea, coffee, and sugar from Java. VOC finances were on the decline in the late 1700s, however, due to internal corruption and mismanagement, costly wars, and subversion of the clove monopoly by the French, who captured clove plants in Ambon and established clove production in the French Indian Ocean colonies. Changes were also underway in the metropole, where the Netherlands had fallen under French domination. In 1800, the VOC was dissolved and the Dutch crown took control of its territories. When the Dutch emerged victorious from the Java War of 1825–1830, they consolidated their rule over the island of Java, and they embarked on a new period of more intensive extraction from their East Indian colony. "Profit from Java was essential," Ricklefs explains. "Not only must it cover the costs of the administration in Java, but it was also needed to bolster the deteriorating financial position in the Netherlands," heavily indebted after the Napoleonic Wars.[5]

To make Java profitable, Johannes van den Bosch, the new governor-general, imposed the infamous Cultivation System (*cultuurstelsel*), which required villages to set aside land for compulsory production of export crops for the government, especially coffee, sugar, and indigo. While the amount of land used for export crops varied, Ricklefs emphasizes that "the labour investment was clearly massive," with a large proportion of the island's population involved in producing government crops.[6] Extraction through the Cultivation System operated not primarily through plundering natural resources (although it degraded ecological conditions of production) but through plundering the local people of Java by appropriating their reproductive labor (energy usually spent on rice agriculture) for the purpose of export and profit. As Lisa Tilley notes, the Cultivation System "was also the first means by which European capital could be extensively drawn into the Dutch East Indies," and "these innovations on Java would ultimately lead to the expansion of European capital investment for the purposes of extraction across the wider archipelago."[7]

As an extractive institution, the Cultivation System was enormously profitable. In the 1830s and 1840s, remittances from Indonesia accounted for nearly one-fifth of Dutch state revenues, Ricklefs reports, and by the 1850s, that proportion rose to one-third: "These revenues kept the Dutch domestic economy afloat: debts were redeemed, taxes reduced, fortifications, waterways and the Dutch state railway built, all on the profits forced out of the villages of Java." In this way, the Netherlands' industrial development depended directly and explicitly on the degradation of the people and environment of Java. The costs of this extraction—in the form of depleted soils, famines, and epidemics—undermined the Cultivation System and helped lead to a phasing out of compulsory cultivation during the 1860s, and the installation in the 1870s of a new set of extractive institutions centered on corporate capital investment.[8]

With the Agrarian Law of 1870, the Dutch moved to a model of extractive investment through private plantations, in a shift that soon reached beyond Java to pull the island of Sumatra, as Ann Laura Stoler puts it, "further into the international vortex of capitalist expansion."[9] The Domain Declaration (*domein verklaring*) that accompanied the Agrarian Law appropriated all land not under clear ownership to the colonial state as "wastelands" and served as a pretext for the expropriation of forests and fallow lands for plantation companies. Sumatra's East Coast became a vast plantation belt of Dutch, British, and U.S. corporate estates. In the early twentieth century, the Franco-Belgian SOCFIN corporation drew on its plantation experience in West Africa to pioneer oil palm cultivation on Sumatra. By 2015, 7 percent of the entire land surface of Indonesia was covered by oil palm.[10] This new extractive configuration after 1870 turned eastern Sumatra, Stoler writes, into "one of the most lucrative ventures of the Western colonial empires. Marshaling internationally procured funds and a massive force of indentured Asian workers, within fifty years the East Sumatran estate industry's production of rubber, oil palm, tobacco, tea, and sisal accounted for one-third of the export earnings for the Dutch East Indies, providing many of the raw materials on which the expansion of industrial capitalism in Europe and America was based."[11] In the twentieth century as in the nineteenth, the wealth and development of the Euro-American capitalist core depended on an extractive regime in Indonesia organized around Indigenous dispossession, coercive labor relations, and ecological destruction.

While late nineteenth- and early twentieth-century plantation development was concentrated in Java and Sumatra, in Borneo the Dutch sought control over areas of coal mining and oil extraction but had very little territorial control over the forested interior.[12] Dutch efforts to control the forest products trade from Kalimantan were a continuation of the "species controls" used by the VOC in Java and the Moluccas, and illustrate the early institutionalization of capitalist extraction in Kalimantan.[13] Key forest products in the Borneo trade included gutta percha—a latex from trees of the *Palaquium* genus used by Indigenous peoples for knife handles and by Europeans for insulating submarine telegraph cables—and jelutong—a tree latex from the *Dyera* genus used in Europe to manufacture fire-resistant plates and tiles. While gutta percha could be harvested by tapping, the logic of the commodity boom encouraged a practice of felling the trees and "bleeding" them for their latex.[14] Helen Godfrey estimates that "around twenty-seven million trees were felled to collect gutta percha in the half century after the first [submarine telegraph] cable was laid" in 1851.[15]

Industrial demand for jelutong boomed in the early twentieth century, and Michael R. Dove recounts how the colonial government moved quickly to seize control of the resource from the Indigenous population:

By 1908 the Colonial Government in parts of Kalimantan was requiring a licence to tap the trees; in 1910 the Government awarded all tapping rights to foreign concessionaires; and in 1913 the Government imposed export levies on the native tappers. The Government justified these measures either in terms of the need to avoid overexploitation of the latex-yielding trees, or of the need to protect the

smallholders against middlemen. But the attendant abuse of
native rights in pursuit of European profit was so glaring
that the Dutch legal scholar, J. van Vollenhoven, called it
a textbook case of the Colonial Government's abuse of its
right to "wastelands."[16]

In short, rapacious industrial demand and colonial resource policies
combined to ensure that raw materials and profits from Kalimantan's forests flowed into colonial hands, with little concern for the
ecological sustainability of the resource.

Extraction does not proceed without resistance, however. The
VOC was continually at war in the seventeenth and eighteenth centuries, and labor unrest was a constant preoccupation for plantation
managers in Sumatra during the nineteenth and twentieth centuries.
The political-economic organization of extraction from the Indonesian archipelago has transformed over time through dialectics of
coercion and resistance, technology and ecology, demand and supply, yet over the course of three and a half centuries, the outcome of
these struggles was the recomposition of extractive regimes.

Following independence in 1945, however, Indonesian president Sukarno sought to challenge the archipelago's position as an
extractive periphery. This challenge was cast within an international
project of Third Worldism (articulated at the 1955 Bandung Conference) that attempted to mobilize newly independent states, Tilley
writes, to "break from Western-centred structures and relations of
extraction, and . . . to cultivate relational political and economic connections without the need to loop back through the old imperial
centre."[17] In Indonesia, this period of "delinking" was marked by
improved labor conditions in the plantation sector and the 1958 nationalization of Dutch businesses in Indonesia. The emphasis was
on challenging "foreign imperialism" but not capitalism per se, preserving a modernist objective of industrial "national development."
In the plantation sector, Stoler notes that "as a vanguard of progressive social change, the labor movement had only partial and dimin-
ishing success. Ameliorating some of the more oppressive features
of estate life, it never challenged the basic relations of production on
which exploitation was based or the class structure in which those
relations were reproduced."[18] The attempt to delink from extraction

and pursue a more productivist national development pathway was ultimately frustrated, however, by domestic political struggles, Cold War geopolitics, and capitalist interests.

While the circumstances surrounding General Suharto's rise to power are complex, the United States had engaged in covert operations to undermine Sukarno since the 1950s due to his anti-imperialism and the empowerment of the Indonesian Communist Party (PKI) under his government. U.S. officials in the 1960s were preoccupied by the threat posed by the PKI and mobilized workers to U.S. rubber and oil corporations in the country.[19] Restricting development aid to Indonesia, the United States continued military assistance programs to strengthen the Indonesian Army as a counterpoint to the PKI.[20] When Suharto and the military seized power in late 1965, the United States, United Kingdom, and Australia supported the ensuing purge in which hundreds of thousands of communists, suspected communists, unionized workers, and other leftists and activists were murdered in one of the worst mass killings of the twentieth century.[21] In the bloodbath of the 1965–1966 killings, Third Worldism in Indonesia was definitively suppressed, to be replaced by Suharto's "New Order" regime of crony capitalist extraction.

Kalimantan Forests Under Suharto's New Order

The political economy of New Order Indonesia was structured around the extraction of multiple resource commodities to fuel regional circuits of capitalist accumulation centered on Japan and global circuits centered on the Euro-American core (while lining domestic elites' pockets in the process). The tropical timber trade was a pillar of the regime, particularly after Suharto bankrupted Pertamina, the state-owned oil company, in the 1970s by using it as a source of off-budget funding for development projects.[22] The New Order timber trade also marked the beginning of large-scale industrial deforestation in Kalimantan, so I focus here on the timber sector to illustrate the workings of the New Order extractive regime and the institutionalization in Kalimantan of industrial forest destruction.

"Forest" in modern usage denotes "an area covered by trees," but H. Gyde Lund observes that the term may refer to an administrative unit, a type of land cover, or a type of land use.[23] In New Order Indonesia, the administrative definition of forest—the areas designated by the state to be governed as "forests"—took on tremendous importance. In 1967, the Suharto government passed the Basic Forestry Law, which designated 74 percent of Indonesia's surface area as "forest estate" (*kawasan hutan*), falling under the control of the central government's Forestry Department (later the Ministry of Forestry).[24] The creation of the forest estate was a direct continuation of the institution of state land control promulgated by the colonial Domain Declaration of 1870. In tandem with the Foreign Capital Investment Law of 1967, the creation of the forest estate worked to similar effect as its colonial predecessor by facilitating corporate land concessions.[25] From the late 1960s onward, industrial-scale logging expanded rapidly through the forests of Indonesian Borneo.

The general pattern of timber extraction involved first the allocation of logging concessions to Suharto's military allies and business cronies and their foreign partners. As Christopher Barr recounts, "Partnerships with the largest [foreign] investors were almost always forged by military interests, politico-bureaucratic powerholders, or private entrepreneurs with close ties to elite officials. In particular, military-owned holding companies, cooperative enterprises, foundations, and pension funds, representing the particular interests of both individual officers and whole commands, frequently acted as 'silent partners' for foreign logging companies."[26] The deep involvement of the military in Indonesia's timber sector helped ensure loyalty to the regime (through personal enrichment), facilitated the repression of any local dissent to logging operations, and guaranteed impunity for violations of harvest limits and other regulations.[27] An emblematic example of the alliances between foreign capital and domestic elites for the extraction of Indonesian timber was the partnership between Georgia Pacific, a U.S. timber multinational, and Bob Hasan, Suharto's longtime business partner. Hasan and Georgia Pacific were awarded a 350,000-hectare concession in present-day Kutai Timur District of East Kalimantan, from which Georgia Pacific exported over 2.2 million cubic meters of raw logs during its first decade of operation, with gross earnings valued at over $470 million in 2020 dollars.[28]

Japan was the primary export market for Indonesian timber, processing raw logs especially into plywood panels for use in construction. In the early 1980s, Indonesia banned raw log exports in order to develop its domestic plywood industry. The ecological perversity of turning old-growth trees into low-value plywood was justified by the necessity of resource exploitation for national "development," but the economic benefits of industrial growth in the timber sector flowed only to a small crony-capitalist elite.[29] State banks financed processing operations, and plywood, sawn wood, and pulp and paper mills proliferated in the 1980s and 1990s without effective government supervision or the guarantee of sustainable timber supplies, leading to structural overcapacity and a timber supply deficit in the wood-processing sector. To manage the competition that developed among heavily indebted processing firms and to boost Indonesia's international market share, Bob Hasan was given control of the Indonesian Wood Panel Association (Apkindo), which he transformed into a marketing cartel. Apkindo then flooded Japan with plywood at below-market prices, undercutting Japan's domestic plywood producers.[30] Through government subsidies and the Apkindo cartel, Indonesia became the world's largest hardwood plywood exporter, providing artificially cheap plywood to global markets and enriching politically connected firms through a vortex of unsustainable old-growth logging.

In a coup de grâce of the extractive regime, in 1989 the Suharto government created a Reforestation Fund (Dana Reboisasi) ostensibly intended to support reforestation and rehabilitation of degraded lands. The Reforestation Fund was supplied by a volume-based levy on timber concessionaires and was the largest single source of government revenues from the commercial forestry sector. The Ministry of Forestry used the fund to support the development of industrial tree plantations, predominantly on forested land and by companies with close ties to political elites that engaged in fraudulent practices to maximize rents from the fund and from the exploitation of forest areas. The fund was also used by the regime to finance unrelated, off-budget development projects, such as a $190 million transfer to the state aircraft company and a $109 million allocation to Bob Hasan's PT Kiani Kertas to finance construction of the company's pulp mill in East Kalimantan's Berau District. A 1999 audit by Ernst & Young documented losses of $5.2 billion from the Reforestation Fund in the five years from 1993 to 1998 due to mismanagement, fraud, and improper diversions of funds.[31]

A web of extractive institutions under the New Order regime thus churned the massive dipterocarps of the Borneo rainforest into pulp and plywood for export markets, with hardly a care for the island's people or environment. Conservation efforts did little to check the destruction. While the Ministry of Forestry was formally tasked with administering forest areas for the protection of biodiversity, erosion control, and other ecosystem functions in addition to making lands available for logging or conversion to non-forest uses, in practice professional foresters in the civil service were subordinate to extractive interests. As Peter Vandergeest and Nancy Peluso write,

> Foresters had little direct or actual control over the military branches with timber concessions and civil administrators who had interests other than implementing sustainable logging or conservation plans. Some foresters collaborated in corruption, a much easier alternative than enforcing legal controls. Foresters, civil service officials and members of the military who protected the companies' operations were commonly known to be corrupt. Indonesian foresters frequently referred to their institution as "the golden ministry," and with good reason....
>
> Overall, the example of Kalimantan demonstrates the irony of professional forestry. On the one hand, the land use planning and other development exercises were intended to render landscapes and subjects visible, legible and "sustainable." On the other hand, the actual practices of foresters (and others) were often illegal and intended to produce illegibility and obfuscation.[32]

The forestry service was absorbed into the New Order extractive regime, and even national parks, that sacrosanct category of international conservation, proved largely incapable of protecting Indonesian forests. Indonesia established its first national parks in 1980 as part of a global wave of park creation supported by international actors such as the United Nations Development Programme, International Union for Conservation of Nature, and Asian Development Bank, but large-scale logging and deforestation still occurred within park boundaries. In Kalimantan, 56 percent of protected lowland forests, an area of 29,000 square kilometers, were deforested from 1985 to 2001, with the expansion of oil palm plantations and decline of timber stock in logging concessions helping to drive industrial logging operations into national parks and areas formally designated by the Ministry of Forestry for conservation and protection.[33]

From Plywood to Palm Oil: Re-Forming Borneo After Suharto

The fall of the Suharto dictatorship in 1998 in the gyre of the Asian financial crisis ushered in the period of "Reform" (*Reformasi*) in Indonesia, but many of the extractive institutions of the New Order regime survived with little alteration in the post-Suharto period. As Vedi Hadiz and Richard Robison observe, "It was crucial to the post-Soeharto trajectory that *reformasi* did not sweep aside the predatory and illiberal social and political forces nurtured by the New Order. In fact, because of the very hesitancy of *reformasi*, these were allowed to reconstitute themselves within new political vehicles and institutions, and therefore remain ascendant."[34] In the forestry sector, Paul Gellert notes that Bob Hasan and Apkindo's "personal, monopoly market power" were attenuated after 1998, "but the sectoral dynamics and structures of accumulation beneath that power were not transformed."[35] The Ministry of Forestry continued to assert its control over the lands of the forest estate. An initial move to decentralize some authority to district governments prompted a surge in smaller-scale district-level concessions, exacerbating illegal logging and forest clearing, and in 2000 the central government moved to suppress district-level permitting. Structural overcapacity in the wood-processing sector and a timber supply deficit persisted, however, and combined with the endemic corruption and cronyism of the forestry bureaucracy to drive what Krystof Obidzinski,

A. Andrianto, and C. Wijaya characterized in 2007 as "massive over-harvesting" and the "spiralling deterioration of Indonesia's forest resources."[36]

By the late 1990s, industrial logging was declining across much of Kalimantan, as most of the accessible lowland forests had by this time been logged. While Sumatra had been a source of cheap agricultural commodities since the colonial period, the first oil palm plantations were established in Kalimantan only in the 1980s. With the rise of transnational agri-food corporations after World War II centered on processed food production (what Harriet Friedmann and Philip McMichael called the "durable foods complex"), West African oil palm (*Elaeis guineensis*) grown on monocrop plantations in Southeast Asia became a key source of cheap oil for everything from cereal to ice cream to toothpaste.[37] Kalimantan forests whose old-growth trees had been shredded into plywood for Japanese construction were now clear-cut and burned to make way for plantations providing cheap calories for the global working class and profits for corporate agribusiness. Oil palm expansion in Kalimantan began under the Suharto regime, and during the *reformasi* period plantation companies spread across the island through similar institutions of corruption, cronyism, illegality, and environmental degradation already established in the timber sector.

Oil palm plantations in Kalimantan are often characterized by low-quality inputs and poor land-use planning, and they expand predominantly through conversion of forests or peatlands in order to avoid tenure conflicts and profit from timber sales during plantation establishment. During the 1990s and 2000s, 90 percent of Kalimantan oil palm expansion came at the expense of forest cover, and as plantations have expanded, local populations have lost access to land and are generally marginalized or "adversely incorporated" as plantation labor.[38] Plantation companies leverage legal ambiguities and institutionalized corruption to establish plantations over land within the forest estate, for example by paying a $100,000 bribe to district government officials for a plantation permit, clearing land, establishing operations, and then paying a $150,000 bribe to forestry officials to legalize their "non-procedural" plantation. Eko N. Setiawan and colleagues report that in just one province, Central Kalimantan, 282 companies benefited from a 2012 amnesty allowing them to legalize nearly 40,000 square kilometers of plantations in the forest estate.[39]

Industrial plantations are frequently represented in Indonesian and global development discourses as vehicles of productivist modernization, yet once established, Kalimantan oil palm plantations are essentially extractive enterprises, operating through what Tania Li describes as a "mafia system" of institutionalized plunder.[40] Revenues do not improve plantation operations (gaps between actual and potential yields on Indonesian plantations are large, and yields have increased only marginally since 1990) nor are they generally reinvested in local or regional value-added production.[41] Oil palm plantations work, as Li explains, through a system of pervasive rent-seeking that monopolizes livelihood resources (land, water, living space) and captures law and governance institutions, transforming entire districts into "plantation zones" of predation and palm oil. Supervisors steal wages, government officials demand bribes, managers bypass regulations, and everyone is absorbed into an infrastructure of predatory extraction.[42] This palm oil from Kalimantan feeds global demand for processed foods and cosmetics—the mass consumption of ecological destruction. More ironically, palm oil expansion was further accelerated by European countries' attempts to "go green," when European Union renewable energy targets led to a fivefold increase in the use of palm oil for biodiesel in Europe from 2010 to 2014: ecological modernization masking a new geography of extraction.[43]

Contesting Extraction in the *Reformasi* Period

After the rise of Suharto and the mass killings of the 1960s, rural society under Indonesia's New Order was heavily repressed and depoliticized. Nancy Peluso, Suraya Afiff, and Noer Fauzi Rachman affirm that "until the 1980s, the New Order state successfully maintained such overwhelming power and control that rural protest was almost unknown."[44] The 1980s and 1990s saw nascent mobilization around environmental justice and Indigenous peoples' discourses, recasting issues of land rights and dispossession that had been a focus for the peasant movement. With the fall of Suharto, civil society in Indonesia gained greater space to organize and to contest the terms of the extractive regime.

Domestic environmental NGOs, Indigenous peoples' associations, agrarian movements, and international environmental organizations have formed shifting alliances during the *reformasi* period. For the purposes of this chapter, I highlight two tendencies with regard to environmental conservation. The first comprises what Joan Martínez-Alier calls "environmentalism of the poor": struggles by local communities to defend their land and livelihoods against corporate extraction.[45] In some parts of Indonesia, these struggles have coalesced into organized social movements, such as the Sedulur Sikep resistance to cement factories in Java and the Bali Tolak Reklamasi movement against land reclamation for tourism development in Bali's Benoa Bay.[46] In Kalimantan, communities have seized logging equipment and blockaded palm oil mills, sometimes halting operations for extended periods, and NGOs and communities in East Kalimantan have come together to demand reclamation of abandoned coal mine pits.[47] At the national level, a notable victory for community land rights came with a 2013 Constitutional Court decision supporting traditional communities' customary rights to their forest lands, though the government bureaucracy has been reluctant to implement the decision, and change on the ground has been glacial.[48]

The second tendency is ecological modernization or "green growth" policy discourse, which seeks to address extractive degradation through improved regulation and "green development." During the late 2000s and 2010s, Indonesia participated in the emerging global framework for Reducing Emissions from Deforestation and Forest Degradation (REDD), as the government joined the UN-REDD Programme, sanctioned domestic pilot projects, and signed an agreement with the government of Norway in which that country pledged up to $1 billion to support Indonesian REDD efforts. Government REDD approaches generally focused on the idea that carbon credits would finance forest protection, and national REDD strategies mostly dissociated the question of reducing deforestation from the question of plantation expansion. Anne Casson, Yohanes I Ketut Deddy Muliastra, and Krystof Obidzinski noted in 2015 that "within Indonesia, climate change policy is rarely consistent with other sectoral policies. For example, policies that promote the expansion of palm oil (both for food and biofuel production) into new areas often conflict with climate change policies designed to reduce emissions from deforestation and degradation."[49] Meanwhile, NGOs and agribusiness corporations have spearheaded initiatives aimed at reducing deforestation for oil palm that center on land-sparing strategies for increasing production while limiting new forest clearing.

Two principal land-sparing strategies emerged in the oil palm sector during this period. The first sought to shift the siting and development of plantations so that forest areas would be spared from conversion. The Roundtable on Sustainable Palm Oil, a multi-stakeholder group of corporations and NGOs convened by WWF in the early 2000s, adopted guidelines against the clearing of primary or "high conservation value" forest, which reflect this logic. Further, during the early 2010s, the World Resources Institute, a U.S.-based NGO, advocated "land swaps" to direct oil palm expansion away from forested areas toward "degraded lands." A pilot attempt initiated by the World Resources Institute in 2009 with support from an oil palm company, an Indonesian NGO, and the local community was not approved by the national government, however, and by 2013 the project had stalled "because of the complexity and cost of the legal process," reflecting how heavily Indonesian institutions favor extractive expansion.[50]

The second strategy sought to intensify or improve the efficiency of oil palm cultivation in order to raise productivity and close "yield gaps," hypothesizing that increasing yields could substitute for plantation expansion and decouple palm oil production from deforestation. (This strategy does not seem to account for the inconvenient fact that thanks to palm oil's multiple industrial uses, global demand is virtually unlimited.) While this latter strategy of increasing productivity represents an archetypical logic of land sparing via agricultural intensification, the former strategy of improved land-use planning is also a strategy for land sparing via land-use intensification. Both strategies seek to increase palm oil production without increasing deforestation and are rooted in a shared belief that industrial agriculture and environmental protection are compatible, so long as industrial production is effectively controlled and managed.

Ecological modernization initiatives like REDD and oil palm land swaps are couched in a logic of green capitalist development. They promise profit, but by curbing deforestation, they threaten the windfall profits of forest destruction enjoyed by logging and plantation companies and their government collaborators. Extractive coalitions of government and business elites have consequently worked vigorously to undermine new forest protections. Indonesian lawmakers and the Indonesian Palm Oil Association (Gapki) vocally opposed a government moratorium on new concessions in primary forest and peatland areas, for example, arguing that it would "incur losses to palm plantation companies that had contributed much to the state income."[51] In 2014, when major oil palm producers announced the Indonesia Palm Oil Pledge to purge their supply chains of deforestation, government officials accused the companies of restricting competition by refusing to buy from deforesting producers and eventually forced them to disband their pledge under pressure from the government anti-monopoly agency.[52] It was this pervasive persistence of forest destruction despite land-sparing initiatives and other conservation efforts that became a subject of my research when I arrived in Indonesia in November 2014.

CHAPTER TWO

Deforesting the "Green Province"

I
CAME TO EAST KALIMANTAN on the trail of The Nature Conservancy (TNC). An environmental NGO founded in 1951 in the United States, TNC began working in Indonesia in the early 1990s. Its Indonesia Terrestrial Program (devoted to forest conservation) concentrated beginning in 1992 on protecting Lore Lindu National Park in Sulawesi. Around 2000, TNC began to shift toward Kalimantan, establishing the East Kalimantan Program in 2001, initially with a focus on orangutan conservation and support for sustainable logging. In 2002–2003, TNC conducted an "eco-regional assessment" study for East Kalimantan, which led the program to identify four priority sites for conservation, primarily in the neighboring districts of Berau and Kutai Timur, as well as a number of "leverage sites" where TNC would encourage conservation by local governments and partners with limited direct involvement.[1] TNC has subsequently been involved in conservation efforts in Kutai Timur and Berau for nearly two decades, and those conservation programs were an entry point for me to learn about forest governance in East Kalimantan and to explore how the "green development" vision and land-sparing strategies of TNC and its partners touched down in different places.

In retrospect, my fieldwork in 2014–2015 came at an inflection point for Indonesian deforestation. Despite UN conferences, Green Province declarations, and billion-dollar pledges, deforestation had

*Fig. 2. Map of Indonesia showing Kutai Timur (Kutai Tim.) and Berau
Districts in East Kalimantan Province (East Kal.).*

been accelerating since the early 2000s, at the national level and in
East Kalimantan. The year 2014 was just short of 2012 as the worst
for primary forest loss in East Kalimantan since the turn of the century. As I departed Soekarno-Hatta Airport in Jakarta in July 2015,
fires were already burning in Sumatra and Kalimantan in what would
become one of Indonesia's worst fire and haze episodes ever. Millions
of hectares burned, at a total cost to Indonesia of over $16 billion
(about 1.8 percent of the country's GDP), and researchers estimate
that haze from the fires resulted in over 100,000 excess deaths across
Indonesia, Malaysia, and Singapore.[2] Following the 2015 fires, the
government implemented a raft of new policies and deforestation
began to decline. My account is of East Kalimantan in the time just
before the burn, a period that appears through the inflection point
of the fires as an apotheosis of extractive deforestation and the frustration of conservation and land-sparing efforts. In this chapter and
the next, I use my window onto this conjuncture to describe how
extractive institutions persisted in East Kalimantan in the *reformasi*
period, effectively stymieing green modernization projects.

A Destructive Blossoming

Awang Faroek Ishak was the first *bupati* (district head) of Kutai
Timur. The district came into being in 1999, just after the fall of

Suharto, through the breakup of the much larger district of Kutai. Kutai Timur joined a nationwide "blossoming" (*pemekaran*) of new district creation that was, more often than not, an occasion for the creation and capture of new rents. "A new district creates seats in a new legislature, a new district budget, new opportunities to appoint family or friends to civil service positions, and lucrative construction contracts to build new government buildings," Edward Aspinall explains.[3] Indeed, districts blossomed so quickly that the national government imposed a moratorium on new districts in 2009.

If the blossoming of new districts was an opportunity for new rent-seeking, then in a certain sense Kutai Timur was destined for extraction from its birth. Yet an extractive regime governed Kutai Timur's territory long before 1999. Kutai District, from which Kutai Timur was carved, was a center for logging, oil and gas production, and coal mining throughout the twentieth century. The 350,000-hectare Georgia Pacific logging concession was located in present-day Kutai Timur and began operating in 1971. Kaltim Prima Coal was formed in 1982 as a joint venture of the oil and mining multinationals BP and Rio Tinto. In the early 1990s, the company began operating the Sangatta coal mine, an open pit operation with some of the world's largest thermal coal reserves, on the outskirts of the town of Sangatta, which is today the Kutai Timur district seat.

The climate of Kutai Timur, to the south of the Sangkulirang peninsula and its karst escarpments, is somewhat warmer and drier than Berau to the north, and the district experienced earlier and more extensive logging and tree plantation development than its northern neighbor. Plantations and logged forests are more susceptible to fire than primary forest ecosystems, and modified forest areas, once burned, become more vulnerable to future fires. During the 1982–1983 and 1997–1998 El Niño years, fires burned vast areas of Kutai Timur. Rona A. Dennis and Carol P. Colfer found that in a 2,000-square-kilometer study area in Kutai Timur, 70 percent of the forest that burned during the 1982–1983 El Niño had ceased to be forest in 2000. Similarly, Florian Siegert and Anja Hoffmann reported that for a test area of 18,500 square kilometers overlapping present-day Kutai Timur, 71 percent of the area burned during the 1997–1998 El Niño, with the most severe damage occurring in more heavily logged areas and tree plantations.[4] These conflagrations, in other words, were not "natural" disasters—earlier severe droughts in Kalimantan did not result in large fires. Only in the 1980s, after industrial loggers and plantation companies had begun to extensively alter the land cover, were forestlands susceptible to large-scale burning.[5]

As Peter Dauvergne argues forcefully, the fires were

> a disaster that arose naturally from the political economy of Indonesian forest mismanagement. Decades of reckless logging have left wide areas degraded and highly susceptible to fires. To "reforest" these areas, companies lit most of the fires to clear land and establish palm oil, and to a lesser extent, rubber and industrial wood plantations. Government policies and international markets provided incentives for these companies. Corruption assisted and protected them. And indifference, low state capacity, inconsistent and weak responses, and a dry El Nino year fuelled these fires.[6]

The fires served as a propellant for forest conversion: logged and burned-over areas of Kutai Timur became prime sites for the expansion of oil palm and tree fiber plantations.

When in 1999 Kutai Timur became a new district, with Awang as its head, it was one of the richest districts in the country, thanks to royalties from oil and gas production and coal mining. The new bupati wasted no time turning Kutai Timur into a hub of oil palm expansion as well. "Around 2000, Kutai Timur was a new district and there were many new permits, the largest number being for oil palm. As a new district, Kutai Timur wanted to grow quickly," a district forestry official told me during an interview at the Kutai Timur government office complex in 2015.[7] There were strong personal, institutional, and political incentives for officials to accelerate "economic growth." A longtime district official recalled,

> When the district was created, there was a need to speed development. There was the old model of HPH [industrial forest concession] management, but it wasn't very good. . . . Permits [on the concessions] were ending, and

what was left? Sixty percent of the district area that hadn't been managed well. Kutai Timur needed to develop the economy and open new areas. The regulations permitted conversion, so the private sector came in to convert land. There wasn't much land use planning from the government: it was the companies that indicated which places were most appropriate for expansion. Many areas were converted to oil palm.[8]

In the early 2000s, as production from industrial logging concessions in Kutai Timur declined, the provincial and district governments issued large numbers of land-clearing permits (IPK). "Expansion of IPK logging over last few years is directly related to Kutai Timur's plans to become the center of agro-business and agro-industry in East Kalimantan," Obidzinski and Andrianto wrote in 2005. "To accomplish this, the district authorities plan to clear 1.3 million ha of land/forest for large-scale plantations, mainly oil palm. As a result, IPK licenses are continuing to be issued by district authorities (even though the central government regulations prohibit this) and the allocated forest areas to be cleared are large." By 2015, the provincial statistics bureau reported that over 424,000 hectares in Kutai Timur had been planted with oil palm.[9]

A Park, Some Oil Wells, and an Airport

The fate of Kutai National Park shows how even strict legal forest protections are subverted by extractive regimes. The park lies in a coastal, lowland area easily accessible for extraction (especially of timber, oil and gas, and coal) and attractive for settlement and agriculture. Originally established as a game reserve by the Dutch in 1936, Kutai National Park was designated by the national government in 1982 as one of Indonesia's first national parks. The government gazetted an area of 198,629 hectares to the park comprising a highly biodiverse lowland rainforest ecosystem that includes charismatic species such as hornbills, orangutan, and proboscis monkeys.

Oil exploitation within the current park boundaries was initiated by the Dutch during the colonial period, and some early migrants

from Sulawesi settled in the park area in the 1950s and 1960s.[10] With
the start of the logging boom in East Kalimantan in the late 1960s
and 1970s, timber companies operated within the park, while Pertamina, the national oil company, built drilling rigs, and the mining
towns of Sangatta and Bontang grew on the park boundaries and
were eventually connected by a road built across the park in 1991.[11]
The El Niño fires of 1982–1983 and 1997–1998 heavily damaged
the park's forests. Almost the entire area of the park burned in
March and April 1998.

After the division of Kutai District in 1999, the new Kutai Timur government, led by Awang Faroek Ishak, sought to "enclave"
(i.e., excise) an area of the park near the Bontang-Sangatta road that
had been heavily burned and encroached. The Ministry of Forestry
did not fulfill the request at the time, and as Bontang and Sangatta
grew during the 2000s and traffic along the road increased, thousands of migrants settled on park land. As Godwin Limberg and
colleagues explain, "People regarded the area as offering economic
opportunities, and the protected area as offering free land."[12] While
most of the settlers were people of the Bugis ethnic group from Sulawesi, their successful encroachments on the park sparked resent-
ment among Dayak and Kutai groups, who felt land was being given
away to "outsiders," and who responded with their own incursions.[13]
Politicians in Kutai Timur, including Awang, played on the conflicts,
allegedly encouraging encroachments and promising land titles to
gain political support or to profit from private land speculation.[14]

In 2007, Awang weathered corruption accusations surrounding
construction of the Kutai Timur government office complex on his
way to becoming governor of East Kalimantan Province (and first
elected successor to Suwarna Abdul Fatah, who was removed from
the governorship in 2006 for a corruption scheme involving 1 million hectares of illegal oil palm permits).[15] From around this time,
"integrated teams" of district officials, park management, and civil
society began meeting to seek solutions to the land conflicts in the
park. The Kutai Timur district government continued to demand
an enclave of over 24,000 hectares from the park, claiming that the
park was constraining the development of the subdistricts of South
Sangatta and Teluk Pandan, which it overlaps.[16] In the 2010s, the
district government also became fixated on the idea of construct-

ing an airport at Sangkima, which lies within the park. The integrated team and forestry officials agreed to recommend an enclave of 17,000 hectares in a revision to the provincial spatial plan, which must be approved by the National Congress (Dewan Perwakilan Rakyat [DPR]), but the final recommendation from the Ministry of Forestry to the Congress in 2013 was for an enclave of just 7,816 hectares, limited to already settled areas, including the area of the Sangkima airport.

Awang, now governor, threw his weight behind the seventeen-thousand-hectare reduction of the park:

> I told the DPR working group [that visited the park], just look at the conditions on the ground, and the working group visited Teluk Pandan, South Sangatta, and Sangkima, which are in the park. They see that Pertamina is there. It's not possible if they only make an enclave of 7800 ha. . . . If DPR approves (the 17,000 ha enclave), then the plan for the Bontang-Sangatta toll road also won't be a problem. PLN [the electric company] can connect the area to the grid. But I'm sure, in accordance with the reality on the ground, DPR will definitely agree.[17]

Only the more limited enclave of 7,816 hectares was approved. By 2021, the status of the proposed airport lands at Sangkima had still not been resolved, and the district government had begun to shift its airport aspirations to a former logging airstrip in the Bengalon subdistrict north of Sangatta.

Although much of the discourse supporting reduction of the national park focused on the need to develop the southern subdistricts of Kutai Timur and to give tenure security and public services to the population living on park land, after agreement on the enclave was obtained, the Kutai Timur government had no compunction in asserting its priorities. The area around the proposed airport at Sangkima was covered in oil palm planted by local people who had settled on park land. Ismunandar, the bupati of Kutai Timur in 2016–2020, declared there would be no compensation for people who settled or were cultivating land that was formerly part of the national park:

> "That land was property of the national government, and
> after the creation of the enclave, it is now fully owned by
> the government of Kutai Timur, and not individual per-
> sons." ... However, he [Ismunandar] continues, the Kutai
> Timur Government does not want to strong-arm people,
> so it will give compensation for the oil palm trees that are
> already planted. "The district government will be generous
> in giving compensation for people's plantings. However, of
> course it will be done with a different calculus because the
> plantings were made on government land," he said. "For
> people who want to have rights to land, they have to follow
> the proper procedures."[18]

Incidentally, Ismunandar and his wife, who was head of the district
assembly, were arrested in 2020 along with three high-ranking officials from Ismunandar's administration in a bribery scandal related
to infrastructure projects in the district.

For government officials, the destruction and reduction of Kutai
National Park has been a question of their political fortunes and opportunities for extractive expansion and personal enrichment. Rents
would be captured from the construction of an airport as surely as
from any other industrial project in Indonesia, though the airport
may also be desired for the personal convenience of the elites who
would use it, or as part of broader goals for expanding coal mining in
the park area. Migrant agriculturalists have been convenient pawns
in elite maneuvers to reduce the park, but the welfare of the population (as Ismunandar's hypocrisy demonstrates) is not the business
of the extractive regime, and neither they nor government forest
protections could be allowed to stand in the way of a new airport.

Kaltim Green

A year before Awang became governor, the 2007 UN Climate Conference took place in Bali, where REDD was integrated for the first
time into negotiations of the UN Framework Convention on Climate Change. The Bali Conference touched off a wave of REDD
activity in Indonesia and internationally. In East Kalimantan, a

Fig. 3. Pertamina oil company billboard in Kutai National Park along the
Bontang-Sangatta road in Sangkima: "Sangkima Eco-Tourism: Pertamina
EP Sangatta Field is fully committed to the preservation of Kutai National
Park," April 2015. (Author's photo)

provincial REDD working group was already in existence, and after
Awang assumed the governorship in late 2008, TNC and other environmentalist actors encouraged him to enroll East Kalimantan in
the Governors' Climate and Forests Task Force (GCF). GCF had
just been founded in 2008 by a group of U.S. states (California, Illinois, and Wisconsin), Brazilian states (including Mato Grosso and
Pará), and Indonesian provinces (Aceh and Papua) to support the
development of REDD at the subnational level. In 2009, Awang
traveled to California, where he met California governor Arnold
Schwarzenegger and participated in the Governors' Global Climate Summit. Awang's personal website recounted the event: "At
the meeting that last week of September 2009 in Los Angeles (LA),
these two men, each important in his respective region, exchanged
souvenirs. Awang Faroek Ishak gave [Arnold] a red ruby ring from
Kalimantan, while Aarnold [sic] gave Awang Faroek Ishak a position

as the eleventh permanent member of the Governor Climate and Forest (GCF) [Task Force]."[19] This meeting with Schwarzenegger motivated Awang to move forward with a green agenda.[20]

In 2010, Governor Awang convened the district heads and mayors of the province to launch the Green East Kalimantan Declaration, which asserted a commitment to environmentally sustainable development and included a clause "recognizing that global warming is happening that causes global climate change, one of the causes of which is deforestation and forest and land degradation, so it is important to prevent forest destruction and improve the quality of forest through restoration, reforestation, and forest and land rehabilitation."[21] "Kaltim Green" ("Green East Kalimantan") became one of the principal slogans of Awang's administration.[22] When I arrived in the East Kalimantan capital of Samarinda in 2015, the slogan was displayed prominently over the entry to the governor's residence.

The role of oil palm in Kaltim Green was never in doubt: oil palm is green. The key distinction for the governor and his staff, I learned, was between nonrenewable and renewable resources. "Coal and forest exploitation have been too rapid," one of the governor's assistants told me, "and areas were becoming degraded. . . . The economy was just oil and gas, coal, and forestry, but these will decline. We need to build renewable, sustainable production."[23] Agriculture was foremost among these renewable sectors, a provincial planning official affirmed to me a couple weeks later, but "agriculture alone can't go very far in replacing oil and gas. There must be processing of renewable resources. For example, palm oil processing must go beyond CPO [crude palm oil] to downstream industries, and coal should be used for petrochemicals."[24] In this way, provincial officials articulated a vision for economic transition from extractive, primary commodity exports to productivist, value-added manufacturing: "We want the province's potential to be realized here," said the governor's assistant.[25] An interesting effect of this discourse is that it renders further coal mining and especially palm oil production justified, and even necessary, but it asserts that these sectors will now be productivist and not extractive. Of course, should value-added industry never materialize, the effect is simply to sanction further extraction under a discourse of productivist development.

In order to limit deforestation for the "renewable" plantation sectors, Awang and his officials called for land sparing. They argued that tree fiber plantations should be expanded to avoid clearing of natural forest areas, suggesting that high-yield fiber plantations could help meet wood demand and reduce deforestation.[26] (Forestry scientists have found, however, that reduced-impact logging of natural forests can be more effective at preserving biodiversity and producing timber than industrial tree plantations, and tradeoffs between logging and fiber plantations are not well captured by a simplistic logic of "forest sparing.")[27] Arguments for agricultural intensification to protect forest land also figured in East Kalimantan's "Environmentally Sustainable Development Strategy," developed between the provincial government and the National Council on Climate Change. The strategy called for boosting yields of smallholder agriculture while limiting the use of fire, and in the plantation sector for "productivity gains to replace some expansion of [oil palm] concessions."[28] The idea that more efficient and higher-yield oil palm plantations could reduce deforestation was embraced by the government's international partners as well: a longtime Indonesian employee of GIZ, the German cooperation program, emphasized in an interview over coffee at a mall in Samarinda that "Indonesia can double its palm oil production without converting forest."[29]

More prominent than arguments for agricultural intensification, land-use intensification was heavily promoted by government officials, local academics, and NGO actors, who called for identifying degraded lands and siting new plantations in degraded areas to avoid deforestation. East Kalimantan's Regional Climate Change Council, an ad-hoc government policy forum, undertook to map degraded or "critical" lands in the province according to biological, chemical, and physical criteria, and in a message to a provincial-level seminar in 2015, Awang declared that there were 7.9 million hectares of degraded land in the province, which would represent roughly two-thirds of the total provincial land area.[30] Similarly, a provincial discussion document on "optimizing land use management" stated that "areas with high carbon values need to be identified and prioritized for conservation," while simultaneously highlighting the need to "ease productive access to degraded land" and noting that "there is a large amount of degraded land in [the] forestry estate that are [*sic*] suitable for oil palm."[31]

As Jun Borras and Jennifer Franco note, however, in their discussion of land grabbing in the Global South, lands classified as "degraded" are rarely empty or unused (despite being perceived as such by government and corporate planners), and advocating for plantation expansion on degraded lands reframes plantation expansion as an essentially positive development model that simply needs to be properly "managed."[32] In Indonesia, where the Dutch appropriated forest and fallow land as "wasteland" under the Domain Declaration, arguments asserting the availability of ample degraded land for corporate plantation expansion have a particularly charged historical resonance. A 2010 letter-writer to the *Jakarta Post* put the matter bluntly: "The term 'degraded' is synonymous with idle, marginal, unproductive, empty or wasted, and is derived from the similar colonial concept and model."[33]

In practice, there were multiple obstacles to redirecting plantation expansion to "degraded" lands. Land swaps to shift existing plantation permits from forests to degraded areas were so administratively complex that most people I spoke with considered them unviable.[34] With existing permits already a loss, the focus would have to be on siting new plantations on degraded lands. While plantation expansion on degraded lands as opposed to forests could have substantial environmental benefits, degraded lands were not generally found in contiguous areas of sufficient size for plantations. Additionally, there were high transaction and regulatory costs for securing concessions on degraded lands since they were often subject to multiple and overlapping land claims, and there were fewer opportunities for rent extraction when opening plantations on degraded lands, since in many cases plantation companies would use profits from timber sales from forest clearing to finance plantation establishment (if they intended to establish a plantation at all). The political-economic incentives were still heavily geared toward deforestation.

In 2013, at the same time that he was pushing for the reduction of Kutai National Park, Awang declared a moratorium on new logging, mining, and plantation concessions in East Kalimantan, ostensibly to give time to inventory and evaluate existing concessions.

Concession permits are issued at the district level but then require a provincial recommendation for approval. The moratorium on new concessions should in principle have laid the groundwork for a provincial land-use transformation, but in practice it did little to slow the expansion of mining or plantations into forested areas. When the moratorium was issued, 2.4 million hectares of the province had already been permitted for oil palm, while only 1 million had so far been planted.[35] As one of the governor's staff observed, "Permits have been pretty much fully issued over East Kalimantan's territory, so now we have a moratorium."[36] Kaltim Green could thus boast no new permits for deforestation, even as vast areas could still be cleared under existing permits for mining and oil palm plantations, in addition to whatever expansion occurred on ostensibly degraded lands. Even then, the bupati of Kutai Timur at the time, Awang's former deputy Isran Noor, sent a letter of protest to the governor, arguing that the moratorium on new mining concessions would reduce district revenue.[37]

A Value-Added Fig Leaf

As for that other piece of the productivist transition, the development of value-added manufacturing, the provincial government launched a new megaproject: construction of a major port facility and creation of a Special Economic Zone at Maloy (KIPI Maloy) in Kutai Timur. Maloy was included in the national government's 2011 Master Plan for the Acceleration and Expansion of Indonesia's Economic Development, which called for massive investments in infrastructure, natural resource sectors, and agro-industry (while initially omitting any consideration of environmental goals). Officials promoted Maloy as a future hub for palm oil, biodiesel, and petrochemical industries that would help spur development in a new part of the province, rather than reinforcing the existing centers of Bontang, Samarinda, and Balikpapan.[38] It was hard not to see a pork barrel, however, in the proposal for massive industrial development in Awang's home district. Awang's moratorium on new permits, meanwhile, included an exception allowing new oil palm concessions that would support the development of KIPI Maloy. One of my interviewees alleged that Awang and his cronies had bought up the land around Maloy on speculation, and that Awang was also involved in land speculation around Kutai National Park, where road projects linked to the Maloy corridor would pass.[39]

Whether or not Awang was involved, megaprojects provide massive opportunities for speculation and corruption. What the project has so far failed to provide is any kind of tangible industrial development. In 2021, eight years after the Maloy project was formally inaugurated, it is well known to local residents, according to a reporter, "not because it's going to become a special economic zone, but as a fishing spot."[40] The roads are barely passable, and private investment has yet to materialize, but provincial officials continue to propagate the myth of Maloy as a hub of private investment and economic transformation.[41] It is a boondoggle, yes, and also a fig leaf for the unchanged business of coal and palm oil extraction.

"Awang declared 'Kaltim Green,' but you can't find it in the regulations," an environmental lawyer told me in 2015, "it's just a slogan."[42] And yet East Kalimantan appeared to be one of the most promising places for forest conservation to succeed in Indonesia. Despite decades of timber and fossil-fuel extraction, East Kalimantan in the 2000s still had substantial remaining forest cover.[43] It had a history of involvement with environmental NGOs, research groups, and bilateral cooperation programs stretching back to the early 1990s. In 2009, it became a member of GCF. Germany's FORCLIME project and TNC's Berau Forest Carbon Program, both in East Kalimantan, were designated by the Ministry of Forestry as two of Indonesia's four official REDD demonstration activities. In 2010, East Kalimantan declared itself a Green Province, and in 2013 Awang imposed a moratorium on new concessions. And during all this time, deforestation accelerated. "Kaltim has been an early adopter of ideas [such as REDD], but slow in implementation," mused an Indonesian who had worked for many years with the German cooperation program in the province. "Before COP13 in Bali we already had a REDD task force, but now on the ground [in 2015] not that much has changed. This phenomenon in itself is political."[44] The phenomenon is political, and it is institutional. Among Awang Faroek Ishak, his provincial officials, environmental NGOs, and international organizations, certainly many if not all were genuinely committed to transforming East Kalimantan from an extractive periphery to a hub of green development. Instead, East Kalimantan's forests were cleared to funnel resources to the productivist core: plywood to Japan, coal to South Korea, palm oil to Europe. Green visions wrecked against an extractive regime with a four-hundred-year legacy.

CHAPTER THREE

Losing the Forest,
Sparing the Trees

ERAU WAS IN MANY respects the most promising district in Indonesia for reining in large-scale deforestation. Not only is it located in East Kalimantan, the self-declared Green Province, but Berau is also the site of a district-level REDD program launched in 2009. Berau had been largely spared the massive El Niño fires that swept across Kutai Timur in the 1980s and 1990s, and as of 2001, primary forests still covered 79 percent of the district (compared to just 31 percent in Kutai Timur), including some of the largest remaining areas of intact lowland forest in Indonesian Borneo. Berau had not been immune to industrial extraction, but it had also been home to international forest conservation programs since the 1990s. If anywhere could transition from extraction to green development, it should have been Berau.

Ruled by a sultanate from the fourteenth century to the early eighteenth century, Berau was then divided under influence of the Dutch into the Sultanate of Sambaliung and the Sultanate of Gunung Tabur, whose wooden palaces lie across the river from each other in what is today Tanjung Redeb, the district seat. Coal mining in Berau began during the 1800s under the sultanates and continued under the Dutch during the first half of the twentieth century.[1] Mining lapsed after Indonesian independence, and Berau's export economy turned to timber, with the allocation of the first large-scale logging permit in the district in 1969.

Major actors in the timber sector included government-owned PT Inhutani I, which in 2015 controlled over 300,000 hectares in the district and during the 1990s controlled as much as 530,000. Companies linked to Suharto's crony Bob Hasan included the Astra Group, which controlled 140,000 hectares through the concessions of PT Sumalindo Lestari Jaya, and the Kalimanis Group, which controlled over 300,000 hectares of logging concessions as well as nearly 200,000 hectares permitted for tree fiber plantations to support the group's Kiani Kertas pulp mill, which came on line in 1997.[2] Kiani Kertas was an exemplary boondoggle of the New Order extractive regime. The mill received heavy subsidies from the Suharto government, including $100 million from the Reforestation Fund, and there was widespread diversion of funds into private hands during mill construction. Tree fiber plantations to supply the mill also received support from the Reforestation Fund, but large areas were never planted, and the concessions served instead as cover for timber extraction. The mill virtually never operated above half capacity and suffered frequent shutdowns.[3] After the fall of Suharto and Bob Hasan's imprisonment, Kiani Kertas faced severe financial problems linked to the overall liabilities of the Kalimanis Group. The mill was sold in 2004 to a consortium led by military and government officials but remained paralyzed by legal and financial problems, and by the time I arrived in Berau, it was effectively shuttered.

By the 2010s, Berau's economy was driven first and foremost by coal. Industrial coal mining resumed under PT Berau Coal in 1983 and expanded significantly during the 1990s. In 2002, mining accounted for roughly a third of the gross regional domestic product, and by 2014 it accounted for nearly two-thirds.[4] A steady stream of coal barges ply the waterfront in Tanjung Redeb, and flying into the district airport, the plane approaches over a chain of open mining pits. Direct deforestation for mining is limited (although indirect deforestation linked to mining can be many times greater than forest loss within concessions), and oil palm was the primary direct driver of increasing deforestation in Berau after 2001.[5] Plantation expansion accelerated dramatically after 2005, and by 2015 the district had 115,000 hectares planted in oil palm.[6] During a meeting over tea and fried snacks at the district Plantations Agency (Dinas Perkebunan) in 2015, officials informed me and a fellow researcher that roughly 300,000 hectares had already been permitted for oil palm, and they viewed the provincial moratorium on new permits as temporary, noting that provincial development plans had asked Berau to allocate even more area for plantations.[7]

Even as the industrial frontier of timber extraction and land conversion expanded in Berau, the district was the site of a number of high-profile forest conservation programs. The STREK (Silvicultural Techniques for the Regeneration of Logged-Over Forests in East Kalimantan) forest regeneration study began in 1989 through a collaboration with French researchers in Inhutani's Labanan concession. (Ironically, while STREK comprised one of the foremost long-term studies of tropical forest regeneration, parts of the STREK plots were damaged in the *reformasi* logging boom after 1998.)[8] In 1996–2002, the EU-funded Berau Forest Management Project (BFMP) conducted forest management research and attempted to support a multi-stakeholder "model forest" management body in the district, even developing a concept for forest carbon trading under the nascent Clean Development Mechanism of the Kyoto Protocol.[9] While an Inhutani manager told me that BFMP may have helped the company develop a "social management" approach in its concessions, most actors working on forest conservation in Berau at the time of my research saw little impact from the project. "BFMP was a good project, there was lots of money, but it was lost," recalled an informant who had worked on forestry in Berau for over two decades. "Whatever they set up, it's not left in the field. There wasn't really ownership with Inhutani and the district government."[10] "The approach of BFMP was hiring European consultants and making studies, but there was not much impact," a former TNC staffer confirmed, but he noted that TNC used BFMP's reports when they set about designing the Berau Forest Carbon Project roughly five years later.[11]

Berau Goes REDD

From its launch in 2009, Berau's district-level REDD program aimed to reduce deforestation by transitioning the district to a pro-

ductivist "green economy." Six years later, the mining and plantation sectors were virtually absent from the program while multiple
activities aimed to reduce deforestation in upland villages by controlling shifting cultivation and intensifying village land use. These
projects in many cases delivered tangible benefits to villagers and
might succeed in reducing their forest clearing. Focusing on village
land use without attending to the massive industrial deforestation
of the landscape, however, seemed quite literally to miss the forest
for the trees. Why did the transformative land-sparing logics of Berau's REDD program take hold at the village level but not across
the broader political economy of the district? What stymied Berau's
green development?

When the 2007 Bali Climate Conference touched off a new
wave of REDD programs, TNC decided to build on its presence in
Berau to launch a REDD pilot program in the district. TNC formed
working groups with partners including the Ministry of Forestry,
an Indonesian NGO, an environmental consultancy, and the World
Agroforestry Centre to develop the technical aspects of the Berau
Forest Carbon Program (BFCP). As a number of informants noted,
the commitment of the district government to BFCP was never more
than lukewarm. Makmur, the bupati of Berau from 2005 to 2015, was
opposed to carbon trading because of the failure of a previous attempt to develop a Clean Development Mechanism forest project in
Berau. TNC promoted REDD to the bupati as a way of improving
district forest governance, eventually securing his assent, if not enthusiastic support.[12] "TNC went deep in Berau, but never had clear
champions there," according to a former TNC staff member.[13]

The plan initially called for BFCP to be funded by a multi-donor
trust fund and overseen by a steering committee, with TNC participating as a donor and steering committee member. TNC was unable to attract donors for the trust fund, however, so "TNC now had
a big design and no money and had to change the implementation
concept," one of BFCP's architects recalled.[14] Thus, around 2009,
TNC decided to "put all its eggs in the Berau basket" and go "all in
on REDD and Berau," reallocating resources to the district and at-
tracting donors to support particular programs.[15] Funding for BFCP
subsequently came from sources including the Anne Ray Charitable
Trust (created by Cargill heiress Margaret A. Cargill), the Bank of

America Foundation, the Grantham Foundation (Jeremy Grantham sat on the TNC Board of Directors), the Norwegian government, the Boeing Foundation, and Xerox.

BFCP's objective was nothing less than a transformation of the district political economy from extractive resource degradation to productivist green development. In his preface to the 2011–2015 BFCP Strategic Plan, Bupati Makmur wrote,

> This program is designed to achieve a sustainable forestry and natural resources management in the District of Berau. With this program, it is expected that the District of Berau can achieve its development goals and manage its natural resources sustainably. We believe that this program carries a positive relevancy in our effort to jointly save the earth from further destruction, which impact is already starting to be felt by us. . . . This is Berau's support to the world.

The eco-modernist framework underlying the bupati's statement is clear: development and sustainability are compatible, and proper management can save the planet. The document is also explicit regarding the magnitude of the transition envisioned by the project. "The District Government of Berau is determined to change the course of its development," the plan reads, "through transformation in its governance of natural resources, strengthening institutions, and capacity building of human resources," and the document goes on to outline a comprehensive framework of "enabling conditions" and "site-based investments" to realize this transformation.[16]

The Nature Conservancy's BFCP activities comprised a combination of these enabling conditions and site-based components. Its work on enabling conditions concentrated on building up the jurisdictional REDD program, including carbon accounting, support for the district REDD working group and BFCP steering committee, and engagement with government policy and planning processes. TNC's other activities focused on endangered species (particularly orangutans), protected areas, corporate engagement (especially with logging concessions), and community-based natural resource management.[17] Work in these areas included projects related to enabling conditions, such as research on reduced-impact logging methods, but the bulk of these activities were site-based, including work in the Sangkulirang karsts for protected areas and orangutan conservation, and support for Forest Stewardship Council certification and collaborative forest management in corporate logging concessions. Finally, TNC's work on community-based natural resource management involved intensive work with two Dayak villages, on the basis of which TNC developed a methodology for community engagement in REDD called SIGAP-REDD+.[18]

Alongside its own heavy investment in BFCP, TNC successfully encouraged Germany's bilateral cooperation programs (GIZ and KfW, the German national development bank) to select Berau as one of the target districts for their Forests and Climate Change Programme (FORCLIME). FORCLIME, like TNC, aimed to develop REDD readiness and demonstration activities, although its field activities operated only in western Berau, whereas TNC took a "wall-to-wall REDD" jurisdictional approach.[19] FORCLIME began work in Berau around 2010 on activities including capacity development for the Berau Forest Management Unit within the district Forestry Agency, sustainable logging practices and Forest Stewardship Council certification in the Sumalindo Lestari Jaya IV concession, and "alternative livelihood" development with villages in the Sumalindo and Inhutani I Labanan timber concessions. These livelihood activities, which launched in 2013–2014, aimed to provide alternative sources of subsistence and income through agroforestry and intensified rice production so that communities would reduce forest clearing for shifting cultivation.[20]

TNC leveraged their community strategy, meanwhile, packaged as SIGAP-REDD+, to secure funding for BFCP within a U.S. government Tropical Forest Conservation Act debt-for-nature swap. Debt-for-nature swaps are run through the U.S. Treasury and U.S. Agency for International Development, and initially focused on protected areas. Around 2009, however, Treasury personnel were interested in incorporating climate change issues into the program and contributing to REDD, according to a TNC director at the organization's headquarters.[21] TNC pitched its SIGAP approach and managed to forge an agreement with fellow international environmental NGO WWF to manage the debt-for-nature program in Kalimantan. TNC would focus on implementation in Berau and WWF would focus on Kutai Barat in East Kalimantan and Kapuas Hulu in West Kalimantan, where it had ongoing programs.

Through this debt-for-nature swap, TNC secured $10 million for BFCP for 2013–2017, which it used to fund local organizations to replicate SIGAP-REDD+ in villages across Berau.

SIGAP is based on the experiences of the two "model" villages of Gunung Madu and Long Kelay, where TNC piloted community REDD projects.[22] The villages are located in forest landscapes in the Kelay River watershed, and each consists of a collection of wooden homes and community buildings, with concrete pathways traversed by people, dogs, chickens, and motorbikes. In the mid-2010s, each village was home to between thirty and sixty households who practiced a variety of livelihood activities in the surrounding village territory, including gold mining, fishing, wage labor for logging companies, and farming through shifting cultivation.

A primary strategy for reducing deforestation in these villages was reducing forest clearing for shifting cultivation (also known as swidden) in favor of more intensive land-use strategies, including limiting swidden to previously cleared areas and establishing permanent rubber gardens. Swidden, or shifting cultivation with fire, has for centuries been a dominant component of agricultural systems across much of the tropics. In upland Borneo, swidden systems center on dry rice production. Generally, a household selects a forested area of roughly one hectare for cultivation, and trees and brush are felled and then burned to enhance soil fertility. The swidden plot (called *ladang* in Indonesian) is cultivated in rice for one or several years, often intercropped with or succeeded by other useful species such as chili, cassava, or banana, and the plot is then fallowed for a period of usually not less than five years. Fruit trees and hardwoods are often tended in the fallows. When sufficient time has passed to restore fertility and reduce the population of weeds and agricultural pests, the plot may again be cleared and returned to cultivation.[23] These swidden plots and fallows are traditionally controlled by the household that originally cultivated them, or by descendants of the original cultivators.

In late 2013, TNC signed conditional grant agreements with Gunung Madu and Long Kelay. The initial grant to the communities, 239 million rupiah each (about $20,000) for the first year of the agreement, included support for forest patrols and forest management, rubber cultivation, chicken raising, vegetable gardening, honey production, fish farming, and capacity building, among other activities. In exchange, villagers agreed to "strengthening the enabling conditions" and "[climate change] mitigation and management of natural resources."[24] Enabling conditions generally related to village financial management and capacity building, while under mitigation and management, villagers agreed to carry out forest patrols and biodiversity and ecotourism surveys, and to limit their practice of shifting cultivation. Villagers agreed to open not more than one hectare per household per year of ladang, and only to open ladang in fallows as opposed to in new forest areas. In Gunung Madu, villagers committed to a maximum of four ladang plots per household (active or fallowed), for a total of four hectares of swidden land each, while in Long Kelay the community agreed to a maximum of seven ladang per household (active or fallowed), totaling seven hectares of swidden land. TNC additionally assisted each village in the development of a village land-use plan, specifying areas for settlement, swidden farming, rubber gardens, agroforestry, and reserve land.

These community agreements thus sought to engineer a land-sparing transition at the village level. Where prior to the agreements villagers would predominantly open ladang in new forest areas, they should now only open ladang in fallows, and permanent rubber gardens and small-animal husbandry would help offset the need for new swidden clearing.[25] This approach combined land-use intensification, by directing swidden clearing to fallow land, and agricultural intensification, by incentivizing permanent cropping over shifting cultivation. A similar village-level land-sparing logic informed FORCLIME's "alternative livelihoods" activities, and the debt-for-nature implementation plan likewise envisioned "supporting intensification of production, increasing use of degraded land for economic activities, and increasing the degree of local processing to capture downstream benefits within the district," a productivist recipe for "forest-related green economic development."[26]

To Stop Swiddening While the World Burns

In practice, Berau's REDD activities worked to transform the political economy of rural development through land sparing, but at the village level. Yet swidden agriculture as traditionally practiced in

Dayak communities is not extractive. It produces primarily subsistence products for household consumption; it maintains high levels of biodiversity, carbon sequestration, and forest cover; and its extent is limited by the availability of household labor. Nonetheless, BFCP "alternative livelihoods" projects suggested that village agriculture needed to be modernized and intensified, at the same time as the modern, industrial land uses responsible for the vast majority of deforestation continued unchecked. What explains this diversion of land-sparing principles?

Recent efforts to limit swidden and encourage production of permanent cash crops like rubber are only the latest in a long history of efforts to control and intensify swidden livelihoods. James Scott describes at length the struggle of Southeast Asian states to fix shifting cultivators and other upland populations in the landscape and to make their livelihoods legible to state systems of territorial control, economic production, and taxation.[27] In Borneo, traditional swidden lands became part of the national forest estate, along with most of the rest of Kalimantan, under the Basic Forestry Law of 1967, and subsequent commercial logging and "development" schemes involved the relocation and sedentarization of many upland groups. Nancy Peluso describes how the Suharto regime promoted smallholder rubber production in Kalimantan as a strategy to tame "wild" shifting cultivators into "governable citizen-subjects" who were "dependent on the market and on the central government."[28] Environmentalist efforts to limit swidden thus dovetail neatly with historical efforts to govern upland populations and control their livelihood activities. While most government and NGO employees I spoke with in Berau did not view swidden as a major environmental problem, many nonetheless saw reforming swidden as desirable and progressive. For example, both a FORCLIME employee and a district REDD coordinator claimed that ladang is the largest source of *illegal* deforestation in Berau, since conversion for plantations and mining occurs under government licenses.[29] This "illegality" of ladang speaks to government efforts to suppress shifting cultivation and facilitates the confluence of government and NGO interests in making ladang "more effective" in the words of a local NGO director, or offering "alternative economies" in the words of the REDD coordinator.[30]

Meanwhile, the oil palm, tree fiber, and mining sectors were conspicuously absent from BFCP. For TNC, engagement with the oil palm sector was delayed in part by changes in BFCP organization and negotiations with funders, a staffer explained to me, but they also lacked a model for reining in plantation-driven deforestation. They had found that "land swaps," where an oil palm company would trade forested areas within its concession for degraded areas within the forest estate, were not feasible in Berau because most logging concessions were still active and there was little degraded forest estate land suitable for oil palm.[31] Limiting oil palm expansion was also politically sensitive given the centrality of oil palm to district and provincial development plans and the payoffs that district officials received from palm oil companies. In 2015, TNC launched a "Sustainable Palm Oil" program with four years of funding from the German Federal Environment Ministry. The program would promote land sparing through land-use intensification by seeking to direct new oil palm plantations toward degraded lands, among other goals.[32] A TNC manager acknowledged, however, that the oil palm sector had been a major gap in their Berau program up to that time.[33]

The focus of land-sparing efforts at the village level through control of swidden, and the failure to control industrial deforestation, show how extractive institutions stymie productivist green development initiatives, even in a "best case" district like Berau. Swidden control gained traction because it was compatible with extractive interests: government officials, NGOs, and concessionaires could all agree on limiting the areas used by forest dwellers while turning them into rubber producers for industrial commodity chains. Rubber-producing villagers become more profitable to global capital, while less land under shifting cultivation means more land for industry—the windfall profits of extraction continue unchecked. Both provincial and district officials viewed "renewable" plantations, however, as the key to economic development, and they had no intention of limiting the overall expansion of plantations in favor of forest conservation. A TNC manager told me matter-of-factly, "BFCP doesn't mean there will be no deforestation. We need to take into account the district development plan. With APL [land zoned for agriculture], it's just a matter of time before they convert it to mining or oil palm. If we had shown up and said, 'You can't have any more clearing,' we would have been kicked out of Berau long ago."[34] Apparently, then, Berau's green transition would have to be compatible with large-scale deforestation.

There is an additional pitfall to focusing on swidden in a sea of oil palm. When you spare the trees and lose the forest, you eventually lose the trees as well. Expanding plantations appropriate Dayak lands, driving speculative forest clearing and land conflicts within and between villages. Long Kelay residents had boundary conflicts with a neighboring village that had been established around 2008 by Dayaks driven from Kutai Timur, partly by land conflicts caused by oil palm concessions. Gunung Madu villagers also had ongoing boundary disputes with a neighboring village, which were exacerbated by the establishment of an oil palm plantation that limited the neighboring village's forest area. Members of both communities would open new swiddens in contested areas to claim land for cultivation and to hedge against further oil palm expansion. Communities have few options for resisting plantations, but those whose ladang or tree gardens are taken by a concession may be able to claim compensation from the company. Gunung Madu villagers feared that if neighboring villagers continued to clear in their forest area, it would be rezoned for conversion to oil palm, and the village government would have no authority to prevent it. By making clearings of their own in the contested area now, they might at least receive compensation if the land was expropriated by a plantation. Following these logics, several Gunung Madu households cleared new forest land in the disputed area, in violation of the village agreement with TNC.[35] Similar speculative clearing by Gunung Madu villagers was said to have occurred in response to a coal company survey some time before. In short, village-level land sparing is undermined by landscape-level industrial extraction. The village cannot be separated from its surroundings.

A Green Dream Deferred

Without leverage or a clear strategy to restrain extractive deforestation, environmentalist actors forged a land-sparing coalition in Be-

rau focused on controlling swidden agriculture to limit deforestation and promote economic development. Industrial deforestation
dwarfs forest loss in swidden systems and undermines village-level
land sparing, however. Even villages that pursue a "green development" pathway are challenged by landscape-level forest fragmentation (which affects biodiversity and species abundance), hydrological and regional climatic changes caused by large-scale forest loss,
and socioeconomic transformations that trigger resource conflicts
and drive speculative deforestation. The inclusion of an oil palm
program in BFCP has not reversed the juggernaut of deforestation
rolling across the district. In 2005–2009, the five years leading up to
the launch of BFCP, Berau lost an average of 89 square kilometers
of primary forest every year. In 2010–2014, the first five years of
the program, average annual primary forest loss nearly doubled, to
166 square kilometers per year. In the next five years, 2015–2019,
primary deforestation accelerated still further, to 186 square kilometers annually.[36] From 2010 to 2019, the first decade of Berau's
green economic transition, the district lost 1,764 square kilometers
of primary forest.

The failure to reduce deforestation in this best-case district in
a best-case province demonstrates the power and persistence of extraction as a political-economic regime. District officials were firmly
entrenched in this regime, where Indonesia's legacy of extraction
filtered through the heritage of the Berau sultanates into a district
government that many of my interlocutors described as hierarchi-
cal, nepotistic, and exclusive. "There's all sorts of deals going on [in
Berau]," a former TNC manager explained. "TNC wanted to get a
deal for conservation. . . . Berau is happy to have the profile and pub-
licity [of BFCP] and to have TNC spending money, but until you
show success, it's hard to get them fully on board."[37] FORCLIME
was viewed more favorably than TNC, some suggested, because
FORCLIME funneled its funds through the government bureaucracy, whereas in the case of TNC, "district officials see, 'oh, TNC
has this money, but it doesn't go to us.'"[38] FORCLIME's financial
coziness with the district government did not make them much more
effective in changing the course of district development, however.
As one former FORCLIME employee recounted, "FORCLIME
shares with DPRD [the local assembly] and the bupati, and they're

enthusiastic, especially about supporting communities with short-term investments, but then they carry out contradictory activities, such as giving APL [land outside the forest estate] over to oil palm. It's the same everywhere."[39]

In the rapidly expanding plantation and mining sectors, the predominance of extraction was clear. "The problem is that oil palm is massive," the same FORCLIME employee lamented, "Oil palm is from the government, so we can't do anything to stop it."[40] TNC staff recounted that when in 2011 or 2012 TNC supported villagers in the Segah watershed to oppose an oil palm concession in the region, the bupati became furious and nearly kicked TNC out of Berau.[41] Since then, the oil palm company had courted some village leaders with money and travel, and succeeded in turning some of them against forest conservation.[42] Concession permits, meanwhile, were a major source of rents for government officials. One informant reported that for an oil palm permit, a company had to pay 25 million rupiah ($2,000) each to nine different people, with the bupati also receiving a cut. Another claimed that district candidates spend at least 10 billion rupiah ($770,000) to get elected, so "once they are elected, they are thinking about returning their investment through natural resource permits [bribery] and district budget markups [overbilling]." This corruption is endemic across the extractive sectors. Officials from the district Forestry Agency allegedly used to demand 300 million rupiah ($23,000) from companies to approve their yearly harvest plans, though since the large-scale timber concessions have declined, the head of the agency reportedly asked a company for only "'modest' bribes, because times are harder now." Informants say that if a company were not to pay bribes, it would not have its permits approved and would be investigated by the district agencies, a process that would be expensive and time-consuming for the company.[43]

Berau's natural resources were generating vast wealth that flowed to companies, shareholders, corrupt officials, and importing economies, degrading the district environment and dispossessing local people with virtually no reinvestment in the district economy. Coal mining was exemplary in this respect. PT Berau Coal provided career opportunities for its employees, many of whom were from other parts of Indonesia, and a corporate social responsibility

(CSR) "slush fund" for the district, but as a company CSR officer stated candidly, "CSR is a strategy to keep operations going and avoid social conflict."[44] As coal was wrested from pits in Berau for boilers in China and the Philippines, hundreds of millions of dollars flowed to the politically connected Bakrie family or to financier Nat Rothschild, and hundreds of millions more were embezzled away.[45] Capital accumulates in Jakarta and London and carbon dioxide accumulates in the atmosphere, leading to more extreme El Niño droughts, more severe fires in Kalimantan, and more deforestation. Meanwhile, between 2006 and 2010, U.S.-based Merrill Lynch arranged buyouts and financing deals for Berau Coal that returned over $1 billion to investors and helped Berau mine millions more tonnes of coal per year. Merrill then advertised its efforts to address global climate change with a $300,000 donation to the Berau Forest Carbon Program.[46] The math speaks for itself.

Erik Meijaard's 2015 letter in the *Jakarta Globe* gave voice to the frustration of conservation under Indonesia's extractive regimes: protected areas and conservation laws were ineffective, government was corrupt, and financial interests overruled environmental law. "We don't need more laws, new laws, or changed laws," Meijaard affirmed. "We need a new system." Until then, "The whole environmental conservation mission in Indonesia is failing in its objectives, year in, year out"—four hundred years of extraction.[47]

Green at Last?

I N THE AFTERMATH OF the 2015 fire and haze disaster, Indonesian president Joko Widodo ("Jokowi") moved quickly to prevent future fires, especially on peat soils that were a major source of smoke and carbon emissions. Among other measures, Jokowi established a Peatland Restoration Agency with a mandate to restore millions of hectares of degraded peatlands, issued a moratorium on peat swamp draining, and threatened to demote military and police officials who failed to control fires in their regions, while the Ministry of Environment and Forestry sought to fine companies for fires in their concessions. Pushback came from parliament, where legislators advanced a bill allowing oil palm expansion on peatlands; from corporations, industry associations, and a Sumatran labor union that fought fines and regulations in the courts; and from officials such as the governor of West Kalimantan Province, who despite his membership in the Governors' Climate and Forests Task Force wrote to Jokowi asking him to allow tree fiber plantations to continue draining peatlands. This resistance from a strong extractive coalition notwithstanding, fires have been more effectively controlled and primary deforestation has declined. In this new wave of government regulation and reform and corporate zero-deforestation commitments, some analysts have seen a "bright spot" of hope for forests.[1]

Jokowi has matched new policies with a discourse of green development drawing on ecological modernization and land-sparing logics, particularly in the oil palm sector. After issuing a three-year moratorium on new oil palm plantation licenses in 2018, Jokowi delivered a speech at the annual meeting of the Indonesian Palm Oil Association (Gapki), calling on producers to use more advanced technologies to increase their productivity, saying, "This is important, so that palm oil does not continuously come under fire from NGOs, or from the left, from the right, from above or from below. Sustainability is really the one aspect that needs serious attention."[2] The president also highlighted the government's replanting program, launched in 2017, which aims to provide oil palm smallholders with higher quality seeds. Indonesia's palm oil production contributes to the UN Sustainable Development Goals, Jokowi told the conference, and "palm oil is the most suitable vegetable oil to meet the world's needs because of its efficiency in land use and productivity."[3] Efficient and productive oil palm plantations would feed downstream domestic industries. "We want crude palm oil to become processed goods. Why not? Or jet fuel or cosmetics, soap," said Jokowi in a 2019 interview, where he asserted that Indonesia should follow Germany's and China's successes in developing their domestic industries. "The direction we're going is we want to build a semi-processed or processed goods industry or downstream industry. No longer raw materials, we want added values," Jokowi affirmed.[4]

Does this rhetoric of sustainability, efficiency, and value-added investment mean that Indonesia is shifting at last from extraction to productivist development? Will it move like China from the periphery toward the capitalist core, buoyed by a land-sparing combination of forest conservation and agro-industrial growth? Large-scale political-economic transformation takes time, and it is too soon to know whether new policies and declining deforestation will endure. A number of countervailing forces suggest that Indonesia's extractive regimes are largely intact, however, and there is much more deforestation still to come. The government biofuel mandate is perhaps the most troubling. Concerns over deforestation for oil palm led the EU to alter its renewable energy directive in 2018 to begin phasing out palm oil–based biofuel, prompting both Indonesia and Malaysia to challenge the restrictions at the World Trade Organization. In the meantime, Indonesia launched a biodiesel transition program to blend palm oil biodiesel into conventional diesel fuel, a move calculated to reduce crude oil imports while propping up demand for palm oil in the face of low prices and environmentalist restrictions. From a mandate of 20 percent palm biodiesel for diesel fuel in 2018 (B20), Indonesia moved to a 30 percent blend (B30) in 2020, with plans to reach B50 by 2025.

The problem with this plan is that replacing Indonesia's conventional diesel consumption with palm oil biodiesel will require millions of hectares of new oil palm plantations. The Indonesian think tank Traction Energy Asia estimated that with Indonesia's low-yield plantations and ratcheting biodiesel targets, demand would outstrip supply by 2023. "This biodiesel program was initially created to absorb excess crude palm oil production, but unfortunately it has become a boomerang as the [biodiesel blend] target kept being increased. What was initially an oversupply will become a deficit," one of the researchers told the environmental news site *Mongabay*.[5] Efforts to increase plantation productivity have fallen short of their targets, while rising palm oil prices have made biodiesel increasingly expensive, forcing the government to allocate hundreds of millions of dollars in subsidies to keep the fuel competitive and driving massive losses for the state-run energy company Pertamina, now a vehicle for Indonesia's biodiesel ambitions.[6] As Hans Nicholas Jong notes,

> A key reason the replanting program [to increase yields] has fallen short is because its funding, raised through mandatory export tariffs slapped on palm oil companies, has largely gone toward subsidizing biodiesel production and sales, to make the fuel more competitive with conventional diesel. The export tariffs are collected by the state palm oil fund. . . . Since its establishment in 2015 until 2019, the fund collected 47.2 trillion rupiah ($3.3 billion) in revenue, and gave 71% of it back to biodiesel producers—and less than 5% to small farmers for the replanting program.[7]

The failure of oil palm intensification and surging palm oil demand are a recipe for a new wave of plantation-driven deforestation, now as a project of strategic national interest for energy independence and under the guise of a green transition from fossil fuels. Indeed, in 2019 an Indonesian firm was already bulldozing rainforest on the island of New Guinea for the Tanah Merah project, which could become the world's largest oil palm plantation.[8]

Not only are these biodiesel policies a boondoggle that seems guaranteed to enrich the palm oil industry at the cost of massive deforestation and public subsidies, but the scheme is also eerily similar to the boondoggle of the Reforestation Fund under Suharto. The Reforestation Fund, like the State Palm Oil Fund, was supported by a levy on concessionaires, and instead of financing replanting, the fund plowed money into new tree fiber plantations and the Kiani Kertas pulp mill in Berau, helping to create overcapacity in the processing sector that drove rampant illegal logging and forest destruction. The use of the State Palm Oil Fund to expand biodiesel processing at the expense of replanting is poised to repeat the process. Why reinvent the wheel when you have a proven recipe for extraction?

Turning to East Kalimantan, the "bright spot" of hope for forests grows dimmer. With fewer peatlands than elsewhere in Kalimantan and Sumatra, the province was less affected by new government regulations. While Indonesia's average annual primary deforestation in 2017–2019 was 56 percent lower than the 2014–2016 average, in Kutai Timur and Berau Districts, primary forests continued to disappear at a historically rapid pace. Annual primary deforestation in fire-prone Kutai Timur for 2017–2019 was down just 21 percent from the highs of 2014–2016, while deforestation in Berau was essentially unchanged, with its 2017–2019 average clearing just 3 percent lower than the previous three years. Meanwhile, the Jokowi government's plan to move the national capital from Jakarta to a new "smart, green" planned city between Balikpapan and Samarinda in East Kalimantan will surely drive massive land-use changes in the province, should the project come to fruition.[9]

Government efforts to protect peatlands after the 2015 fires seem somewhat effective, but as Brazilian environmentalists had discovered over the previous decade, it is easier to reduce deforestation with command-and-control measures than it is to transform the political-economic drivers of forest clearing, and repression without transformation works at best temporarily. Rather than marking the beginning of Indonesia's ecological modernization, Jokowi's green development discourse may be another iteration of the developmentalist discourse of the New Order regime, through which, Paul Gellert observes, "predatory accumulation strategies . . . can be legitimated through practices that appear developmental."[10] Not only does Jokowi claim that palm oil benefits the public good; he also claims that it benefits the environment, providing another green layer of legitimation for ongoing extraction. Oil palm is called a godsend, but for the people and forests engulfed by plantations, it appears a damnation.

Extractive Regimes in Indonesia

Extractive institutions in Indonesia are unique—because of the particularities of history, geography, culture, and ecology—but they are also paradigmatic. Across the tropics and beyond, political and economic institutions extract resources and appropriate labor, channeling materials and energy to centers of wealth and consumption, leaving behind landscapes in ruins. The extractive regime concept emphasizes the organized, institutional character of social and ecological degradation and the dialectic relation between extractive degradation and productivist "development." The preceding chapters provide empirical examples of extractive regime organization in Indonesia and demonstrate the utility of the concept for analyzing both the dynamism and persistence of capitalist political-economic orders. Expanding on Gellert's definition, we can see that extractive regimes in Indonesia encompass both resources (e.g., timber) and labor (e.g., compulsory cultivation of export crops); they have existed over the *longue durée* of historical capitalism, from the 1600s to the present; and they are organized and contested at and across multiple territorial levels, including the district, province, and nation.

Moreover, the Indonesian experience substantiates an understanding of political-economic regimes as hybrid, enacted, sticky, and contested. The extraction-production dialectic is a hybrid relation, not a polar binary, and political-economic regimes in Indonesia combine both extractive and productivist tendencies. At the national level, for example, Indonesia's raw log export ban in the 1980s led to the growth of the domestic wood processing industry, but profligate financing, corruption, and unsustainable logging practices turned the productivist project of value-added wood processing into an accelerator for elite rent capture and ecological destruction. At the provincial level, Governor Awang made declarations like Kaltim Green and championed productivist "green growth" projects like Maloy, but he also used Maloy to create loopholes for new oil palm expansion and supported the reduction of Kutai National Park. At the district level, the Berau government joined the Berau Forest Carbon Project but continued to champion coal and oil palm expansion. In these district-, provincial-, and national-level regimes, extraction and production are both present, but policies and institutions ultimately support predominantly extractive processes.

The extractive character of these regimes is not the inevitable and predetermined effect of some geographical, historical, or economic feature, however. Regimes are enacted and contingent and must be continually reproduced through political decisions and collective and individual conduct. For example, oil palm production in Kalimantan is primarily extractive, but that extractive character is institutionally determined, and more productivist oil palm economies are also possible. As Tania Li observes,

> Independent smallholders who are not tied to plantations can grow this crop [oil palm] successfully, so long as they have access to good planting material, roads, mills and credit. Although there are significant challenges, many studies have shown that the social, ecological and economic impacts of smallholder oil palm are much less damaging. . . . [But] an oil palm sector dominated by independent smallholders would cut off the income streams of many parties that currently benefit from plantation expansion, and vigorously promote it. It is not the technical superiority of plantations but their lucrative system of on-the-books profit and private predation that leads companies, investors and state officials

to argue that only orderly, efficient plantations can meet global demand.[11]

Oil palm extraction, and extraction in Indonesia more broadly, is continually enacted through people's behaviors that reproduce extractive institutions, but behaviors and institutions can also be transformed.

Nonetheless, regimes are sticky, and transformation is difficult. There are powerful, institutionalized interests in the extractive oil palm economy that militate against an alternative, independent smallholder economy, as Li describes. Similarly, as The Nature Conservancy discovered at the district level in Berau, it is no small matter to transform an extractive political-economic regime into a productivist regime of "green" modernization, especially when that extractive regime is nested in higher-order extractive regimes at the provincial and national levels. At the national level, too, regimes are sticky and a productivist transition is difficult, as demonstrated by the frustration of Sukarno's Third Worldism by domestic and international actors committed to maintaining Indonesia as a zone of extraction.

Despite this stickiness, regimes are always contested. Internal contradictions and transformative projects from above and below challenge regime configurations and the prevailing mode of production. Indigenous rebellions against the Dutch, Third Worldism, and land sparing may not have succeeded in overthrowing or transforming extractive regimes in Indonesia, but they have pushed the reconfiguration of political-economic institutions, and perhaps sown the seeds for future transformations.

Specters of Displacement

Over the course of four centuries of capitalism in the Indonesian archipelago, extractive regimes have time and again been challenged and reconfigured, but at each critical juncture, the mode of extraction prevailed. This Indonesian experience demonstrates, first and foremost, the continuous social and environmental destruction that has always been the necessary foundation for global illusions of capitalist "development." In this light, it seems remarkably facile to think that land-sparing policies driving a productivist transition in the Brazilian Amazon could be transferred effectively to Indonesia—not because Indonesia cannot change but because the political-economic transformations required for a productivist transition are so complex, fundamental, and historically contingent.

I have suggested that Indonesia's post-2015 productivist transition is dubious, but let us imagine, nonetheless, that it will succeed exactly as Jokowi, Awang, TNC, and other land-sparing advocates have professed: with more productive oil palm plantations expanding onto degraded lands, sparing the forests and feeding vibrant downstream domestic industries. The end of extractive deforestation in Indonesia would not be the end of global extraction. The problem is displacement: when the opportunities for extraction in one place are foreclosed, extractive actors move to new frontiers.

At a previous moment of potential transformation, when Sukarno's national developmentalism threatened foreign corporations, plantation companies did not simply resign themselves to a less exorbitant rate of profit. As Ann Laura Stoler writes, "Efforts of foreign owned companies to protect their capital investment in Indonesia were accompanied by long-term schemes for investment elsewhere in the Third World. . . . In the 1950s, in greater or lesser degree, they shifted their holdings to more secure and profitable terrain," especially in Africa and South America.[12]

Today, it is Southeast Asian palm oil corporations that are expanding their plantations in Africa and South America. For example, FELDA, a Malaysian-government-controlled palm oil and agribusiness conglomerate, owns oil palm plantations in Indonesia and employs thousands of Indonesian migrant workers on its plantations in Malaysia, where investigations have documented egregious labor abuses.[13] FELDA's global holding company raised over $3 billion in its 2012 initial public offering, which it planned to plow into land purchases across Southeast Asia and West Africa.[14] FELDA had also planned a 100,000-hectare oil palm plantation in the Brazilian Amazon, but that project was called off in 2009. According to a company chairperson, the reversal was due to "several technical and environmental issues . . . which also includes return on investment."[15] "The payback period is too long and we received protests, which are unhealthy to the company, accusing us of polluting the air when in reality somebody else wanted the land to grow soyabean. So it is wiser for us not to proceed," he affirmed. Instead, they would look to Africa, where "we might start planting an initial 100,000ha [1,000 square kilometers] and if there are no trouble we can increase the hectarage."[16] Palm oil companies will move across the tropics, where protests and environmental issues are no trouble and returns on investment are favorable. By a thousand square kilometers here and a thousand there, and then a thousand more, forests will be bull-dozed for palm and profit.

Whatever the outcome of this new conjuncture, Indonesia in the first decades of the twenty-first century showed the power and persistence of extractive regimes, swallowing up forest conservation efforts and green development initiatives to funnel materials and energy to the capitalist core. Jeremy Campbell, working in the Brazilian municipality of Novo Progresso in southwestern Pará, described the political economy of Brazil's Amazon frontier as a system "rigged for theft and destruction."[17] He could just as easily have been describing the political economy of Indonesian Borneo, or of any other periphery of the capitalist world system governed by a regime of institutionalized plunder. And yet, in the Brazilian Amazon in the decade after 2004, plunder seemed to give way to productivity as a complex of government, agribusiness, and environmentalist actors came together to intensify agricultural production and spare forest lands for conservation.

A Modernist Transition
in the Brazilian Amazon

An Amazonian Success Story

A HERON SWOOPS ACROSS A bank of trees, and tribal drums pulse. "The Amazon is one of our most important environmental assets," a voice intones. An eight-minute video produced by the Brazilian Development Bank opens a session on Brazil's Amazon Fund at the Global Landscapes Forum, a two-day gathering on the sidelines of the Paris Climate Conference in December 2015. "Brazil is proud to have significantly reduced deforestation in its area of the Amazon," the voice continues, as the camera pans across a forested floodplain. "This decrease is one of the main contributions, across the world, towards countering climate change." At the end of the video, another shot of flooded forest provides a backdrop for the Amazon Fund logo, and the voice reads out the Fund's motto: "Brazil protects it. The world supports it. Everybody wins."[1]

Since the beginning of large-scale deforestation in the 1970s, representations of the Amazon have been dual and dueling. On one hand, in the eyes of many environmentalists, it is a tropical Eden, the "lungs of the world," whose Indigenous peoples and biodiverse rainforests must be protected. On the other hand, in the eyes of many Brazilian military officers, development planners, farmers, and politicians, the Amazon is a "green hell" where the expansion of modern agriculture is essential for the sovereignty and development of the nation. What if these two visions were not dueling but compatible?

What if environmental protection and agricultural industrialization could work together to build state capacity, conserve forests, and drive economic development? What if everybody could win?

The land-sparing hypothesis claims this reconciliation is possible, and in the Brazilian Amazon after 2004, government agencies, environmentalist organizations, and agro-industrial actors began working together to make that land-sparing vision a reality. Over the next decade, they appeared to succeed. Deforestation declined to historic lows, even as the Amazon region became a hub of Brazilian agribusiness.

Environmentalists, government officials, and the promotional video I saw in Paris all trumpeted Brazil's Amazon transition as among the largest contributions of any country to addressing climate change, and "one of the great conservation successes of the twenty-first century."[2] Not only that, but Brazil seemed to provide a blueprint for ending deforestation across the tropics. "Brazil has waged a successful war on tropical deforestation," declared a 2015 news feature in the journal *Nature*, "and other countries are trying to follow its lead."[3] The Brazilian Amazon, much like Indonesian Borneo and other tropical forest regions, was for centuries an extractive periphery of the capitalist world system. In the first decades of the twenty-first century, a new model of productivist eco-modernism seemed finally to gain ground against Amazonian extractive regimes. How did this transformation occur, and what does it tell us about the prospects for sustainable capitalist development?

A Green Path from the Periphery?

Extractive regimes are enduring political-economic formations, as the case of Indonesia underscores, but geographies of extraction and production are also dynamic and evolving. Classical world systems and dependency analyses, by focusing on conditions that reproduce underdevelopment in the periphery, can give the impression that the periphery is trapped in an indefinite, extractive equilibrium, perpetuated by seemingly insurmountable structures of political, economic, and ecological inequity. "Core" and "periphery" are not immutable properties of particular regions, however. Extractive institutions militate against productivist processes of reinvestment and value-added industrial development, but regimes can change, and regions can move from the periphery toward the core—from extraction to production. Analyzing these transitions can open up a richer understanding of the process and contingency of political-economic and environmental change. When and how might an area move from being an extractive periphery to a productivist core? How do transitions between extraction and production at different levels interact and spread through systems? And to what degree can policy catalyze these transformations? The following chapters look to Brazil for some answers to these questions.

In the Brazilian Amazon, government, environmentalist, and agribusiness actors united by land-sparing logic deployed environmental regulation to promote agricultural intensification and state-building in a way that inverted the territorial logics of the extractive regime. The resulting deforestation reductions and agro-industrial growth were dramatic but also contested, uneven, and regionally bounded. Regulation, technification, and capitalization of agro-industrial operations were coupled with smallholder dispossession. Small farmers left for the cities or for new frontiers, or in some cases found a profitable foothold producing cash crops like cacao for global supply chains. Cattle and soy production boomed, and dusty frontier towns acquired asphalt, apartment blocks, and air-conditioned supermarkets.

Industrial agriculture is high-input agriculture. Exporting cattle or soy requires an infrastructure of roads, slaughterhouses, soy crushers, and ports. Meeting government and corporate environmental and sanitary standards is expensive. Farmers and ranchers needed to produce large quantities of crops or cattle to profit in this supply chain, so they intensified their agricultural practices with investments in machinery and warehouses, cattle genetics and transgenic seeds, fertilizers and pesticides. These high levels of capitalization drove up land values, especially where controls on deforestation limited the amount of available land.

The increasing concentration of value in the regional agro-industrial economy was "green" in that it did not depend directly on new Amazonian deforestation—to the contrary, intensification was driven in part by limitations on deforestation that forced increased investment in existing agricultural lands. But productivist growth depends always on expanded extraction. First, because of increasing throughput: producing and exporting more cattle and more soy required more energy and materials—fossil fuels, phosphorus, steel, petrochemicals—primary inputs imported from elsewhere. Second, because of displacement: land appreciation, capital accumulation, and the (partial) closing of the Amazonian deforestation frontier drove a search for cheap land and windfall profits on new forest frontiers. While unequal exchange of energy and materials to supply economic throughput, the first mechanism, is typical of core-periphery relations in general, the second mechanism of displacement, "leakage," or "spillover" highlights how productivist policies in one region can propel new extractive frontiers elsewhere. Ultimately, the transformation of the political-economic regime in the Brazilian Amazon was only partial, and the "sparing" of forests was reversible. With the rightward shift of the Brazilian government after 2015 under Michel Temer and then Jair Bolsonaro, the political consensus on land sparing was shattered, and the land grabbers and cattle launderers, slaughterhouses and local strongmen, launched a new wave of deforestation and resurgent extraction.

CHAPTER FOUR

The Amazonian
Extractive Economy

"WHAT IS NOW CALLED the environmental destruction of the Amazon is merely the latest surge in a long epic of annihilation," wrote Susanna Hecht and Alexander Cockburn in their 1989 classic *The Fate of the Forest*.[1] Understanding the drivers of forest destruction in the Brazilian Amazon—and how land-sparing policies began, after centuries of extraction, to transform the Amazonian economy—requires some familiarity with that "long epic of annihilation."

In 1534, forty years after Portugal and Spain carved up the Western Hemisphere in the Treaty of Tordesillas, King John III of Portugal created fourteen hereditary captaincies (*capitanias*) through which members of the Portuguese nobility would develop the territories of coastal Brazil. The capitanias reached the eastern edge of the Amazon, which became a source of forest products and Amerindian slaves, while the coastal economy revolved around sugar and trade in both African and Amerindian slaves. Beginning in the second half of the eighteenth century, the Companhia Geral de Comércio do Grão-Pará e Maranhão, a chartered trading company, expanded the commercial linkages between Europe and the Amazon Basin. The principal commodities of the Amazonian trade were cacao and various "spices" (known as the *drogas do sertão*, "drugs of the

hinterlands"), including clove-bark (*Dicypellium caryophyllatum*), co-
paíba oil, and achiote (*urucu*), as well as gums and latex (particularly
rubber), and timber, pelts, and brazil nuts (*castanha-do-pará*). The
Amazonian region, known as Grão-Pará, integrated uneasily into
the new Brazilian state after independence in 1822, exploding in the
Cabanagem Rebellion of the 1830s. This rebellion undermined
the landed elite of the colonial period, who were then supplanted
by the commercial elite that rose with the Amazon rubber boom.[2]

Fine Pará rubber, coagulated from the latex of *Hevea brasiliensis*
trees endemic to the Amazon, was an important product in Amazonian trade from the mid-eighteenth century onward. Already in
the 1750s, army boots and knapsacks were being sent from Lisbon
to the city of Belém, at the mouth of the Amazon River, for wa-
terproofing. By 1800, Belém was exporting rubber shoes to New
England, and an industrial factory for making rubber goods opened
in the United Kingdom in 1820, followed by the first rubber factory
in the United States in 1828.[3] With the patenting of vulcanization
by Goodyear in 1845 and the advent of steam travel on the Amazon River after 1850, the stage was set for the massive expansion of
rubber extraction from the second half of the nineteenth century
into the early twentieth century. Rubber proliferated in industrial
applications and in tires for the "bicycle craze" of the 1890s, as well
as in the automobile industry that emerged in the 1900s, driving a
boom that brought vast quantities of rubber to Europe and North
America and fabulous wealth to the "rubber baron" elites of Manaus
and Belém.

The boom in wild rubber production drove the first establishment of a non-Indigenous population in many parts of the Amazon.
Latex is extracted from rubber trees by tappers (*seringueiros*), who
traditionally work "trails" of trees in the forest, walking the trail
early in the day to slash the trees and returning in the evening to
collect the latex, which they later coagulate into a ball of rubber. By
the late nineteenth century, Indigenous populations in the Amazon
had been decimated by centuries of violence, disease, and enslavement. The rubber boom touched off a new wave of disruption of
Indigenous societies, as they faced incursions by thousands of non-
Indigenous rubber tappers or were drawn into tapping themselves
through enslavement or debt relations. The rubber boom also in-

creased the extraction of other forest products, such as cacao and brazil nuts, which were collected by tappers during the wet season when rubber extraction became more difficult.

The rubber economy was structured through an institution of debt relationships known as *aviamento*, which subjected tappers to oppressive living and working conditions and forced them into permanent extractive production.[4] Meanwhile, in Manaus and Belém, the rubber barons built opera houses, decorated their homes with Portuguese tiles, and are said to have sent laundry to be washed in Paris. The rubber boom finally came to an end in the 1910s, when the successful domestication of *Hevea brasiliensis* on British plantations in Asia broke the Amazonian rubber monopoly. Brazil nut extraction expanded after the rubber crash, but it was not until World War II that the Amazonian extractive economy again intensified, when Japanese action in the Pacific isolated the United States from Malayan rubber plantations, and Brazil was called upon to fill the gap in exchange for millions of dollars in foreign aid. More than 55,000 Brazilians—mostly poor northeasterners—were sent as "rubber soldiers" to the Amazon, where nearly half of them perished from disease or animal attacks before the Japanese surrender in 1945.[5]

The extractive regime of the rubber boom dramatically altered the socioecology of the Amazon Basin, yet it depended on forest products such as cacao and brazil nuts, in addition to rubber, and its impact pales in comparison to the extractive institutions that arose in the region after World War II. As Barbara Weinstein wrote in the early 1980s:

> True, the rubber era left the Amazon substantially altered from the preboom period, bringing in new settlers by the hundreds of thousands, populating remote corners of the valley, wiping out whole tribal cultures in the search for new laborers, and creating an extensive network of commercial elites. Yet if the present course of events in the Amazon continues unhindered, we can expect the impact, both in human and ecological terms, to be far greater, far more distressing, than anything witnessed by the region during the rubber boom.[6]

In the years after World War II, a whirlwind of loggers, miners, farmers, and ranchers descended on the Amazon. Brazil nut extraction intensified in eastern Pará under a system of concessions (*aforamentos*), while gold mining expanded in the Tapajós basin of western Pará (a center of "artisanal" placer mining to this day). Road building, especially the construction of the Belém-Brasília highway in 1956–1960 and completion of the BR-364 highway to Porto Velho in 1968, opened vast new areas for extraction and colonization. Logging in the Caribbean and Central America had depleted most commercial stocks of mahogany in those regions by the early twentieth century, but access to new populations in the Brazilian Amazon touched off a "mahogany rush" in the 1970s. Seventy-five percent of mahogany exports from 1971 to 1992 went to the United States and United Kingdom, and by the early 1990s regional mahogany stocks were virtually exhausted.[7]

The Brazilian federal government directed financing toward agriculture and ranching in the Amazon with the creation of the Superintendency for the Valorization of Amazonia (SPVEA), founded in 1953.[8] Support for agricultural development in the region redoubled after the 1964 military coup, when the generals replaced SPVEA with the Superintendency for Development of the Amazon (SUDAM). The land-owning elites of the Amazon had long objected to the forest economy of the region, favoring agriculture as the basis for economic growth—a modernist perspective that also happened to suit their economic and political interests.[9] The rubber boom had drained labor away from the agriculture and transport sectors and created an "autonomous population of quasi-independent producers" illegible to state control and with a surplus that could not be appropriated by the landed classes.[10] Hecht and Cockburn recount,

> The grand families of Belém yearned for the dignified stability of agricultural empires to rival the sugar estates of the Northeast, the pastoral fortunes of Recife, but their wealth was amassed from products dragged out from the forest by slave or peon. . . . For decade after decade, agricultural ambitions expired as both labor and capital chased off upriver on yet another extractive jaunt. . . . This was a mercantile and bureaucratic elite in the traditional style of the Por-

tuguese empire, set in its ways down the centuries. Hopes that Amazonia would gracefully submit to the paradigms of development and shun the raffish temptations of extraction survived into the 1950s when the Superintendency for the Valorization of Amazonia—the initial post-war development agency for the Amazon—proclaimed that the region's vulgar past would finally be extinguished and it would become a cornucopia of respectable crops.[11]

The developmentalist military government that came to power in the 1960s sought finally to "inundate the Amazon forest with civilization."[12] With a mixture of tax credits and subsidies coordinated by SUDAM and financed by the regional development bank, Banco da Amazônia S.A., the federal government drove the massive expansion of cattle ranching in the Amazon during the 1970s and 1980s, alongside programs encouraging large-scale migration of small farmers to the region. The brazil nut concessions of eastern Pará were converted to pasture, and a new frontier opened in northern Mato Grosso and western Pará with the 1971–1976 construction of the BR-163 Cuiabá-Santarém highway.

Mining also expanded during this period. Industrial-scale mining in the Amazon was driven by the state-owned Companhia Vale do Rio Doce. Vale (as the company is known today) took over development of the Carajás mineral deposits from U.S. Steel in the late 1970s to create the world's largest iron ore mine. The mine's operations are powered principally by the Tucuruí hydroelectric dam, constructed in 1975–1984 on the Tocantins River, a tributary of the Amazon. Financing for the Carajás Iron Project came from the World Bank, the Brazilian National Development Bank (BNDE, today BNDES), the European Community, Japan, and eventually also American commercial banks and the USSR.[13] In this way, the world's largest iron mine was developed in the Amazon Basin with investments by a virtually complete list of the financial capitals of the global industrial core.[14]

The construction of a new agricultural economy in the Amazon was coupled with a reordering of property institutions in the region. Colonial extraction had operated initially through land grants and concessions, but agrarian legislation passed prior to Brazilian independence in 1822 recognized private land rights accrued through occupation and effective use (*posse*), allowing for independent land claims on undesignated state lands (*terra devoluta*). By the end of World War II, there was already a long history of often overlapping land claims by both small and large landholders in the Amazon. The military government, on coming to power, seized control over vast areas of land from the Amazonian states and sought to facilitate land distribution to private investors.

Far from creating a modernized, productivist tenure regime in the Amazon, however, the military government's interventions intensified tenurial chaos, for several reasons. First, the cadastral optic of agrarian tenure was layered over past forest-based land claims such as the aforamentos, and federal development programs clashed with elites such as brazil nut concessionaires (*foreiros*), who fought to maintain and expand their control of land. Second, the military's promotion of agriculture and ranching was beset by an internal tension between support for smallholder colonization programs and promotion of large-scale ranching and agro-industrial investments. As Marianne Schmink and Charles Wood observe, "The crux of the matter was the incompatibility between two opposing sets of priorities. On the one hand, there was an emphasis on private property and on incentives to capital accumulation and technological change; on the other, there were the provisions for state intervention to reduce poverty and to make land available to those who worked it. The contradiction lay at the heart of the so-called 'agrarian question,'" and generated a contentious agricultural frontier characterized by a mixture of actors and land uses.[15] Third, existing structures of power and patronage in the Amazonian extractive regime and the advent of new, capitalized private investors to the rapidly expanding frontier created a fertile environment for corruption, rent-seizing, and all manner of plunder.

The developmentalist interventions of the military government failed to transform the Amazon from a zone of extraction to a center of productivist modernization. Instead, the Amazonian extractive regime was reconfigured during the 1970s and 1980s through the rise of a new extractive elite of large ranchers (*fazendeiros*) and land grabbers (*grileiros*), who ruled the *Faroeste* (Wild West) of the

Amazonian frontier through networks of institutionalized corruption and patronage, waging "land wars" with hired guns to dispossess small farmers, Indigenous peoples, and forest-dependent communities.[16] Land titles were multiple times forged or fraudulently issued and subsequently revoked, and SUDAM, the Amazonian development agency, became a vehicle for corruption.

One emblematic figure at the national level among the Amazonian extractive elite of this period is Jader Barbalho, who since the 1970s has served multiple terms as federal deputy, senator, and governor of Pará. (He was elected to his third term as senator in 2018.) He has been accused of massive corruption linked to the operation of SUDAM in Pará, where he allegedly coordinated the diversion of over a billion reais, and probably an amount several times greater, almost certainly exceeding US$1 billion.[17] Barbalho was forced to resign from the Senate in 2001 in the midst of the SUDAM corruption scandal, yet he has continued to be elected to national political offices. In 2014, Barbalho turned seventy years old, at which point Brazilian law reduces the statute of limitations by half, and criminal proceedings against him were dropped.[18]

As recently as 1978, less than 2 percent of the original forest area of the Brazilian Amazon had been cleared.[19] Between 1978 and 2004, roughly 600,000 square kilometers of forest were lost, an area larger than metropolitan France. Cattle ranching, which occupied an estimated 60–80 percent of this deforested land, was established in an extractive mode reinforced by speculation.[20] The productive value of the herd was often secondary to the ability to profit from future land sales and government tax breaks and subsidies. Where this exchange value of land far exceeded its productive value, land managers had few incentives to invest in sustainable practices.[21] Ranchers consolidated large properties, frequently through coercive or illegal land grabbing; extracted the fertility of deforested land through unmanaged or excessive grazing; and then as pastures became degraded moved on to grab and clear new areas. From the mid-1980s, cattle ranching also became widespread among smallholders, intensifying cycles of land degradation and frontier expansion. Insecure land tenure, especially for smallholders, was an additional institutional factor promoting deforestation (to establish ownership through "productive use") and inhibiting agricultural intensification (by hindering credit access and discouraging capital investments).

This extractive regime in the Brazilian Amazon persisted throughout the later decades of the twentieth century, as loggers, ranchers, miners, and land grabbers used networks of patronage and corruption, lack of tenurial clarity, and frequent violence to extract windfall profits through deforestation and the dispossession of Indigenous and traditional populations and small-farmer colonists. This continued extractive "underdevelopment" of the Amazon region was integrally linked with the productivist development of the Brazilian core regions of the South and Southeast, and later the Center-West, as well as growth in the industrialized Global North. During the 1960s and 1970s, agriculture in southern Brazil mechanized and intensified, driven particularly by the expansion of soy, which was increasingly in demand for animal feeds in Europe and North America. This agricultural industrialization in the Brazilian South and Southeast displaced hundreds of thousands of small farmers, giving impetus to colonization programs in the Amazon and leading eventually to the founding of the Landless Workers Movement (Movimento dos Trabalhadores Rurais Sem Terra) in 1984. Cattle ranching had been the principal agricultural land use in the Brazilian backlands since the sixteenth century, knitting together the plantation economies of the Atlantic coast with the mining regions of the interior.[22] With the expansion of industrial field cropping into former pasture areas in South and Southeast Brazil, cattle production in those regions intensified as well, and low-input, extensive ranching was displaced toward the Amazonian frontier.

Agricultural intensification in southern Brazil combined with broader processes of productivist industrialization to produce the "Brazilian economic miracle" of the 1960s and 1970s, and this rapid growth of the Brazilian core relied on the "internal colony" of the Amazonian periphery.[23] Colonization of the Amazon served to relieve social pressures brought about by poverty and dispossession in the southern core and the stagnant Northeast, while energy and materials extracted from the Amazon in the form of timber, metals, electricity, and cattle supported industrial investments and growth in the core. Amazonian extraction also fed productivist growth in the Global North, both directly through exports of Amazonian resources and indirectly through relations mediated by the Brazilian core. From 1971 to 1980, annual exports from Brazil more than quintupled, growing from under $4 billion to over $20 billion, driven especially by exports of soy, iron, and machinery, and trade grew from 14.6 to 20.4 percent of GDP.[24] During the 1980s and 1990s, the "intensive frontier" of industrial agriculture, led by soy cultivation, expanded into the Cerrado biome in the Center-West, continuing to push extensive ranching ever deeper into the Amazon.

Twentieth-Century Forest Conservation: Protected Areas and Socio-Environmentalism

Although the political economy of the Amazon through the end of the twentieth century was geared toward extraction, various coalitions attempted to conserve forest areas and to moderate extractive expansion, especially as deforestation accelerated after 1975. These coalitions and the policy models they developed were important precursors to the land-sparing policies of the 2000s, though their interests were not necessarily the same as those that later motivated land sparing.

Twentieth-century forest conservation efforts operated largely within a protected areas model through which scientists and environmentalists interested in wilderness preservation found common cause with state efforts to control people and resources. The Brazilian government began to create protected conservation areas after the promulgation of the first Federal Forest Code in 1934, and the earliest designations were made in the Atlantic Forest Region, where protection of forested mountainsides also served important hydrological functions by limiting erosion and regulating stream flow.[25] The first national park in the Amazon biome, Araguaia National Park in present-day Tocantins, was created in 1959, followed by the designation of Xingu National Park in 1961, which was subsequently converted to an Indigenous territory. Protected area creation expanded dramatically during the 1970s and 1980s, during which time the National System of Conservation Areas (Sistema

Nacional de Unidades de Conservação) was developed and several
large parks were declared in Amazonas State.

Protected area creation in Brazil contains a number of different
designations in addition to national parks and has developed through
historical processes driven by several different assemblages. Strictly
protected conservation areas—including national parks, biological
reserves, and ecological stations—prioritize wilderness preservation. "Sustainable-use" conservation areas and Indigenous territories (which have a distinct legal status) allow occupation by local or
Indigenous populations, and their creation has generally resulted
from advocacy by coalitions of local and Indigenous people, Indigenous rights and environmental NGOs, and government Indigenous and environmental agencies.[26] Prior to the 2000s, strictly protected areas in the Amazon were located mainly in remote regions
far from the deforestation frontier, whereas Indigenous territories
and sustainable-use areas were often created in direct response to
frontier expansion.[27]

Sustainable-use conservation areas such as Extractivist Reserves
(*Reservas Extrativistas*) and Sustainable Development Reserves were
the product of a socio-environmentalist movement that coalesced
in Brazil in the 1980s in opposition to government development
projects and extractive ranching, logging, and mining.[28] In 1981, the
federal government began work on the Polonoroeste project, a development program to pave the BR-364 highway to Porto Velho in
Rondônia and provide infrastructure for colonization areas. World
Bank financing for the project included provisions for the protection of Indigenous territories and conservation areas. The immediate effects of Polonoroeste included a surge of new migrants to the
southwestern Amazon and corresponding spikes in deforestation
and invasion of Indigenous lands and conservation areas. Anthro-
pologists working with Indigenous peoples in the region spoke out
against the project, and their protest was joined by environmentalists in the United States seeking to use multilateral development
bank lending as a lever for environmental protection in the Global
South.[29] The campaigners succeeded in prompting the U.S. Congress to hold hearings on development bank lending practices, and
in 1985 the World Bank suspended Polonoroeste funding due to

violations of protections for Indigenous territories and conservation areas.

In Acre, to the west of Rondônia, rubber tappers led by Chico Mendes had been organizing since the mid-1970s to defend their livelihoods from expanding cattle ranching. Following the intense mobilization against Polonoroeste, environmentalist activists focused on the Rio Branco-Porto Velho Road Improvement Project, a plan financed by the Inter-American Development Bank for paving the BR-364 between Rondônia and Acre. Supporters of the Acre rubber tappers and American environmentalists formed an alliance, and the first meeting of the National Council of Rubber Tappers (Conselho Nacional dos Seringueiros) in 1985 launched a new proposal for Extractivist Reserves in the Amazon. The reserves, partially inspired by Indigenous territories, would guarantee tappers' use of the land and ensure protection of the forest. Chico Mendes's visit to Washington, DC, in 1987 and his subsequent assassination in 1988, coupled with growing public concern over Amazonian forest destruction, helped popularize the rubber tapper cause and reinforce the environmentalist framing of rubber tappers' struggle to preserve their livelihood.[30]

The Polonoroeste conflict and the environmentalist–rubber tapper alliance consolidated a discourse of socio-environmentalism (*socioambientalismo*) in Brazil, linking forest conservation with the livelihoods of local peoples and contesting the modernizing "development" discourse driving forest clearing and agricultural expansion. Socio-environmental advocacy gained further organizing space with Brazil's democratic opening, which was marked by return to civilian rule in 1985 and a new democratic constitution in 1988. Prior to the 1980s, virtually all protected areas had been designated by the federal government, but after 1985 the Amazonian states began to create conservation areas as well.[31] The first Extractivist Reserves were created in Acre, Amapá, and Rondônia in 1990. In 1992, Brazil hosted the UN Conference on Environment and Development in Rio de Janeiro, which helped consolidate global sustainable development discourse and strengthened environmentalist advocacy in Brazil and linkages between environmental NGOs in the Global North and South. The Pilot Program to Conserve the Brazilian

Rainforest, a multilateral cooperation program of the G7 countries, became operational in 1994 and directed support over the next decade to protected area creation and environmental governance institutions, including the Extractivist Reserve model.[32] Also in 1994, the Brazilian NGO Instituto Socioambiental was formed out of a network of environmentalist and Indigenous rights activists, and in 1996 the first Sustainable Development Reserve was created in Amazonas State.

Socio-environmentalist coalitions thus succeeded in carving out territories for forest-dependent livelihoods through the designation of "sustainable-use" areas, and they played a key role in the subsequent dramatic expansion of the Amazonian protected areas network in the mid-2000s. This socio-environmentalist movement was not sufficient, however, to transform the political economy of agricultural expansion that continued to drive large-scale deforestation in the Amazon Basin. Only when forest conservation became a question of agro-industrial development, with the emergence in the 2000s of a modernist, land-sparing policy coalition, did the tide of extractive deforestation begin to ebb.

CHAPTER FIVE

The Logic of Brazilian
Land Sparing

FAVORITE ACTIVITY IN SCHOLARLY accounts of Brazil's Amazonian conservation "success story" is to enumerate the many proximate factors that helped reduce deforestation in the region. While macroeconomic and climatic factors play an important role in changing deforestation rates, studies primarily attribute Amazonian deforestation reductions after 2004 to new governance institutions and practices. Researchers have highlighted especially the effects of supply-chain sustainability initiatives for "zero-deforestation" soy and beef; the expansion of conservation areas and Indigenous territories; and policies supporting compliance with environmental regulations, including enhanced environmental enforcement, agricultural credit restrictions, and funding for sustainable agriculture.[1] A 2014 review in the journal *Science* listed fifty-one different policies and programs that "may have influenced the decline in deforestation" in the Brazilian Amazon.[2]

These accounts share a predominantly "technical" approach to policy, either attempting to quantify effects of specific policy interventions on deforestation or listing policies and processes out of whose interactions deforestation reductions emerge.[3] Largely absent from these studies is a systemic political-economic perspective that looks beyond proximate policies to the actors and institutions

that generate the policy environment.[4] This chapter moves beyond
that technical approach to a more systemic account. Understanding the Amazonian political-economic regime as a set of ruling institutions and practices, I show how the dozens of policies that combined to drive deforestation reductions emerged from a confluence
of government, NGO, and agribusiness interests that linked territorial control, agricultural intensification, and forest conservation in a
project of political-economic transformation through land sparing.

Multiple factors converged in the mid-2000s to align opponents
of the extractive economy, including local populations, environmentalists, and productivist elements of the Brazilian government and
transnational capital. By the early 2000s, infrastructure spending,
agricultural research, and global commodity-chain development
had brought industrial soy and cattle production to the southern
and eastern Amazon. The increasing role of corporate agribusiness
in Amazonian forest clearing alarmed environmentalists and the
Public Ministry, who began to pressure transnational corporations
to control deforestation in their supply chains. Mainstream environmental NGOs, meanwhile, had moved during the 1980s and 1990s
from oppositional politics toward a neoliberal approach of "partnerships" with governments and corporations, which facilitated a
"politics of agreement" among powerful actors.[5] Remote sensing
and GIS technology for monitoring deforestation had also advanced
during the 1990s, and the National Institute for Space Research
(INPE) emerged in Brazil as a center of technological capacity, offering tools for more active and targeted regulation.

As annual deforestation in the Brazilian Amazon surged from
18,165 square kilometers in 2001 to 27,772 square kilometers in
2004, international attention to the role of forests in climate change
was growing rapidly (leading to the inclusion of REDD in UN
climate negotiations in 2005), and land-sparing arguments were
gaining prominence in academic discourse. Domestic concern over
climate change in Brazil was also heightened by the extreme heat
and drought of the 1997–1998 El Niño. When Luiz Inácio Lula
da Silva was inaugurated as president of Brazil in 2003, he brought
to power an administration with ties to socio-environmental movements, installing rubber tapper activist Marina Silva as minister of

environment. At the same time, the administration's alliances with agribusiness demanded a conciliation of environmental protection with agricultural production. Under these conditions, productivist elements in the Brazilian executive linked with environmental and enforcement agencies and NGO and civil society networks to craft a new environment and development agenda for the Brazilian Amazon.

Land sparing has global popularity as a scientific hypothesis and a policy prescription. The Brazilian Amazon after 2004 is the single most prominent example of a purportedly successful large-scale implementation of land-sparing policy. How did land sparing materialize as policy in Brazil, and what does the logic of Brazilian land sparing reveal about the actors and interests behind this policy discourse?

An Action Plan for the Amazon

In 2004, the Brazilian federal government launched the Action Plan for the Prevention and Control of Deforestation in the Legal Amazon (PPCDAm), bringing activities of thirteen federal ministries under coordination of the president's office. Under PPCDAm, anti-deforestation efforts developed along three axes: (1) "territorial ordering," including protected area creation and land tenure regularization; (2) monitoring and enforcement, including enforcement of the Federal Forest Code, which required preservation of areas of natural vegetation on rural properties; and (3) support for sustainable production, including technical assistance and financing for agricultural intensification.[6] In a pattern typical of neoliberal governance interventions, government policies within PPCDAm formed the backbone for a new environmental order, but mechanisms for achieving government policy goals frequently depended on non-state actors. PPCDAm thus became a substrate over which diverse coalitions at multiple territorial levels built the institutions for a productivist political-economic transition in the Brazilian Amazon. This chapter describes the regional-level development of PPCDAm strategies and explains the theoretical architecture of Brazilian land-sparing policy, while the following chapters show the uneven implementation of these strategies across the Amazonian Arc of Deforestation.

"Territorial ordering" to prevent and combat deforestation included strategies of protected area creation and land tenure regularization. In 2004–2007 under PPCDAm, nearly 20 million hectares of new conservation areas were created. Illustrating the role of non-state actors in this process, protected area creation in the Terra do Meio region of Pará, between São Félix do Xingu and Novo Progresso municipalities, was driven by a socio-environmental coalition anchored by smallholder farmers, who sought to halt the expansion of large-scale ranches. The planning process for Terra do Meio was facilitated by domestic and international environmental NGOs, including Instituto Socioambiental, Greenpeace, and the Woods Hole Research Center.[7] During the same period, Indigenous peoples and activists secured designation of 10 million hectares of Indigenous territories. Crucially, these new protected areas were located primarily in zones of high deforestation pressure in the eastern Amazon, signifying a new territorial logic of protected area creation. Since protected area status in Brazil (particularly strictly protected status or designation as an Indigenous territory) substantially reduces the likelihood of deforestation, these new protected areas acted as "green barriers" to agricultural expansion. By one estimate, protected area creation was responsible for 37 percent of the decrease in Amazonian deforestation in 2004–2006.[8]

Secure land tenure, meanwhile, is a foundational institution of productivist political-economic regimes. Advocates argued that tenure regularization would prevent deforestation by combating predatory land grabbing and small-farmer displacement, while also encouraging investments in agricultural intensification on properties with secure tenure.[9] In this way, tenure regularization appeared to be a consummate land-sparing intervention. In 2009, the Brazilian government launched the Terra Legal (Legal Land) program to support titling for Amazonian settlers. This program was a late addition to PPCDAm, and its initial performance was weak. Against a goal of titling nearly 150,000 properties, by November 2015 fewer than 20,000 titles had been issued.[10] Some NGOs also sought to support tenure regularization, but land titling depends ultimately on the government, and the NGOs made little headway.

While tenure regularization was promoted as an enabling condition for agricultural investment, it is neither sufficient nor absolutely necessary for intensification. Formal title may not be strictly necessary for intensification, since untitled producers, especially large landholders, may have fairly secure tenure even without legal title, and therefore may still invest in intensification when economic conditions are favorable.[11] Meanwhile, smaller producers who lacked title but complied with environmental regulations were still eligible for agricultural credit. On the other hand, a study of over ten thousand landholders who received titles through Terra Legal found that small and medium landholders actually increased deforestation after titling, underscoring that there is no guarantee that agricultural investment in titled properties will result in land-sparing intensification.[12]

The military government passed a new federal Forest Code in 1965, which was subsequently modified by presidential decrees. At the beginning of the 2000s, the Forest Code required rural landowners to maintain "permanent protection areas" along water courses and on steep slopes, and to maintain an additional percentage of the property as a "legal reserve" of natural habitat, which in the Amazon biome was set to 80 percent of the property area. These requirements went largely unenforced, and by 2012 achieving compliance would have required restoration of 50 million hectares nationally.[13] Under PPCDAm, the federal government intensified Forest Code enforcement through enhanced monitoring and sanctioning of illegal deforestation and the development of new environmental registration systems to regulate property-level Forest Code compliance.

The Rural Environmental Registry (Cadastro Ambiental Rural, CAR) exemplifies the close but contingent and sometimes conflicted interactions among the Brazilian municipal, state, and federal governments, NGOs, and corporations behind Brazil's Amazonian transition. CAR developed out of the System for Environmental Licensing of Rural Properties (SLAPR) in Mato Grosso, a registry funded by international donors that used remote sensing and

Fig. 4. Pastures and forest in southeastern Pará show the landscape created by Forest Code compliance, with permanent protection areas of forest along watercourses and larger blocs of forest that could be a legal reserve or protected area, July 18, 2014. (Author's photo)

GIS to manage rural environmental licensing (which regulates land use, including forest cover, on private properties). In 2006, spurred by a Greenpeace campaign, transnational soy traders agreed to a moratorium on purchasing soy from newly deforested areas in the Amazon. The Soy Moratorium and environmentalist pressures motivated the municipal government of Lucas do Rio Verde (Lucas) in Mato Grosso to partner with The Nature Conservancy (TNC) to pursue compliance with environmental regulations, including SLAPR registration of all rural properties. The Lucas project began in 2006, but in 2008 the federal environmental enforcement agency (IBAMA) fined landowners in Lucas for violations. The fines damaged the project's credibility with producers and led to lobbying by municipal leaders, TNC, and the state environmental agency, culminating in a state law creating CAR in Mato Grosso.[14] CAR divided environmental licensing into parts: producers would first voluntarily register their properties with state environmental authorities through CAR and then were granted a period to achieve compliance without incurring fines for past illegal clearing.

CAR spread regionally and nationally. In 2008, the Ministry of Environment published a "priority list" of Amazonian municipalities for combating deforestation that subjected priority municipalities to strict monitoring and enforcement. A requirement for exiting the list became completion of CAR in 80 percent of a municipality's private property area.[15] TNC, other NGOs, and the federal government developed CAR registration programs across the Amazon, and in 2009, under pressure from environmentalists and public prosecutors, meatpacking corporations in the Amazon began requiring CAR from producers in order to purchase their cattle. Pará launched a Green Municipalities Program in 2011 to encourage CAR registration, and at the federal level CAR entered the 2012 Forest Code revision as a requirement for all rural properties in Brazil.

While CAR may not have been sufficient independently to reduce deforestation or promote forest restoration on registered properties, the new institution worked in combination with other policies, such as enhanced monitoring, fines for illegal clearing, and credit and commercial restrictions on properties with illegal deforestation.[16] Collectively, these enforcement policies were responsible for major reductions in deforestation. Policies targeting priority municipalities, for example, may have avoided over ten thousand square kilometers of deforestation just in 2009–2011.[17]

The final axis of PPCDAm was support for "sustainable production," including agricultural intensification. In 2011–2014, the Brazilian government provided $2.7 billion in credit through its Low-Carbon Agriculture Program to support activities such as restoration of degraded pastures and integrated ranching-cropping-forestry systems.[18] The federal agricultural research corporation, Embrapa, promoted intensive ranching through improved pasture management and environmental compliance, while the executive's Secretariat for Strategic Affairs worked to expand credit access for ranching intensification.

At the same time, environmental NGOs expanded beyond their traditional focus on natural areas, developing programs to support ranching intensification and agricultural production on degraded lands. Brazilian NGO Instituto Centro de Vida, for example, promoted ranching intensification in northern Mato Grosso, with funding from Fundo Vale, the foundation of Brazil's Vale mining company. In Pará, TNC developed a sustainable beef project in São Félix do Xingu, supported by meat processor Marfrig and retailer Walmart, as well as a Cargill-funded program promoting cacao agroforestry on degraded lands.

Sparing the Forest and Building the State

PPCDAm, and the projects that coalesced around it, provide an example of land-sparing policy in practice in Brazil's Legal Amazon—a territory of more than 5 million square kilometers. This Brazilian experience of implementing land sparing as policy highlights a key dimension of the land-sparing project often unmentioned by academics and conservationists celebrating agricultural intensification: land-sparing policy builds state power. When scientists move beyond calculating "tradeoffs" between agricultural yields and biodiversity, they are quick to acknowledge that "yield increases cannot be depended upon to result in land sparing without active measures to protect natural habitats."[19] Moreover, investments to increase yields are unlikely to occur spontaneously so long as economic incentives favor expansion, as in the Brazilian Amazon, where extensive ranching has been particularly profitable as a form of land speculation. Accordingly, land sparing in Brazil relied heavily on government regulation to protect natural habitats and drive intensification through territorial constriction, imposing political limits on the land area available for agricultural production. Agribusiness and conservation interests were reconciled, in other words, with a central role for the Brazilian state.

State actors were well aware that land sparing was a form of state-building. Technicians from the federal government's Secretariat of Strategic Affairs wrote in the Brazilian trade magazine *Agroanalysis* that ranching intensification and "the growth of agricultural production with preservation" (i.e., land sparing) was central to "strengthening Brazil as an agricultural and environmental power."[20]

Likewise, environmentalists, academics, and business interests supporting land sparing often labeled their efforts as contributions to "environmental governance," understood as a modernist project of territorial control and development that presupposes and reinforces state authority.[21] Brazil's policy model of agricultural intensification and forest conservation through territorial constriction bolstered state power in several specific ways. Territorial constriction through protected area creation and Forest Code enforcement served to fix spaces of settlement and economic activity, rendering the territory and population legible for state administration. Forest conservation protected natural capital and helped to guarantee ecosystem services necessary for subsistence and production, while agricultural intensification raised profits and expanded infrastructure, which increased state revenues and capacity.

The PPCDAm land-sparing model merged these state-building processes with agribusiness and environmentalist interests (table 1). Agro-industrial corporations, in particular, favored intensification to improve supply-chain productivity and integrate producers into markets for inputs and financial products like credit and insurance, while territorial constriction benefited landowners by raising property values. The agribusiness sector as a whole stood to benefit from a "green" production model that could alleviate environmentalist criticism. For environmentalists, territorial constriction would secure forest conservation, while support for intensification allowed them to demonstrate the compatibility of economic and environmental goals and their commitment to benefiting local people with "green development."

In short, PPCDAm was a blueprint for transforming the Amazonian political-economic regime from extraction to productivism. Protected area creation and Forest Code enforcement would conserve forests and close the extractive frontier through territorial constriction, while support for sustainable production and tenure regularization would facilitate agricultural intensification and productivist socioeconomic development, and implementation of these productivist policies would feed back into strengthened productivist governance institutions (fig. 5).

In the decade after 2004, Brazil's Amazonian transformation surpassed all expectations. Veteran Amazon scholar Susanna Hecht

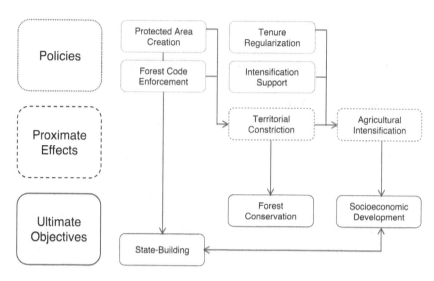

Fig. 5. The Brazilian Land-Sparing Model. This model depicts the simplified, ideal relationships motivating land-sparing advocates. Protected area creation and Forest Code enforcement contribute to state-building through territorial ordering and produce territorial constriction. Territorial constriction guarantees forest conservation while inducing agricultural intensification, which is also supported by tenure regularization and agricultural policy. Agricultural intensification catalyzes socioeconomic development, and development and state-building are mutually reinforcing.

Table 1. Sectors and Interests in Amazonian Land Sparing

	Interests in Land-Sparing Policy		
Sector	Territorial constriction	Agricultural intensification	Forest conservation
State	Legibility and control	Revenue and infrastructure	Natural capital and ecosystem services
Agro-industrial capital	Increasing land values	Productivity and supply-chain integration	Ecosystem services
Environmental NGOs	Forest conservation	Green development	Biodiversity and ecosystem integrity

marveled in 2011 that Brazil's plummeting deforestation rates would have been "unimaginable even a decade ago," while a group of eighteen prominent scientists and conservationists wrote in 2009 that Brazil's forest policy successes "finally make feasible the end of deforestation in the Brazilian Amazon."[22] Despite aggregate statistics showing declining deforestation and increasing soy and cattle production, political-economic change over such a vast and diverse territory was highly varied, and different policies were implemented with different levels of efficiency and effectiveness. While command-and-control actions clamped down on illegal deforestation, support for sustainable production and tenure regularization languished, leaving especially smallholders in dire straits, unable to expand and unable to intensify. Territorial constriction, meanwhile, was contested at multiple levels by persistent coalitions of extractive actors, and the "ruralist bench" of the Brazilian Congress pushed back by passing a new Forest Code in 2012 and moving to weaken protected areas.

In 2013, when I arrived in Belém, Pará's steamy capital on the banks of the Amazon estuary, Brazil's Amazonian deforestation was at a historic low. It became clear, however, as I spent time in the "interior" of the Xingu and Tapajós River basins of southern Pará and northern Mato Grosso, that the transition from extraction to a productivist economy was far from complete and profoundly uneven. Industrial soy production and intensive ranching were making inroads on these extractive frontiers, while the indirect social and ecological effects of land-sparing policies and agro-industrial development—small-farmer dispossession and frontier displacement—swirled beneath the surface of triumphant narratives of Brazil's deforestation "success."

When I returned to the Amazonian interior four years later in 2018, tensions had heightened. With the ascension of agribusiness interests and cuts to environmental programs during Dilma Rousseff's administration, and especially under Michel Temer's right-wing government that took power after Rousseff's impeachment, federal support for land sparing was rapidly eroding. When Jair Bolsonaro took office in 2019, Brazil's conservation success went up in smoke.

For land-sparing advocates, the collapse of the Brazilian policy model does not invalidate the land-sparing hypothesis. Faced with resurgent extraction, they call for a return to the "successful" policies of the 2000s. But what did these policies look like on the ground, in the frontier municipalities that one NGO worker called "the eye of the hurricane" of Amazonian deforestation?[23] And what do the experiences of these municipalities say about the viability of land sparing as a project for "green development"?

CHAPTER SIX

Greening the Soy Complex
in Nova Ubiratã

T HE STATE OF MATO Grosso lies in the Center-West region of the Brazilian interior and occupies the transition zone between the Cerrado tropical savanna biome
in the eastern and southern parts of the state and the
Amazon biome in the north and west. The Pantanal wetlands biome
lies in the state's extreme south. Cuiabá, present-day capital of Mato
Grosso ("Capital of the Pantanal and of Agribusiness," proclaims a
highway sign), became a center of gold mining in the eighteenth
century, and extensive cattle ranching connected interior mining areas with the agricultural economies of the southern Brazilian coast.

Because much of Mato Grosso is a savanna region and historically connected by land with the Brazilian South and Southeast,
it has a history somewhat distinct from the history of the broader
Amazon Basin that centered on river networks. During the 1970s
to 1990s, Mato Grosso experienced rapid infrastructure development, population growth, deforestation, and agricultural expansion. SUDECO (the Superintendency for the Development of the
Center-West) was established in 1967 as the Center-West counterpart to SUDAM and supported infrastructure and development
programs in the region. Construction of the BR-163 highway began
in 1971, linking Cuiabá with Santarém on the main trunk of the

*Fig. 6. Map of Brazil showing Nova Ubiratã in Mato
Grosso State and São Félix in Pará State.*

Amazon and opening a vast new frontier in northern Mato Grosso
and western Pará. Both the federal government and private firms
launched colonization projects to attract small farmers to the state.
At the same time, agricultural subsidies provided by developmentalist programs including Polocentro (the Center-West counterpart to
Polonoroeste) and the Japanese-financed PRODECER supported
the growth of large-scale ranching and row crop cultivation. Research by Embrapa, the Brazilian Agricultural Research Corporation, identified fertilizer and lime applications to counteract the
acidity and aluminum toxicity of Cerrado soils and developed new
soy cultivars. Meanwhile, agricultural intensification in southern
Brazil raised land values and displaced small farmers, pushing migration and investment into the Center-West. These processes drove

the coupled soy and cattle frontiers far into northern and western Mato Grosso and transformed the state into the epicenter of Brazil's agro-export economy.

During the 1990s and early 2000s, Mato Grosso was the state with the highest annual deforestation rate in the Brazilian Amazon, comprising roughly 40 percent of Brazil's total Amazonian deforestation. Mechanized soy production requires high levels of investment, and its expansion in eastern and central Mato Grosso integrated these parts of the state into transnational commodity chains, providing a foundation for articulated agro-industrial development through the provision of infrastructure and inputs and through the production of value-added outputs such as soy meal, biodiesel, pork and poultry, and processed meat products. With the conversion of pasture to row crops and rising land values due to soy expansion, remaining ranching operations in soy areas were also forced to intensify. Contrary to descriptions of industrial soy production elsewhere in South America as a form of "agrarian extractivism," this Brazilian "soy complex"—an economic assemblage of mechanized production of soy and associated crops (e.g., corn and cotton), intensive ranching, and small livestock production—drove a state-level productivist transformation in Mato Grosso.[1]

In the north and northwest of the state, however, an extractive political economy persisted centering on logging, mining, and extensive ranching. Lisa Rausch writes that the State Environmental Foundation (FEMA), Mato Grosso's environmental regulatory agency, was "plagued by corruption and inefficiencies. . . . Therefore, farmers' willingness to comply with its regulations, given that compliance usually came at the expense of profits, was also low. Farmers knew that if they were to be fined (unlikely, in any case, due to the expanse of the state and the few resources available to FEMA agents); the going-rate for a bribe to have the fine disappear was around 10 percent of the total value of the fine." The effective payment rate of environmental fines in Mato Grosso was around only 6 or 7 percent, and in 2005 the president of FEMA, the superintendent of IBAMA in Mato Grosso, and some eighty other officials, loggers, and timber traders were arrested in a bust of an illegal logging ring.[2] This scandal led to the dissolution of FEMA, which was replaced by the State Environmental Agency (SEMA).

In 2004, the year that deforestation in the state peaked and nearly twelve thousand square kilometers of primary forest were cleared, Mato Grosso produced 29 percent of Brazil's soy harvest and supported 13 percent of the national cattle herd.[3] Expanding soy production and rapid deforestation during the late 1990s coincided with the increasing power of soy producers and agro-industrial interests in state-level politics and changes in state-level forest governance institutions. Governance in Brazil was marked by a general trend of decentralization during the 1990s, which included decentralization of some environmental governance responsibilities to the states. The Mato Grosso State Environmental Code was approved in 1995, and in 1999 the federal government devolved control over forest management and environmental licensing to FEMA, though monitoring and enforcement powers remained with federal agencies.

In 2000, with support from the Pilot Program to Conserve the Brazilian Rainforest administered by the World Bank, Mato Grosso launched the System for Environmental Licensing of Rural Properties (SLAPR). SLAPR was built as a novel system for managing rural environmental licensing, monitoring, and enforcement related to the Forest Code using remote sensing and GIS technology. Registration in SLAPR occurred on a voluntary, property-by-property basis. There were numerous problems with the system, including low-resolution monitoring technology, reluctance of landowners to "turn themselves in" and be fined for illegal clearing, but also reluctance of state authorities to fine those who registered to avoid deterring people from the system.[4] Rausch explains that SLAPR was intended by the state government as a way to leverage funding for other development programs, and licensing (which would legalize further agricultural expansion) was favored over monitoring (which would detect illegal clearing).[5] SLAPR ultimately did little to constrain deforestation, though it was nonetheless strongly opposed by rural agricultural interests. To the contrary, deforestation was higher on licensed properties than on those properties without licenses, supporting the claim that SLAPR was intended more as an economic project than an environmental one, aimed at legitimizing Mato Grosso's agricultural production for external markets.[6] As one rancher told me in Nova Ubiratã, environmental registration was a way for the government and agro-industry associations to "put a stop to the environmentalists."[7] Deforestation continued to increase after the introduction of SLAPR, and opposition to the system may have contributed to the election of Blairo Maggi, Brazil's largest soy producer, as governor of Mato Grosso in 2002.[8]

Maggi's election led many environmentalists to fear the worst for forest conservation in Mato Grosso. Deforestation in the state increased over 13 percent from 2003 to 2004, and in 2005 the NGO Greenpeace bestowed on Maggi its "Golden Chainsaw" award, calling him the person "most responsible for Amazon destruction."[9] During 2005, however, deforestation in Mato Grosso began to decline precipitously, and by the time Maggi left the governor's office in 2010, he had even come to be viewed as an "unlikely hero of the environmental movement" for his efforts to combat illegal deforestation.[10]

Of course, the reduction in deforestation is not attributable solely to Blairo Maggi. After 2004, deforestation in Mato Grosso was checked by new governance interventions and declining soy profitability due to a downturn in global commodity markets. Lowered economic incentives for expansion and the potential economic benefits of certified legal compliance during times of reduced profitability contributed to a willingness of Mato Grosso soy producers to engage in new governance initiatives in the 2005–2007 period.[11] Blairo Maggi's company, Grupo Maggi, had already in 2002 begun to develop an "environmental and social management system" for its supply chain under the conditions of a loan from the International Finance Corporation, to which it agreed in part with the objective of achieving "legitimacy and recognition for adhering to environmental and social standards that other soy exporters could not claim."[12] In 2006, in response to a Greenpeace campaign, the major transnational soy traders agreed not to purchase soy produced on newly deforested land in the Amazon, and Maggi's company was well-prepared to comply with the moratorium.

Also in 2006, TNC began to collaborate with the municipal government of Lucas do Rio Verde, a soy-producing municipality on the BR-163 to the north of Cuiabá, to support landholders working toward compliance with the Forest Code, allowing the municipality to promote an image of "environmentally responsible" production. The project received support from major national and transnational agribusiness corporations with operations in the municipality, as well as from the rural producers' syndicate, State Public Ministry, and SEMA. Spiking commodity prices in 2007 drove an increase in deforestation across the Amazon, and the federal government responded in 2008 by creating the "priority list" of municipalities for combating deforestation and imposing credit restrictions on properties not compliant with environmental regulations. The tightening of the federal enforcement regime posed an impediment to agro-industrial expansion in Mato Grosso and threatened the reputation of the state's producers in international markets. These new pressures led to a public spat, with the *New York Times* reporting that "Governor Maggi was exercised enough by the [INPE deforestation] report—which led to harsh measures stifling business in his state—that he asked for, and was granted, a meeting with the president, Luiz Inácio Lula da Silva," and the state government went so far as to submit a formal refutation of INPE's findings.[13]

In Lucas do Rio Verde, the fining of fifteen property owners by IBAMA in September 2008 triggered intense lobbying by municipal leaders, TNC, and SEMA. This lobbying, and the general dissatisfaction with the federal enforcement regime, culminated in a state law that officially created CAR in Mato Grosso, modifying SLAPR by breaking environmental licensing into stages and granting producers who completed CAR a grace period to bring their properties into compliance without being fined.[14] CAR was promoted by the Maggi government at the state level through the creation of a "Legal Mato Grosso" program (Mato Grosso Legal), and was taken up by the federal government as a condition for municipalities to exit the priority list and eventually as a requirement for all rural properties in Brazil in the 2012 Federal Forest Code.

In addition to his support for environmental registration as a strategy for "legalizing" agricultural production, Maggi became a strong advocate for Mato Grosso's participation in an international REDD mechanism, enrolling his state as one of the founding members of the Governors' Climate and Forests Task Force (GCF) in late 2008. Support for REDD initiatives continued under Maggi's successors, including through the passage of a state REDD+ law in January 2013, a part of which highlighted the potential climate benefits of agro-industrial development (such as improved pasture management and cattle genetics) in supporting deforestation reductions.[15]

In sum, under pressure from international- and national-level actors, state-level politicians and bureaucrats in Mato Grosso joined with international and domestic NGOs, multinational and regional agribusiness companies, and proactive municipal governments, farmers, and ranchers to negotiate responses to federal environmental regulations and implement a land-sparing agenda centered on territorial constriction and intensive agro-industrial production. With the exception of relatively minor increments in 2008 and 2011, annual deforestation in Mato Grosso declined steadily from 2004 until it bottomed out in 2012 at 757 square kilometers. Especially during the period of increased agribusiness profitability after 2007, these declines are attributable to the governance institutions that emerged through the operation of land-sparing coalitions across multiple levels.

From "Guts and Money" to a "Greener Nova Ubiratã"

The municipality of Nova Ubiratã, in north-central Mato Grosso, takes its name from the Fazenda Ubiratan ranch, whose owner planned the municipality's urban center.[16] While Nova Ubiratã was thus not named for Ubiratã, an agricultural town in the southern Brazilian state of Paraná, the history of Nova Ubiratã, at the boundary of the Cerrado and Amazon biomes, is nonetheless intertwined with the history of Ubiratã in the southern Atlantic Forest biome.

In the 1950s, the present-day municipality of Ubiratã, in western Paraná, was settled by a private firm: the Northwest Paraná Real Estate Company, or Sociedade Imobiliária Noroeste do Paraná (SINOP). The firm sold lots in the settlement to small farmers from across southern Brazil and beyond, who planted various crops from corn and beans to mint and coffee. Ubiratã's population grew precipitously to over fifty thousand inhabitants in the early 1970s, then just as quickly declined as mechanized soy and wheat production drove small farmers and laborers off the land and the national government promoted colonization projects to the north and west in the Cerrado and Amazon.[17] In 1971, SINOP, the colonization firm, set its sights on Mato Grosso, where it organized colonization of an area of 6,450 square kilometers that today comprises the municipalities of Sinop, Santa Carmem, Cláudia, and Vera (which borders Nova Ubiratã). Thus, agricultural intensification in southern Brazil displaced capital and migrants to new frontiers. SINOP, which had profited from Atlantic Forest destruction, now profited from the conversion of Cerrado woodlands and Amazon rainforest to agriculture. Small farmers and farmworkers who had settled Brazil's southern interior were now displaced by the industrial soy complex to forest frontiers in Mato Grosso and beyond. In Nova Ubiratã, a territory of 12,707 square kilometers in the upper reaches of the Xingu watershed, the drama of capitalist development would be repeated.

The area that today comprises Nova Ubiratã municipality lies in the transition zone between the Cerrado and Amazon biomes. Colonization of the area began in the 1950s, directed by private colonization companies that settled nearly two hundred Japanese families with the idea of promoting rubber and pepper production. Many of these initial settlers perished in a malaria epidemic, and those that survived migrated to more developed areas. Land speculators from the south also established holdings in Nova Ubiratã during this period, but it was not until the mid-1970s that a wave of permanent colonization began, directed by a new set of colonization companies that attracted settlers from southern Brazil. The colonization process followed a pattern common to Amazonian frontiers of land grabbing and violent land conflicts between large and small landholders. Land was cleared by logging operations, ranchers, and colonists who established rice and soy farms.[18]

The "urban center" of the municipal seat was established in 1986, and in 1995 Nova Ubiratã became an independent municipality. The municipal seat lies on the BR-242 highway just over eighty kilometers to the east of Sorriso, which during the 1990s became a major center of soy production on the north-south BR-163 corridor. The municipal territory falls between the municipalities of the BR-163 to the west and the Xingu Indigenous Park to the east, with the far northeastern tip of the municipality overlapping thirty thousand hectares of the park. Roughly 25 percent of Nova Ubiratã is classified as Cerrado, while the remaining 75 percent is in the Amazon biome.[19]

Between 1996 and 1999, the federal government created four agrarian reform settlements covering over 77,000 hectares, primarily in the southwest and northeast of the municipality, where over 900 small-farmer families were settled. The Rio Ronuro Ecological Station, a state-level protected area, was created in 1998 in the eastern part of the municipality over an area of 131,795 hectares. During this period, the population of Nova Ubiratã grew quickly, registering 5,654 residents in the 2000 census.[20] By 2000, nearly 20 percent of the municipal territory had been deforested, an area of 2,400 square kilometers.

During the early 2000s, soy cultivation expanded rapidly in Nova Ubiratã, linked with the regional soy boom along the BR-163 corridor. In 2005, the Rio Ronuro protected area was reduced by nearly thirty thousand hectares to exclude four large landholdings in the southern part of the reserve, an early "reconciliation" of agriculture and conservation in favor of agro-industry. The municipal population continued to grow with the soy boom, reaching 7,782 in 2007.[21] Sorriso and Lucas do Rio Verde, lying to the west of Nova Ubiratã on the BR-163, had transformed into major agro-industrial centers, with Sorriso becoming the largest municipal producer of soy in Mato Grosso. Smaller ranchers sold their land, pastures were converted to soy (usually rotated with corn or cotton), and forest was felled either for direct conversion to soy or for new pastures and land speculation.

Deforestation in Nova Ubiratã spiked along with soy expansion, peaking in 2004 when 383 square kilometers of forest were cleared. After 2005, deforestation declined steeply, reined in by PPCDAm and a slump in commodity prices. The new land-sparing model of PPCDAm was imposed in Nova Ubiratã on a municipal economy where the agro-industrial soy complex was already well-established. The primary goal in Nova Ubiratã, from a land-sparing perspective, was therefore to consolidate agro-industrial growth in cleared areas while avoiding new deforestation.

When commodity prices rebounded in 2007, forest clearing jumped again in the municipality (fig. 7), and Nova Ubiratã was

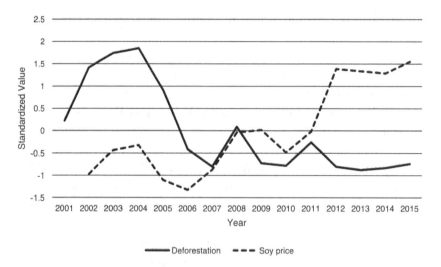

Fig. 7. Commodity-driven deforestation in Nova Ubiratã. Deforestation and soy prices (standardized for comparison) appear closely correlated until 2011, after which deforestation remained low despite spiking commodity prices. Standardized soy prices were calculated from the Brazilian reais price per sixty kilograms in Paraná. Sources: CEPEA, http://www.cepea .esalq.usp.br/br/consultas-ao-banco-de-dados-do-site.aspx; PRODES, http://www.dpi.inpe.br/prodesdigital/prodesmunicipal.php.

included in 2008 in the federal priority list, subjecting rural produc-ers to credit restrictions and intensified enforcement. Speaking with me in 2014, a technician with the municipal Environmental Sec-retariat affirmed that enforcement "comes down heavily, it's rigid," and a former municipal official reflected that "before, Nova Ubiratã was at the end of the world. [You could deforest and] no one would know, no one would do anything. Now the regulatory deadlines are pressing."[22] Family agriculture was particularly affected by the enforcement actions, and the entire agrarian reform settlements of Boa Esperança, home to nearly four hundred families, were embar-goed by IBAMA, meaning they could not legally access credit or sell their cattle or crops. Residents also reported that Nova Ubi-ratã's status on the priority list may have deterred some agribusiness companies and businesspeople from investing in the municipality.[23] These tightened enforcement measures caused most landowners in Nova Ubiratã to cease deforestation on their properties.[24]

In an effort to remove the municipality from the priority list and help landowners "disembargo" their properties, the mayor of Nova Ubiratã, Osmar Rossetto (known as Chiquinho), sought out TNC. People in Nova Ubiratã knew of TNC's work in the neighboring municipality of Lucas do Rio Verde, and Chiquinho hoped to implement a similar project in Nova Ubiratã. At first TNC had no funding for a project in the municipality, but when TNC received a 16 million reais grant from the Amazon Fund to support environmental registration (CAR) in twelve municipalities in Mato Grosso and Pará, Nova Ubiratã was included in the program.[25] The TNC project in the municipality, called "Greener Nova Ubiratã" (Nova Ubiratã Mais Verde), was implemented in partnership with the municipal government and the rural producers' syndicate (the large landowners' association). TNC hired a municipal manager to begin a process of mapping and database development, as well as communication and awareness-raising regarding Forest Code compliance and environmental management. Soon thereafter the project also contracted a forestry engineer who was certified to formally register properties in CAR.

The project principally supported CAR registration for small landowners and residents of agrarian reform settlements, since most large landowners were already registered or in the process of CAR registration.[26] The municipal government also sought to use CAR to support broader governance goals. A former municipal official described how data collection in support of CAR registration facilitated everything from environmental enforcement to tax collection to spatial planning to transportation for schoolchildren. They suggested that a comprehensive database of municipal properties could also be used to market the municipality and attract business. "You can't do public sector work today without planning," the official told me, and the CAR process helped build this municipal capacity.[27] More specifically, the municipal government attempted to leverage the CAR database to advance land titling in Nova Ubiratã. In 2012, Nova Ubiratã established a municipal council for tenure regularization that became a pilot for regularization efforts led by the Mato Grosso Inspector General's office (Corregedoria Geral da Justiça).[28]

Under the heavy enforcement regime of the priority list, there was little deforestation in Nova Ubiratã after 2008. Most areas in the municipality that could legally be cleared were already deforested by the time the priority list came into effect.[29] As a municipal environment official explained in 2014, "What was there to be deforested was already deforested. . . . The timber has already been taken out. The *fazendas* [large estates] are already industrialized."[30] There were two groups responsible for the deforestation still occurring in Nova Ubiratã, according to a former contractor for the TNC project: "those with no option, who must produce to survive and have no choice but to deforest; and those who have lots of money and can pay fines without any trouble."[31] An official with the local property registry (*cartório*) confirmed, "Remaining deforestation is either large actors who want to open more areas to produce more—they know that they can defend themselves in the courts and the profit they make will be greater than the costs of resolving the legal issues; or [agrarian reform] settlements where people deforest because they do not have conditions to develop sustainable activities."[32]

"Those with no option" felt the brunt of federal enforcement measures. A local news outlet reported that in the embargoed agrarian reform settlements, "Family farmers had their access to official financing blocked and were unable to produce. As a consequence, they were unable to sustain themselves from their land. Many families were obliged to abandon their lots to seek employment and income in the city."[33] In 2012, the municipality negotiated with IBAMA to disembargo lots in the settlements that completed CAR, but when a new IBAMA superintendent arrived that year, he refused to disembargo any more lots due to a dispute between IBAMA and the State Environmental Secretariat, SEMA.[34] (IBAMA objected to SEMA's approving CAR registrations without investigating a property's on-the-ground Forest Code compliance.)[35]

Among "those who have lots of money," the protagonist of continuing large-scale deforestation in Nova Ubiratã was Vademilso Badalotti. Badalotti is a large landowner who lives in Paraná. He owned thirty thousand hectares in Nova Ubiratã alone, and in 2011 he was responsible for six of the ten largest illegally deforested areas in Mato Grosso.[36] Badalotti illegally cleared nearly six thousand hectares of forest in Nova Ubiratã using an outlawed practice known as *correntão*, where two bulldozers are connected by a chain and driven forward together to fell all vegetation that comes between them. Deforestation by Badalotti, along with large-scale clearing by other landowners, brought a federal enforcement task force to the municipality in May 2011.[37] Badalotti was known to be engaging in land speculation by buying and clearing areas in Nova Ubiratã, with the intention of renting out deforested areas for rice or soy production.[38] "Speculators get fined, but it is still financially worth it," a former municipal official explained. "They clear the land, and then fight in the courts. They are carpetbaggers [*aventureiros*] with guts and money. . . . If someone has an area that they don't want to or can't legalize, they may sell it to an *aventureiro* to clear and speculate on."[39]

"Have you heard of Badalotti?" a technician in the municipal Environmental Secretariat asked me during an interview in 2014. "Yes," I answered. "How did he deforest such a large area?" The technician rubbed his fingers together: "money and guts."[40] Even as agro-industry in Nova Ubiratã consolidated and intensified in the early 2010s, the productivist municipal economy could not be wholly separated from processes of extractive speculation and illegal forest clearing.[41]

Despite the efforts of the municipal government and the Greener Nova Ubiratã project, the municipality failed to exit the priority list, principally due to difficulties in completing CAR in agrarian reform settlements, bureaucratic delays by SEMA in confirming CAR registrations, and deforestation by land speculators such as Badalotti.[42] Annual deforestation remained low after 2011, however. At the end of the TNC project in December 2013, 55 percent of the private property space in Nova Ubiratã had been registered in CAR.[43] The 2012 Forest Code revision made CAR a requirement for all rural properties in Brazil but also changed the character of CAR in Mato Grosso. The Mato Grosso registry originally required documentation of land rights for completion of full environmental licensing, but the 2012 Forest Code instituted CAR as an unconfirmed declaration by property holders, which was the more flexible model that had been deployed in Pará. By 2017, an area of 1,212,389 hectares in Nova Ubiratã had been registered in CAR, which was nearly 100,000 hectares greater than the area legally open to registration in the municipality. These registries include over 4,000 hectares overlapping Indigenous territories and nearly 74,000 hectares overlapping designated conservation areas.[44]

The municipal government in Nova Ubiratã, and in particular Chiquinho, the mayor, played a key role alongside TNC in implementing environmental policies to "green" the productivist economy. One TNC staff member recalled that "Chiquinho was the most involved of all the mayors. With any question he would pick up the phone and call TNC."[45] The local forestry engineer noted that Chiquinho "knew how the whole process worked, including the software," and another TNC employee recalled that Chiquinho would check for fire alerts every day on his cellphone to monitor new deforestation.[46] After leaving the mayorship, Chiquinho went on to become a functionary with the federal land agency (Instituto Nacional de Colonização e Reforma Agrária, INCRA) in Cuiabá, and during our interview in the INCRA offices he frequently turned to his computer to pull up GIS and Google Earth files to illustrate his points. Bernadete Rechmann, Chiquinho's secretary of environment during most of the project period, was also an active promoter of the project, particularly in the agrarian reform settlements.[47]

In my 2014 visit to the municipality, there was general agreement among the people I spoke with linked to TNC, the municipal government, and the rural producers' syndicate that the Greener Nova Ubiratã project had been worthwhile, deforestation was largely under control, and CAR registration had advanced. A former municipal government employee noted that national-level debates around the Forest Code revision had hindered the project, since industry associations had counseled landowners to wait for the new legislation before completing CAR. With the passage of the new Forest Code and harmonization of state regulations, however, "the situation has been clarified," and even industry associations were advising farmers and ranchers to complete CAR.[48] Nova Ubiratã's position between the Cerrado and Amazon biomes added a wrinkle to environmental compliance, since properties in the Cerrado biome are only required to maintain 35 percent of their area as a Legal Reserve, while properties in the Amazon generally must maintain 80 percent. While most large landholders know in which biome their property falls, there were stories of small producers who deforested beyond their legal limits because they believed themselves to be in the Cerrado when in fact they were in the Amazon.[49]

Environmental licensing and tenure regularization remained mired in the inefficient bureaucracies of SEMA and INCRA, but after 2012 Nova Ubiratã became fully consolidated as a post-frontier agricultural zone under productivist political-economic regimes at the municipal, state, and national levels that emphasized environmental compliance, tenure regularization, and agro-industrial development. The president of the rural syndicate, a local rancher, described to me this transformation:

Production has increased through the restoration or transformation of degraded pastures, primarily into [field crop] agriculture. The pasture area diminished. Ranchers became farmers, and many farmers also came from outside the municipality, including from Sorriso and Lucas. Technology increased and people invested a great deal. . . . The character of the cattle herd changed. Cattle breeding [*recria*] diminished, but finishing [*engorda*—literally, "fattening"] stayed at the same level. Producers are now using feedlots [*confinamento*]. . . . Some ranchers who became farmers are doing integrated [soy/maize and cattle] production. Pastures were very degraded, so the ranchers were going to have to take up agriculture. With the end of deforestation, ranchers realized they needed to intensify. Ranchers themselves sought out new technologies. . . . Old, extensive ranching is very rare today. Old ranchers had to give space for technology to enter.

The expansion of production into degraded areas is going to cease eventually [for lack of additional degraded areas], and further expansion will have to be from the opening of currently embargoed areas. After that, production will stagnate. Production costs have increased greatly. Oil and diesel are very expensive, and producers can't clear new areas. Throughout Mato Grosso, production will stagnate unless there are increases in technology. Since there is great demand, there will be new technologies. It's the natural process of production. Instead of opening new areas, producers will have to produce ever more within the same area. They will increase production and diminish costs with technology.[50]

This rancher's narrative provides a remarkably complete recapitulation of the land-sparing logic of intensification as a response to the "end of deforestation," Esther Boserup's classic logic of intensification as the result of land scarcity, and modernization discourse that views agricultural development as a process of productivist investment and technological intensification.[51] His description of the land-use transformation in Nova Ubiratã is borne out by statistics showing the expansion of soy production over an ever-greater proportion of the deforested area of the municipality (fig. 8), which implies that the continuing increase in the municipal cattle herd concurrent with declining deforestation and increasing soy area came from the intensification of ranching operations (fig. 9). The land-use

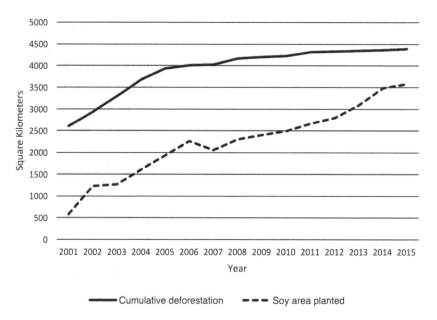

Fig. 8. Soy expansion in Nova Ubiratã. Soy and associated row crop cultivation has occupied an increasing proportion of the total deforested area of the municipality. Sources: "Produção Agrícola Municipal," IBGE, http://www.sidra .ibge.gov.br/bda/pesquisas/pam/default.asp?o=29&i=P; PRODES.

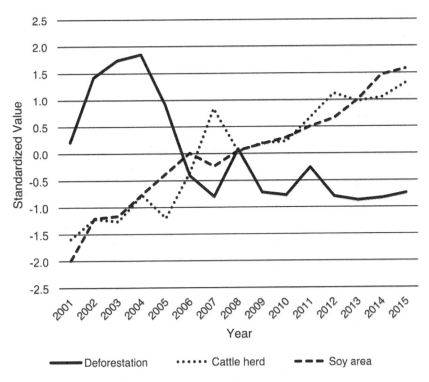

Fig. 9. "Decoupling" of agricultural production and deforestation in Nova Ubiratã. While deforestation has declined, the cattle herd and soy area have continued to increase. All values standardized for comparison. Sources: "Produção Agrícola Municipal"; "Pesquisa Pecuária Municipal," IBGE, https://sidra.ibge.gov.br/pesquisa/ppm/quadros/brasil/2016; PRODES.

transition in the municipality mirrored the state-level transition in Mato Grosso that land-sparing advocates heralded as the "decoupling" of deforestation and soy production. A member of the municipal government confirmed that ranching operations were now working with feedlots and devoted to finishing cattle, while breeding operations had moved northward toward the border with Pará.[52]

A former president of the rural producers' syndicate similarly affirmed this productivist, land-sparing vision, saying, "Production does not depend on deforestation: we don't have to cut down a single tree. There is degraded pasture available, and technology. Ranching is no longer extensive. It needs to be intensive, with pasture rotations and management. Degraded pasture can be used for agriculture. New techniques are changing the profile of agriculture and ranching, . . . and there are various credit lines . . . and agencies that help support intensification."[53] With territorial constriction through environmental enforcement and an inflow of investment linked to the burgeoning soy complex, Nova Ubiratã had transformed almost completely from a zone of extraction to a zone of production, moving from the periphery of logging and extensive ranching toward the expanding agro-industrial core. Behind the modernist triumph of the soy farmers and intensive ranchers, however, lay the displacement of smallholders, squeezed by environmental regulations imposed without corresponding support for compliance and agricultural investment. This unevenness of the Amazonian transition comes into sharper focus farther north in São Félix do Xingu (see chapter 7), where land-sparing policies were imposed over an economy still rooted in extensive agriculture. In Nova Ubiratã, land-sparing regulations came when productivist "development" was already well underway, and so rather than catalyzing economic transformation, land-sparing policies served largely to "green" the fait accompli of the destruction of a biodiverse forest landscape for "development" in the guise of cattle feedlots and soy farms.

Green Successes, Green Fictions

In 2018, I traveled south on the BR-163 from Pará into northern Mato Grosso. I spent the night in a small hotel near the bus station in Sinop and caught a bus the next morning from Sinop to Sorriso. It was easy to see why people in southern Pará and northern Mato Grosso so often point to Sinop as an emblem of development. The city is clearly organized, with wide streets, attractive buildings, and bustling commerce, from tractor sales to beer bars. Between Sinop and Sorriso, massive grain elevators lined the highway, emblazoned with the names of transnational agribusiness corporations: Bunge, Amaggi, ADM, Cofco. Instead of castanheiras, power lines and cell towers dotted the fields.

In Sorriso, new luxury apartment high-rises looked out over the warehouses and silos, announcing a city on the up. On the drive from

Sorriso to Nova Ubiratã, I talked with my taxi driver, a migrant from Paraná who used to be a farmworker but said he stopped because of the toxic agrochemicals. We passed the Bunge and Cargill grain elevators in Caravágio, a depot in eastern Sorriso municipality near the border with Nova Ubiratã. Turning at last to follow the BR-242 into Nova Ubiratã, there were now four grain elevators at the entrance to the municipal seat, where four years before there was just one. The town, too, showed signs of Nova Ubiratã's continuing development. Wooden houses in the center of town were being replaced by contemporary construction, and an entirely new neighborhood was growing up to the east of the town center, anchored by a new municipal government building (*prefeitura*). Near the main plaza in the town center, where four years earlier there was little more than a few small restaurants selling meat skewers, people sat drinking at tables outside a new gas station and convenience store, while the beverage distributor on the plaza had a live *forró* singer and keyboardist who on Sunday night could be heard through half the town.

The modernizing urban center, and the forest of warehouses and silos sprouting up at the gateway to town, were signs of a municipal agricultural economy that had grown increasingly intensive and industrialized. At the rural producers' syndicate, the new president, another transplant from Paraná, told me, "In the past four years, producers have been investing more in technologies for production and attaining higher levels of production. . . . We are attaining higher production in soy and also in corn, using fertilizer more heavily and fungicide." Some ranchers were using feedlots, doing rotations of soy and pasture, and using soy residues and corn silage for cattle (a set of intensive ranching practices known as agriculture-ranching integration—*integração lavoura pecuária*). Farmers were also beginning to plant cotton and invest in center-pivot irrigation systems, and large properties had invested in increased warehouse capacity. These on-farm investments were coupled with growing value-added industry in the local economy. The syndicate president said that an American company was producing corn ethanol in Lucas do Rio Verde and would soon build an ethanol plant in Sorriso, which would increase corn prices. "From what I've seen, it's going to be very good," he smiled. Pig and chicken farms were starting to appear in the municipality, though the slaughterhouse was in Sorriso, which is rather far for transporting chickens.[54] Investments in transportation infrastructure were also in the offing, however, with the gradual completion and paving of the BR-242 highway. This highway, when finished, will improve connections between Sorriso and the BR-163 corridor with ports on Brazil's Atlantic coast. Improved logistics and increased traffic through Nova Ubiratã would fuel further growth in the municipality and across the region.

Not only was Nova Ubiratã on a trajectory of rapid productivist development, but this development was also purportedly "green" and decoupled from new deforestation. In September 2017, the Ministry of Environment removed Nova Ubiratã from its priority list, declaring it a municipality "with deforestation monitored and under control."[55] Ten months later, it seemed as though the municipality's exit from the famous "blacklist" had gone virtually unnoticed. "I wasn't involved in leaving the list," the new secretary of environment told me in 2018. "I entered [the Secretariat], and we exited the list—it fell in my lap." He said he had seen no direct effects from exiting the list, though probably credit lines would improve.[56] "We exited the list?" the surprised cartório official asked when I brought up the topic during our interview in the sleek new cartório building. "I think even the mayor might not know that!" he exclaimed, and he asked me to send him the Ministry of Environment's announcement.[57]

After the 2012 Forest Code revision, which decreased forest restoration requirements for many properties, CAR and environmental compliance became so normalized and the momentum of the soy complex became so powerful in developing the productivist municipal economy that the federal priority list—and large-scale deforestation itself—had become an afterthought. "There is awareness that you have to comply now, you have to regularize yourself," the environment secretary explained. "People are no longer interested in being outside the law. Everything that you're going to buy and sell has to be legal, especially for large producers."[58] The saga of the environmental embargo on the Boa Esperança agrarian reform settlement was still unresolved, with attendant limits on credit and market opportunities for smallholder settlers, but from 2015 to 2018 municipal deforestation averaged less than thirty square kilometers per year, and Nova Ubiratã's days as a hotspot in Brazil's Arc of Deforestation seemed well in the past.

In Nova Ubiratã, a coalition of federal, state, and municipal government actors, TNC, and the rural producers' syndicate implemented land-sparing policies focused on Forest Code compliance in a municipality undergoing a productivist transformation driven by the developing soy complex. With intensification already underway, reductions in deforestation turned Nova Ubiratã into a "successful" land-sparing municipality in a "successful" land-sparing state. By 2018, Nova Ubiratã had become the fifth largest municipal soy producer in Mato Grosso, while 43 percent of the municipal territory remained under primary forest cover. But what were the ecological relations underpinning this new political-economic regime? How "green" was this land-sparing success?

The center-pivot irrigation systems proliferating in Nova Ubiratã require large amounts of water and energy. A municipal environment official observes that these systems consume water twice—both directly for irrigation and indirectly through energy demand that is supplied primarily by Brazil's controversial hydropower dams.[59] Local agricultural water withdrawals place pressure on the upper Teles Pires River, a tributary of the Tapajós, while the loss of Amazonian forest cover to agriculture has shortened the rainy season, altering water and energy availability at both local and regional levels, with the potential for long-term negative effects on agricultural productivity.[60] As water stress increases, fires from land clearing pose an additional threat to crops and to remaining forest areas. Fires that catch in corn straw can spread very quickly, and the president of the rural producers' syndicate recounted how "last year a fire began along the BR [highway] and entered the forest reserve of a property owner. The property owner tried to put out the fire with his tractor, the fire burned his tractor, and he got fined for the fire. . . . If the forest gets burned, you get fined."[61] Furthermore, intensive agro-industry in Nova Ubiratã depends on inputs extracted or manufactured elsewhere, including phosphorus and lime, and other fertilizers, pesticides, and machinery, and these inputs generally require fossil fuels for their production, transportation, and application. The ecological footprint of agro-industry in Nova Ubiratã thus extends far beyond the municipal boundaries, as productivist growth drives extractive expansion.

At the same time, much of the production within the municipality occurs on land that was deforested illegally. Vademilso Badalotti, environmental villain in 2011, cut a deal with the authorities, and by 2018 his formerly forested properties were just another soy field. Meanwhile, small farmers unable to remove embargoes on their properties would sell their soy to their legalized neighbors, from where it would enter the supply chains of the transnational commodity traders, winding up as animal feed in Europe or China. Many legalized properties still had unmet forest restoration requirements, even after the amnesty of the 2012 Forest Code revision. Properties with a forest debt require an environmental restoration plan (PRA) for their environmental registration (CAR) to be approved, and restoration plans can then be implemented over a period of up to twenty years. A technician at the municipal Secretariat of Environment explained that the State Environmental Agency (SEMA) was unable to monitor restoration progress directly. "At the end of the PRA, will SEMA verify the restoration?" he queried. "Possibly. But there are few people who are going to do all the restoration they ought to. In principle, then, their CAR should be suspended again."[62] Environmental compliance may then be more procedural than material—indeed, a study of Mato Grosso and Pará found little effect of CAR registration on deforestation, and reported that only 6 percent of registered landowners were taking steps to restore illegally cleared areas.[63]

Not only is ecological modernization in a "greener" Nova Ubiratã built on a past of forest destruction and a present of rising energy and material imports, but the municipal economy also profits directly from ongoing local and regional deforestation. While logging in Nova Ubiratã has diminished greatly, over a dozen logging companies were still operating in the city in the late 2010s, and much of the logging took place along the border with the municipality of Paranatinga, near the boundaries of the Xingu Indigenous Park.[64] In other words, as the environment secretary acknowledged in 2018, "The deforestation from there comes here [*desmate de lá vem pra cá*]," and Paranatinga (which also straddles the biome boundary) has been included since 2012 in the Ministry of Environment's priority list of municipalities for monitoring and controlling illegal deforestation in the Cerrado.[65]

Another instance of displaced deforestation features Cláudio Bratz, who in 2013 succeeded his brother Fabio as president of the Nova Ubiratã rural producers' syndicate and in 2016 was arrested in a federal operation targeting illegal deforestation and land trafficking along the BR-163 corridor in southern Pará. Bratz was alleged to have rented ranchland in Altamira municipality from a criminal organization specialized in illegal deforestation and land trafficking, and to have taken advantage of a chainsaw gang operated by the organization to deforest additional areas on the property.[66] Bratz's case illustrates concretely how capital from legal, "green" agro-industry in Nova Ubiratã can help drive illegal deforestation in Pará or elsewhere, and then windfall profits from illegally cleared land can be reinvested in legal, "green" properties in Nova Ubiratã or other productivist centers.

Fig. 10. BR-242 highway near Nova Ubiratã, July 2018. (Author's photo)

There is relatively little new primary deforestation within the municipal boundaries of Nova Ubiratã, but even in this exemplar of successful land sparing and green agro-industry, the ecological contradictions and displacement effects of the productivist municipal economy are easily detected. The "greenness" of productivist development, it turns out, is sustained by a series of fictions and occlusions—greenwashing past forest destruction and ignoring contemporary connections and feedbacks that transcend the municipal territory. Nova Ubiratã is well on its way to being a major agro-industrial center. Around the municipal seat, grain elevators loom and fields of soy and corn stretch away to the horizon, where at last, some dark smudges mark where a legal reserve or a streambed has spared a forest remnant. The Nature Conservancy has departed, and Nova Ubiratã's forested past feels like a distant memory. In the far corners of the municipality, around Rio Ronuro and the Xingu Indigenous Park, the last stretches of rainforest survive, beneath the fragile mantle of legal protections. As I left Nova Ubiratã in 2018, bound for the BR-163 and Cuiabá, updrafts picked up corn straw, rustling and swirling above the dry fields. Not far from the highway, a lone emu picked its way across the endless farmland.

CHAPTER SEVEN

Development and Dispossession
in São Félix do Xingu

ROM ITS LOCATION AT the mouth of the Amazon River, the state of Pará has been a conduit for the development of the entire Amazon Basin. Belém was a capital of the rubber boom, and southeastern Pará was a major center of mahogany and brazil nut extraction.[1] Logging has been a mainstay of the economy since the colonial period, and mining, carried out by large companies such as Vale (most famously at the Carajás iron mines) and by prospectors (most famously in the Serra Pelada gold rush), has been a dominant economic sector especially since the 1970s. Extensive ranching supported by government credits and subsidies drove large-scale deforestation in Pará from the 1970s onward. Between 1988 and 2016, Pará lost 143,159 square kilometers of forest, comprising 34 percent of total deforestation in the Brazilian Amazon, and since 2006 it has been the Amazonian state with the highest annual deforestation rate.

The extractive political-economic regime in Pará was bolstered by systematic corruption and violent dispossession of Indigenous peoples, other traditional populations, and small-farmer colonists. Jader Barbalho, who has served as governor, federal deputy, and senator of Pará, is accused of having coordinated the diversion of billions of reais from SUDAM, and a former state secretary of environment claimed in 2011 that half of timber production in the state was illegal and that corruption in SEMA, the Environmental Secretariat, was endemic.[2] Loggers, ranchers, and their hired guns expanded timber extraction and consolidated large ranches through violent land grabs, gaining infamy for southern Pará as "Brazil's most dangerous badland."[3] The 2005 murder of Dorothy Stang, an American-born nun who since the 1970s had been an advocate for small-farmer land rights in Pará, provided a stark reminder of the dangers of challenging extractive interests in the region. Sister Dorothy's murder gave additional impetus to the implementation of PPCDAm and the creation of protected areas in the Terra do Meio (the Land in the Middle), between the Xingu and Tapajós Rivers.

With the launch of PPCDAm and the rise of land-sparing policy coalitions, the Pará state government adopted policies to limit deforestation and support a productivist transition, though extractive coalitions continued to exercise considerable power in state-level politics. State-level protected areas were designated alongside federal areas, including the Triunfo do Xingu Environmental Protection Area in São Félix, created in 2006. In 2007, as deforestation ticked upward with the rise in global commodity prices, Valmir Ortega, director of ecosystems at IBAMA, was brought in as state secretary of the environment. Ortega cracked down on illegal logging and sought to root out corruption in the Environmental Secretariat—more than seventy SEMA employees were removed for corruption during his two years as secretary—but he was opposed and undermined by logging interests to the point where he resigned in mid-2009.[4] In 2008, Pará became one of the founding members of the Governors' Climate and Forests Task Force (GCF).

Pará did not have Mato Grosso's early experience with environmental registration through SLAPR, but after the creation of CAR in Mato Grosso, Pará also developed an environmental registry from 2007 onward. The Ministry of Environment's priority list was created in 2008, and the municipality of Paragominas, in northeastern Pará, launched a municipal initiative to exit the list, with support from TNC and Imazon, a Brazilian environmental NGO based in Belém. Paragominas succeeded in negotiating with the Ministry of Environment to accept CAR in lieu of a full review of land titles as a criterion for leaving the priority list, and in 2010 Paragominas became the first municipality to exit the list. The example of Para-gominas's "Green Municipality" project was then heavily promoted by the state and federal governments and environmental NGOs, including TNC, as a model for combating deforestation and supporting municipal environmental governance.[5] In March 2011, Pará launched a Green Municipalities Program, based on the Paragominas model, to combat deforestation and promote sustainable rural activities through CAR implementation and municipal capacity building. Other state programs were made conditional on adhering to this program, such that by December 2015, 107 out of 144 municipalities in Pará had joined.

Prosecutors for the Federal Public Ministry (MPF) in Pará, in particular Daniel Azeredo, became key actors in promoting environmental governance in the state and throughout the Amazon region. In 2009, MPF began requiring slaughterhouses to purchase cattle only from properties with CAR, which substantially increased CAR registration by ranchers.[6] MPF also required municipalities to agree to municipal "pacts" for controlling deforestation in order to extend environmental compliance deadlines for rural producers, and in 2012 Azeredo brought a civil action against INCRA, the federal agency responsible for tenure regularization and agrarian reform, for its failure to ensure environmental compliance in agrarian reform settlements.

Annual deforestation in Pará declined 80 percent from its 2004 peak to its lowest point in 2012 (compared to a 94 percent decline in Mato Grosso), but after 2012, deforestation began again to accelerate, calling into question the completeness and durability of Pará's land-use transition. The experience of São Félix do Xingu municipality, in southeastern Pará, illustrates the workings of a land-sparing coalition at the local level and highlights the uneven and contested trajectory of the productivist transition this coalition pursued. Rather than imposing land-sparing policies over an existing agro-industrial economy, as occurred in Nova Ubiratã, land-sparing advocates in São Félix encountered a stubbornly extractive cattle economy dominated by extensive ranchers and land grabbers. Could land-sparing policies engineer a productivist transition in a zone of extraction? Could land sparing fulfill its promise to both conserve and develop at once?

São Félix do Xingu and the Land in the Middle

My first trip to São Félix, in January 2014, featured bone-jarring van rides from Marabá, a boomtown on the Tocantins River in eastern Pará, south over patchy pavement to the cattle town of Xinguara, and then west along the PA-279 state highway to Tucumã, where the asphalt stopped. Another hundred kilometers to the west, I arrived at last in São Félix, where the Rio Fresco meets the Xingu River. I checked into the Jacaré Palace Hotel, a low bungalow located a block from the municipal market, where vendors with wooden stalls sold fruits, vegetables, meat, and fish.

The city of São Félix do Xingu was established as a rubber trading post in the early twentieth century, and it was only reached by road in 1983, when the PA-279 finally arrived after a turbulent seven years and 260 kilometers of construction. The Jacaré Palace, whose sign featured its namesake alligator (*jacaré*), was on the edge of the old part of town that had been built before the arrival of the road. Now, in 2014, the area felt like the city center. Motorcycles and pickup trucks zipped by from the ferry crossings on the Fresco and Xingu nine blocks to the west to the PA-279, which began one block to the east as the two-lane Avenida Rio Xingu, divided by a file of dusty trees.

New neighborhoods had grown up along the roadway, and during those first three weeks that I spent in São Félix, I would walk most mornings to the market to catch a motorcycle taxi to the municipal Secretariat of the Environment, located on a dirt block north of the PA-279, about two kilometers east of my hotel. In the evenings, as the heat of the day began to dissipate, I would run up and down the Avenida, joining São Félix residents out for their evening exercise along the city's only unbroken stretch of sidewalk. I left São Félix in late February, returning again for ten days in July 2014. Four years then passed before I saw São Félix next.

In June 2018, I found myself once again van-hopping on the PA-279—from Xinguara to Agua Azul to Ourilândia to Tucumã—through mile after mile of cattle pasture interspersed with babaçu palms and *juquira* (secondary scrub), and the bright yellow of ipê flowers. Some nearby hills were bare or covered in palm or scrub, while more distant hills, looking toward the Indigenous reserves to the north and south, were still blanketed with forest.

"Where are we?" asked a woman as the van arrived in Tucumã.

"End of the line," an old man grumbled as he exited. But in fact, the end of the line was yet another van ride away. Thirty-five years after the completion of the highway, the PA-279 was now paved the whole way to São Félix, though the van was occasionally forced to swerve to avoid potholes. Arriving in town, I checked back into the Jacaré Palace. While the bustle around the Jacaré in 2014 had marked a shift away from the river where the older parts of town were located, it became clear within a few days of my return that in the last four years the city's center of gravity had shifted even farther up the roadway. The heart of São Félix was now around the Praça Cultural, where municipal buildings, a concrete soccer court, and a skate park abutted the Avenida Rio Xingu, a block up from the local branch of the Banco do Brasil. Nearby, the Brasa Viva restaurant, a popular spot for skewered meats, was lined with ads for a butcher shop ("much hygiene and quality!"), a ranch selling bulls with "high quality genetics," and Lacoste, the clothing brand of choice for wealthy ranchers. Completing the city center was the massive, gleaming new Supermercado Roma (whose motto proclaimed it *O Império da Economia*—The Budget Empire). The well-stocked, clean, and organized Supermercado Roma was an emblem of urban convenience compared to the small groceries with wilted produce that had provisioned São Félix until recently. It seemed as though modernity was coming at last to this city at the "end of the line."

The municipality of São Félix do Xingu is almost impossibly vast. At 84,213 square kilometers, it is nearly as large as Portugal. The colonized zone of the municipality is more limited, however, centering on an area of some 15,000 square kilometers to the east of the Xingu River—stretching north and south from the PA-279 to the Apyterewa, Xikrin do Cateté, and Kayapó Indigenous territories—and another 11,000 square kilometers of more sparsely settled land across the river from São Félix city, in the area between the Xingu and Iriri Rivers known as the Terra do Meio, the Land in the Middle. In this colonization zone, construction of the PA-279 catalyzed rapid population growth and land cover change beginning in the late 1970s, a story recounted in Marianne Schmink and Charles Wood's classic 1992 text, *Contested Frontiers in Amazonia*.[7]

While there has always been some mining around São Félix—in recent years, Vale has operated a copper and nickel mine on the municipality's eastern border with Ourilândia, and *garimpeiros* (wildcat miners) extract cassiterite in the central region of Taboca—São Félix is not a mining town. The municipal economy is built on beef. In the 1990s–2000s, the expansion of cattle ranching in São Félix drove large-scale deforestation, and almost all occupation occurred without formal land title. From 2000 to 2007, the population of São Félix jumped from 35,000 to 60,000, the municipal cattle herd grew from 682,000 to 1.6 million head (becoming the second-largest municipal herd in Brazil), and deforestation averaged a staggering 1,200 square kilometers per year.[8]

Forest clearing in São Félix pushed westward, as small farmers and large ranchers moved into the Terra do Meio west of the Xingu River, threatening to break through to the BR-163 Cuiabá-Santarém highway in western Pará. In the early 2000s, São Félix do Xingu was synonymous with frontier violence and forest destruction, known internationally as Brazil's deforestation "champion." By the time I arrived in São Félix in 2014, however, The Nature Conservancy was trumpeting the municipality as a "champion in the reduction of environmental damages."[9] São Félix's transformation into a "green municipality" highlights local experiences of land-sparing policy in Pará and reveals the dynamics of an incipient municipal productivist transition. My visits to São Félix came at two different moments in this process. My time in São Félix in 2014 coincided with the apogee of land-sparing policy in the municipality, when a broad coalition of government, NGO, and private-sector actors backed a common agenda of agricultural development with forest conservation. By the time of my 2018 visit, agro-industrial modernization continued apace, but the goal of eliminating deforestation in São Félix seemed more and more a fantasy. I examine first how land-sparing policies reduced deforestation after 2004 and then briefly describe the subsequent fracturing of the forest conservation agenda.

When the federal government launched PPCDAm in 2004, westward expansion of large-scale, extensive ranching along the PA-279 in São Félix and into the Terra do Meio constituted one of the most rapidly advancing deforestation frontiers in the Brazilian Amazon. To forestall that expansion, small farmers along the Transamazon highway north of the Terra do Meio found common ground with environmentalists in Brazilian and international NGOs to work with the Brazilian government to create a giant mosaic of protected areas.[10] In addition to existing Indigenous territories, which today cover 53 percent of São Félix, the federal government in 2005 created two new strictly protected conservation areas in the municipal territory west of the Xingu: Serra do Pardo National Park and Terra do Meio Ecological Station. Large ranchers, meanwhile, organized to oppose protected area creation. They succeeded in altering some conservation area boundaries and in ensuring that the Triunfo do Xingu protected area, created in 2006 by the state of Pará, was designated as an Environmental Protection Area (APA), allowing private occupation and "sustainable use."[11] Nonetheless, properties in federally protected zones were expropriated and cattle grazing within the areas were seized. With the new protected areas, 19 percent of São Félix's municipal territory fell under conservation areas, virtually all territory west of the Xingu had protected status, and just 28 percent of the municipality remained unprotected private property space.

Protected area creation and enhanced enforcement under PPCDAm drove significant deforestation reductions in São Félix after 2005. Deforestation declined 37 percent, from 1,268 square kilometers per year in 2003–2005 to 800 in 2006–2008, and logging activity, which had been closely linked to frontier expansion, also declined significantly. In 2008, the Ministry of Environment's priority list was created, accompanied by credit restrictions and robust enforcement targeting illegal deforestation. In 2009, TNC and IEB, a Brazilian NGO, launched projects aimed at reducing deforestation with support from Frigol, a local slaughterhouse, and Fundo Vale. The large ranchers initially were hostile to the NGOs, but when public prosecutors began forcing slaughterhouses only to receive cattle from properties that had completed environmental registration with CAR, the rural producers' syndicate (the large ranchers' association) began to work with the NGOs and government to achieve environmental compliance. Annual deforestation in São Félix bottomed out in 2011 at 140 square kilometers, a 90 percent reduction from 2005. That year, CAR registration in the municipality exceeded 80 percent of private property space, and a Pact for the End of Illegal Deforestation was signed by stakeholders including municipal, state, and federal government entities; local, national, and international NGOs; and ranchers', farmers', and community organizations.[12] In signing the pact, rural producers committed not to deforest illegally and to adopt more sustainable practices, while government agencies and NGOs committed to provide technical assistance and credit for sustainable production, to maintain infrastructure, and to facilitate environmental licensing and tenure regularization.

As this history shows, territorial constriction was central to land-sparing policy in São Félix. Protected areas closed the western frontier, limiting and encircling the available area for agricultural expansion. Heavy enforcement rendered constriction effective, as fear of punitive measures led many to reduce or cease forest clearing. Ranching intensification was almost universally considered the necessary response to this new land constraint. Although government officials, NGO activists, ranchers, and small farmers all recognized the necessity of increasing productivity on already-deforested land, intensification did not occur automatically with constriction. Almost all properties lacked formal title, which might have facilitated investment, and by November 2015 Terra Legal had issued just twenty-six titles in rural São Félix.[13] Some larger ranchers with access to credit or capital reserves adopted more intensive practices, such as restoring degraded pastures and implementing pasture rotations, but many land managers lacked access to necessary capital, equipment, and knowledge to intensify. The collateral effect of deforestation reductions thus became a freeze in the agricultural sector in São Félix. Residents spoke of economic stagnation, and real municipal GDP per capita declined from 2006 to 2011. During an interview in 2014, Paulo, a small farmer living in the APA, west of the Xingu River, explained,

> We are isolated, and anything we do is repressed. We have been bound in place.... Until the new regulations, we worked normally. We received financing from the bank to buy cattle, and everything was going well until 2009.... Before, smallholders might sell their properties under pressure

from larger property owners, although in my region this was not the case, but now smallholders are selling to larger producers out of necessity. Just in my region eight small-holders have sold and only one person has bought all their properties.[14]

Farmers could not deforest new land to expand nor did they receive assistance to intensify: a rural exodus loomed.

Realizing intensification might not occur spontaneously, TNC launched initiatives in São Félix to support new production prac-tices. The organization's sustainable ranching project, established in 2013 in partnership with Walmart and Brazilian meat-processor Marfrig, initially supported around twenty primarily medium and large ranchers to intensify and pursue tenure regularization. TNC's sustainable cacao project, begun in 2013 with financing from Cargill, worked with several dozen smallholder families to recover degraded lands with cacao agroforestry. These projects were intended to be replicable and scalable, TNC staff affirmed, and were comple-mented by support for sustainable production from IEB and the Ministry of Environment, but this support for intensification still reached only a small proportion of the ten thousand rural properties in São Félix. Support promised by federal and state governments for infrastructure, technical assistance, credit, and land titling mostly failed to materialize.

Without substantial investments supporting intensification, and with incomes stagnating, two trends emerged. First, deforestation began to rebound, climbing from the 2011 low of 140 square kilo-meters to 223 in 2013. As the municipal secretary of environment told me, "People are afraid of enforcement actions, so they wait for public policies, but when public policies don't come, they decide to run a risk and deforest."[15] Second, as small farmers struggled under the new enforcement regime, there was an increasing tendency for smallholders to sell their properties and move to cities or other parts of the frontier, and this tendency further concentrated land in the hands of large ranchers.[16]

São Félix in the early 2010s featured a relatively strong land-sparing coalition of government, NGO, and corporate actors, but their web of policies and programs attempting to reconcile conservation and agricultural development generated a series of contradictions across the patchwork forests and pastures of the Xingu and Iriri Basins. Command-and-control measures, including protected area creation and Forest Code enforcement, dramatically reduced deforestation. Credit restrictions, regional legal action against slaughterhouses, and NGO and government projects also succeeded in bringing over 80 percent of private property area into CAR. Pressure under territorial constriction for a transition from an extensive mode of extraction to an intensive mode of production was widely felt. Without substantial financial support or technical assistance, however, ranching intensification remained incipient and uneven, favoring more productivist management among large ranchers while smallholders struggled to adapt. Territorial constriction through environmental regulation delivered conservation without development, and while conservationists, scientists, and policymakers proclaimed Brazil's land-sparing policies a success, for thousands of small farmers in São Félix, land sparing was a promise unfulfilled.

If in 2014 the political economy of São Félix tended toward conservation without development, by 2018 the tendency was toward development without conservation. Signs of modernization went beyond the Supermercado Roma and the new asphalt on the PA-279. Across the Rio Fresco, north of town, where four years before there had been only cattle pastures, now fields of corn and sorghum lined the dirt road. Mechanized agriculture had come to São Félix, as ranchers began to plant row crops of corn, sorghum, and soy to provide feed and fodder for their livestock. This integration of agriculture and ranching (known as *integração lavoura pecuária*) is a form of intensification that lowers feed costs and raises ranching productivity. These intensification practices are in part a response to territorial constriction. With the closure of the frontier, ranchers' paths to legal profit lay through increasing productivity on existing agricultural land. While land scarcity helped to induce intensification, it also raised land values through both direct and indirect pathways. Territorial constriction raised land values directly by increasing demand for already deforested land. In June 2018, I sat in the low green building that houses the São Félix small farmers' syndicate, speaking with the three members of the syndicate directorate. They explained that increased demand for land came both from families dislocated by protected area creation and from large ranchers who switched from buying and clearing forest areas to buying up open and degraded lands.[17] Territorial constriction also raised land values indirectly by encouraging agricultural investments in land improvement (e.g., removing stumps from fields, grading fields for row crops). In two communities in the consolidated agricultural area of São Félix east of the Xingu, the Center for International Forestry Research found that the high sale price for a hectare of good agricultural land rose from 2,000 reais in both communities in 2011 to 3,100 reais in one community in 2014 and 3,305 in the other, increases of 55 and 65 percent, respectively.[18]

Land titling, touted by land-sparing advocates as a catalyst for smallholder productivity, had come to be viewed by a number of small farmers and their allies as a vehicle for smallholder dispossession. The small farmers' syndicate leaders said they were initially happy with promises of land titling but soon realized that titling was feeding land concentration: "[Small farmers] get title, sell on, and the *fazendas* get larger. It's going to put an end to family farming," one warned. They noted that titling also increases land values, and saw titling initiatives serving large agricultural interests seeking to consolidate land. "They are titling with an objective," they affirmed.[19] A member of the Pastoral Land Commission, which supports small farmers in the municipality, was more blunt, calling the Terra Legal program legalized land grabbing: "With Terra Legal," he said, "a poor person sells their land."[20]

These ambivalent effects of rising land values and land titling initiatives compounded highly uneven smallholder experiences within São Félix's nascent productivist transition. "For the universe of family agriculture, things have not improved," an NGO worker told me in 2018, reflecting on the four years since our last encounter, but for the 350 or so families connected to the "family agriculture collective" of NGO projects and small-farmer cooperatives, there had been advances.[21] Under the Lula and Rousseff governments, smallholders were constrained by Forest Code enforcement, but they also received support from government purchasing programs and education and extension initiatives for family agriculture. By 2018, the Temer government had substantially weakened these support programs with budget cuts and institutional changes. In areas more distant from the municipal seat, particularly in the Terra do Meio, a rural exodus was underway.

I spoke again with Paulo, the small farmer from the APA, who told me that conditions for him and other smallholders in the area had worsened: NGOs had pushed things forward but then retreated, the price of fuel had increased, they had no electricity and could not afford to buy generators to conserve their produce, and as neighbors sold their land to large ranchers, smallholders became more isolated and their community associations weakened. In the areas close to town, small farmers could access government purchasing programs and received better public services, while in the APA, with falling incomes, high transport costs, lack of energy, and lack of financing, ranches were growing larger while the outlook for smallholders was negative. "At my age, the tendency is to get tired," Paulo sighed. "Things did not move forward."[22]

The smallholder exodus from the APA contrasted with improved conditions for a set of small-farmer families nearer to the municipal center, who were able to access resources and support from NGO projects and government services. I spoke with Mariana, the daughter of one of the small farmers participating in TNC's sustainable cacao project. Mariana had studied at the Casa Familiar Rural, an NGO-run education and training program for youth from smallholder families, and she was now around nineteen years old and studying agronomy. Her family had received government support for dairy cattle, and support from TNC and the municipal Secretariat of Agriculture to plant cacao. In Mariana's eyes, the future was bright:

> Before, people were trying to have a lot of land, but now they see that they can produce a lot with little land. It is sustainable and viable. Today is very different from four or five years ago. Four to five years ago, it was just beef cattle, but now people have agroforestry systems, fruit production, and milk cattle. Now in the markets you can find lettuce that was produced locally instead of imported, and there is a dairy that picks up milk production from the properties and produces cheese and other products. If the NGO and Secre-

tariat projects continue, the future will be good. If we continue producing and preserving [the environment], it will be
a promising future, and it will come quickly.[23]

The contrast between Mariana's and Paulo's experiences illustrates
the unevenness and inequality underlying the productivist transition in São Félix. Life for small farmers in São Félix has never been
easy. Extensive ranching became pervasive among smallholders in
the 1990s in part as a response to government incentives for cattle
ranching and a lack of support or market opportunities for small-
scale crop production. Small farmers would raise cattle, degrade the
land, and move on to clear a new property. With environmental enforcement after 2004 and then weakened support programs after
2016, thousands of smallholders were being pushed from rural São
Félix to the city (where "they don't have a profession, and they suffer," according to a syndicate leader) or to new frontiers in western
Pará.[24] The emerging productivist geography of São Félix agriculture would comprise a smaller number of diversified family farms
producing vegetables, cash crops, and dairy products near the city
center, mixed with intensifying medium and large ranches, while
large-scale extensive ranching consolidated in more distant areas.
Figure 11 shows the decline in smallholder agriculture in São Félix
after the 1990s and the rise in cacao cash cropping during the 2010s.

Industrial ranching and market-oriented smallholder intensification were "developing" São Félix, driving increasing capital cir-
culation through local businesses from agricultural services firms
to supermarkets to furniture stores. This agro-industrial transformation was taking place without the extreme levels of deforestation associated with the extensive ranching boom of the early 2000s,
yet São Félix was far from achieving the "zero-deforestation green
development" propagated by environmental NGOs and corporate
sustainability initiatives.[25] Annual deforestation in the municipality
averaged 283 square kilometers per year in 2016–2018, as ranchers
and land grabbers continued to speculate and profit through primary
forest clearing. Indeed, just as agro-industrialization was arriving in
São Félix, environmental restrictions were relaxing, with loosening
regulations and cuts to environmental agency budgets. "The weak-
ening of national policies left the producer in the countryside who

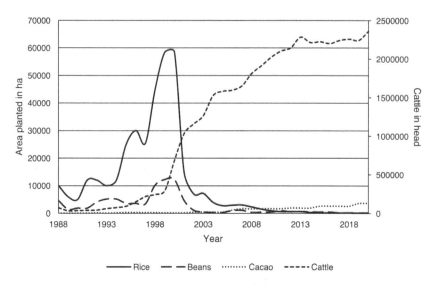

Fig. 11. Smallholder agriculture and cattle in São Félix. Smallholders migrated to the municipality in large numbers beginning in the mid-1980s. They shifted from agricultural crops such as rice and beans to cattle ranching after the 1990s. With environmental restrictions after 2008, many smallholders left the rural zone, while a small but increasing number took up cacao agroforestry. Cattle production data are municipal totals and dominated by large-scale ranches. Sources: "Produção Agrícola Municipal"; "Pesquisa Pecuária Municipal."

wants to deforest more free to do so," reflected a TNC employee in 2018. "The Federal Government is signaling that it is not interested in the socio-environmental agenda. IBAMA is not carrying out strong enforcement. So people sneak around CAR, and producers continue deforesting."[26]

As for TNC, their project working with Indigenous territories in São Félix was coming to an end, and their remaining programs were fully focused on "sustainable production" on private properties. "The deforestation that continues in São Félix is in public areas," a TNC manager explained during an interview in the organization's regional headquarters in Belém, a blue-and-white *belle époque* building from the time of the Amazon rubber boom: "TNC's work should not depend on [command and] control. . . . Public areas are subject to high levels of speculation due to the land question. We won't be able to eliminate speculative deforestation so long as the land is not regularized."[27] And so São Félix was transformed from a frontier zone for limiting deforestation to a "post-frontier" zone for cacao-based forest restoration and "sustainable" intensive beef production, even as large-scale deforestation continued in the western part of the municipality. Elsewhere in the Amazon, TNC was replicating its São Félix forest restoration models to the south and east, in Mato Grosso and Maranhão, while Amazonian deforestation accelerated to the north and west in Pará and Amazonas. The eco-modernist narrative of "green" agro-industry depended, even at the regional level, on ignoring or discounting ongoing processes of extractive deforestation.[28]

São Félix was modernizing, but the land-sparing ideal of unified conservation and intensification never quite materialized, and deforestation reductions and agricultural industrialization were mediated by ongoing processes of smallholder dispossession. Rather than apply land-sparing policy to "green" an already industrializing economy, as was done in Nova Ubiratã, the land-sparing coalition in São Félix attempted to engineer a productivist transformation in a zone of extraction, seeking to catalyze forest conservation and agricultural intensification simultaneously. While command and control measures were effective in reducing deforestation rates after 2004, the policies and resources mobilized in the municipality were insufficient to trigger broad-based economic transformation, and the municipal economy stagnated. While insufficient, programs supporting ranching intensification and smallholder agroforestry were not necessarily ineffective. A growing minority of the smallholder population practiced cacao agroforestry, and intensifying ranchers provided models that spread more broadly with the arrival of the "intensive frontier" of expanding agro-industrial supply chains in the late 2010s. Intensive practices like agriculture and ranching integration began to take hold around 2014, and the first substantial experiments with soy cultivation began around 2018, at a time when deforestation in São Félix was again on the rise (fig. 12).

In short, a productivist transition in São Félix depended on the arrival of the intensive frontier of Brazil's "soy complex." The soy complex was engineered in part by Brazil's national-level productivist regime beginning in the 1970s, but it arrived in São Félix in the late 2010s more as a function of supply-chain expansion than

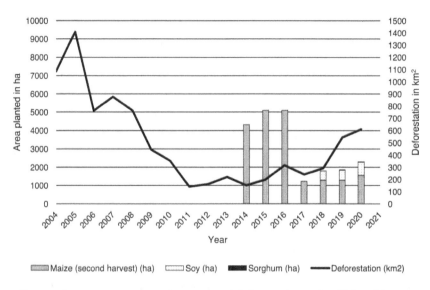

Fig. 12. Intensive row-crop cultivation and deforestation in São Félix. Adoption of intensive integrated ranching-and-agriculture systems coincided with rising municipal deforestation. Sources: "Produção Agrícola Municipal"; PRODES.

as a function of new policy incentives.[29] Land-sparing policies, meanwhile, though initially effective in reducing deforestation, ultimately lacked permanence. Agro-industrial modernization in São Félix did not eliminate extensive ranching in more remote areas of the municipality or the drive for speculation and windfall profits. Even at the territorial level of the municipality, a growing productivist core could not fully decouple from extractive expansion and primary forest destruction. The enduring linkages of modernization with ecological destruction became abundantly clear when extractive coalitions gained the upper hand in the federal government, and the Temer and Bolsonaro administrations opened the floodgates to a new wave of extractive deforestation in the Brazilian Amazon.

A Day of Fire

AS I TRAVELED ACROSS Pará and Mato Grosso in June and July 2018, the image of Brazil as a land-sparing success had already begun to fray. The Temer administration that took over after Dilma Rousseff's impeachment was rolling back environmental protections and support for family farmers, and Amazonian deforestation was ticking upward. When Jair Bolsonaro assumed the presidency in January 2019, the land-sparing policies that reconciled agricultural development with forest conservation were blown wide open. Bolsonaro appointed as minister of environment Ricardo Salles, who in 2018 was convicted for his role in modifying maps and allowing illegal activities in an environmental reserve during his time as secretary of the environment for the state of São Paulo.[1] Bolsonaro, Salles, and Bolsonaro's "ruralist" allies in Congress set about the "systematic dismantling of Brazilian environmental laws," slashing environmental agency budgets, replacing functionaries, and attacking protections for conservation areas and Indigenous territories.[2] Extractive coalitions that had been restrained by federal policies and enforcement now surged across the Amazon, invading protected areas, felling forests, and assassinating activists who stood in their way. Deforestation in Amazonian Indigenous territories nearly doubled from 2018 to 2019, when 498 square kilometers were cleared, including over 85 square kilometers in the Apyterewa Indigenous Territory in São Félix do

Xingu. A similar spike occurred in Amazonian conservation areas, where deforestation in 2019 jumped 46 percent to over 1,100 square kilometers. Over a third of that clearing was in the APA Triunfo do Xingu in São Félix, where 436 square kilometers of primary forest were destroyed. In 2019 alone, at least twenty-four land and environmental defenders were killed in Brazil, twenty-one of them in the Amazon.[3]

The ascendance of extractive interests in the federal government was mirrored in Pará at the state and municipal levels. Helder Barbalho, whose father, Jader Barbalho, allegedly diverted billions of reais from SUDAM, was inaugurated governor of Pará on the same day Bolsonaro assumed the presidency. Under Helder Barbalho (who faced a case for his removal from office for improperly benefiting from his father's media network during his election campaign, among other illegalities), the state of Pará ended police support for IBAMA operations in June 2019, which forced the environmental agency to reduce enforcement actions at the beginning of the dry season, when fires and deforestation are at their highest.[4]

Emboldened by reduced enforcement, incitement from the highest levels of government, and runaway deforestation, ranchers and land grabbers in Pará planned a coordinated act of environmental destruction that became known throughout Brazil as *Dia do Fogo*—the Day of Fire. Claiming that "we need to show the President [Bolsonaro] that we want to work and the only way to do that is by deforesting," the conspirators lit hundreds of fires across central and western Pará on August 10 and 11, 2019.[5] While the Day of Fire centered on the BR-163 corridor in Novo Progresso and Altamira, ranchers in São Félix do Xingu also apparently participated. Satellites detected 288 fires in São Félix from August 9 to 11, an increase of 329 percent over the previous three days. In APA Triunfo do Xingu, thousands of hectares burned.[6] The Day of Fire was one of the most brazen acts in a fire season that darkened the skies of São Paulo and brought domestic and international condemnation of Bolsonaro's policies. Bolsonaro responded by blaming the fires on NGOs and environmentalist actor Leonardo DiCaprio, and turning environmental enforcement over to the military, under whose watch deforestation continued to rise.[7]

Despite police investigations, no one was indicted in the Day of Fire conspiracy. Novo Progresso rancher Gelson Dill, who was twice fined for illegal deforestation and is a suspected organizer of the Day of Fire, was elected mayor of Novo Progresso in 2020.[8] In São Félix do Xingu, the 2020 elections saw João Cleber de Souza Torres return to the mayor's office. A logger and rancher whose properties have been embargoed by the federal government for illegal deforestation, Torres is widely believed to have ordered the killings of multiple people in land disputes.[9] In 2012, he was elected mayor of São Félix do Xingu. As the federal and state governments pushed land sparing and "green development," Torres played along, and his administration cooperated with the government and NGO environmental projects in the municipality. In the 2016 elections, he was defeated by Minervina, a rancher who was considered to represent a more technified, productivist approach to the sector.[10] Municipal politics appeared to be aligning with the productivist transition shifting the broader political economy of the Amazon region. In April 2018, Torres was arrested and spent a month in jail for allegedly having embezzled municipal tax payments while mayor.[11] A second operation in May 2018 revealed that while mayor, Torres had pressured members of the municipal Environmental Secretariat to accept bribes from a rancher attempting to avoid federal environmental enforcement.[12]

Any declaration of Torres's political demise, like any declaration of the end of deforestation in the Brazilian Amazon, would have been premature, however. In 2020, as Bolsonaro and Barbalho cultivated a culture of impunity in the Amazon and ranchers, loggers, miners, and land grabbers in São Félix set fires and cleared forest in APA Triunfo do Xingu and the Apyterewa Indigenous Territory, Torres defeated Minervina to once again lead the municipal government. Extractive coalitions were resurgent at the municipal, state, and regional levels, and forests that had been "saved" during Brazil's land-sparing decade now burned to ash in a spasm of destruction.

The violent surge of Amazonian deforestation under Bolsonaro toppled Brazil from its green pinnacle in the international community. Nonetheless, Brazil's decade of land-sparing policy continues to hold sway with scientists and policymakers as a global forest governance model, for Indonesia and beyond. In 2021, when more primary forest was lost in the Brazilian Amazon than in any year since 2006, David Gibbs, a research associate at the World Resources Institute, told the *New York Times:* "What Brazil did to reduce deforestation could happen in other countries, and has happened to some extent in Indonesia . . . but those reductions in deforestation are always potentially temporary and can be reversed." "So in that way," he added, "Brazil is both a hopeful tale and a cautionary tale."[13]

   This nostalgia for Brazilian land sparing is misplaced. A full understanding of "what Brazil did" and what the actual implementation of land-sparing policies looked like for the people and landscapes of the Amazon region is illegible to a global policy discourse based on aggregate deforestation statistics for an area of over 5 million square kilometers. The preceding chapters show how forest governance in the Brazilian Amazon after 2004 comprised a comprehensive project for transforming the region from a zone of extraction into a hub of productivist "green" development, and they reveal the partial and uneven implementation of that project between the very different state and municipal political-economic regimes of Nova Ubiratã in Mato Grosso and São Félix do Xingu in Pará. Here I reflect on these municipal experiences to draw out further insights into the realities of land-sparing "success" in the Brazilian Amazon and its implications for ecological modernization and green development.

   1. *Land sparing succeeded by "greening" existing intensification.* In the areas of the Amazon where they appeared most successful (at the state level in Mato Grosso and the municipal level in Nova Ubiratã, in this study), land-sparing policies institutionalized an economic shift already underway. Brazil's national-level productivist regime had supported the emergence of a soy complex centered on Mato Grosso since the 1970s, and the intensive agricultural frontier generated by this complex expanded through territorial logics internal to grain and livestock supply chains, in a dialectical relation with changing economic and land policy configurations.[14] Sometimes this intensive frontier synchronized with forest protection policies, and sometimes not. In Mato Grosso, layering forest protections on top of the growing productivist economy turned

"greening" into a project that helped protect and expand the existing soy complex, transforming environmental villains like Blairo Maggi into heroes of "environmentally responsible" production.[15] In Pará, and especially on extractive deforestation frontiers like São Félix, land-sparing policies attempted to both conserve and develop at once—to both stop extractive clearing and catalyze agricultural intensification. Because of these mismatches between the "governance frontier" of land-sparing policy implementation and the intensive frontier of soy complex agro-industry, "green" development occurred in some places more than others, as the rural economy of Nova Ubiratã continued to grow after its inclusion in the priority list, while São Félix went through a period of stagnation.[16]

2. *Land-sparing "success" depended on social and ecological displacement.* Second, as land-sparing "success" and "green" development concentrated in some places, displacement effects and expanded extraction materialized in others. These contradictions of the land-sparing model are simultaneously social (displacing small farmers) and ecological (displacing deforestation). Displacement effects are evident at the micro-level, when a Nova Ubiratã farmer or rancher like Cláudio Bratz rents illegally deforested land farther north in Pará, or when small farmers in São Félix sell their land to a large rancher and move to new frontiers to the west. Displacement effects are also detectable at more aggregate levels. At the state level, Nikolas Kuschnig and colleagues find that even as direct forest conversion to agriculture was negligible in Mato Grosso in 2006–2017, spatial spillovers between municipalities meant that agriculture—especially soy production—remained a major driver of state-level deforestation through indirect effects.[17] Land appreciation is a primary mechanism of indirect deforestation, as rising land values increase incentives for forest clearing, and Peter Richards, Robert Walker, and Eugenio Arima find evidence for this effect at the national level as well. They calculate that new soybean production in Brazil indirectly caused one-third of Brazilian Amazon deforestation in 2002–2011 (a loss of over

thirty thousand square kilometers of primary forest), and that soy expansion in the southern Brazilian agro-industrial core (the states of Rio Grande do Sul, Santa Catarina, and Paraná) was responsible for a third of this indirect deforestation.[18] In other words, the apparent land-sparing success of agro-industrial growth and forest recovery in the Atlantic Forest biome of the Brazilian South in fact drove massive deforestation in the Brazilian Amazon, and the apparent land-sparing success of deforestation reductions and agricultural intensification in the Brazilian Amazon after 2004 masked similar displacements.[19] Environmental enforcement and productivist development pushed deforestation to new frontiers within the Amazon itself, as deforestation hotspots shifted to the north and west, but displacement also materialized regionally, through increased clearing in the Brazilian Cerrado, and internationally, as Brazilian actors and capital flowed into neighboring countries, including Bolivia. A growing core requires an expanding periphery.

3. *Primitive accumulation persists within productivist economies.* The Brazilian experience underlines that even as productivist economies rely on extraction elsewhere, there are ongoing processes of primitive accumulation internal to productivist economies themselves. Political-economic regimes are always hybrid. Under land-sparing policies in São Félix, large-scale ranching operations consolidated through processes of small-farmer dispossession. In Nova Ubiratã, annual deforestation fell 95 percent from 2004 to 2007, but every year since, speculators, ranchers, and farmers have cleared hundreds of hectares of rainforest for ranching and row crops. In 2018–2020, the three years after Nova Ubiratã was declared a municipality with deforestation monitored and under control, seventy-five square kilometers of primary forest in the municipality were destroyed. Most deforested land in Nova Ubiratã is converted to productivist, intensive agriculture. Agro-industrial development, and broader processes of capitalist modernization, are not necessarily "green"—indeed, they are fundamentally ecologically destructive, since they rely on irreversible processes of material and energy consumption. The question for

land sparing, and for ecological modernization generally, is not whether deforestation or other forms of environmental degradation are eliminated but rather the degree to which those processes are displaced to create a localized illusion of green development.[20] In Nova Ubiratã, ongoing deforestation and ecological feedbacks of agro-industrial land, water, energy, and chemical use demonstrate that the illusion of green capitalism is never quite complete.

Productivist development implies a constant demand for extractive inputs, both as materials and energy for industrial production and as windfall profits to maintain growth. Thus, the global political economy depends on extraction, but whether that extraction occurs in one place or another is determined by political-economic regimes at multiple levels. In the Brazilian Amazon, coalitions of government, NGO, and agribusiness actors attempted to limit deforestation and transform Amazonian political-economic regimes through land sparing. Policy innovation and institution-building were crucial to this project, from PPCDAm and the federal priority list to municipal anti-deforestation pacts and sustainable agriculture programs. The productivist agro-industrial sector that expanded in the Amazon region during the land-sparing decade of 2005–2015 did not suddenly disappear with the rollback of land-sparing policies and institutions, even if spiking agricultural deforestation makes it difficult to sustain the narrative that agro-industrial growth is saving forests. In the longer run, however, the dismantling of productivist institutions that encouraged environmental management and agricultural intensification, and the resurgence of extractive coalitions in the Amazonian political economy, threaten the survival of productivist agro-industry in the Amazon.

Feedbacks from resurgent extraction that may undermine productivist sectors include environmental sanctions, climate and ecosystem disruption, and economic instability. Sanctions for forest destruction may come from the public and private sectors, as well as civil society. In the face of spiking fires and deforestation in 2019, media reported that "European leaders threatened to cancel a major trade deal, protesters staged demonstrations outside Brazilian embassies and calls for a boycott of Brazilian products snowballed on social media," while VF Corporation, a major buyer of Brazilian leather, threatened to cancel purchases from the country.[21] Less immediate, but more ineluctable, climate and hydrological disruptions from Amazonian deforestation drive up energy costs by reducing hydropower generation and increase temperature and water stress, degrading the long-term productivity and profitability of Brazilian agro-industry.[22] Further, at the macroeconomic level, the Bolsonaro administration's pork-barrel approach to economic management resulted in dramatic currency depreciation, inflation, and collapsing domestic economic growth.[23] While these trends may encourage agro-exports in the short term, in the longer term they could undermine domestic linkages of labor, production, and consumption that make Brazilian agro-industry a driver of productivist development.

Capitalism requires extraction, but institutions determine where extraction is suppressed and where it is enabled. The Brazilian Amazon has for centuries been a zone of extraction, but in the decade after 2004, land-sparing policies pushed the region toward a trajectory of productivist development. This political-economic transformation was uneven and incomplete, and has subsequently been challenged by resurgent extraction. Nonetheless, the Brazilian experience demonstrates that policies can shift the geography of extraction. This result is still heralded by land-sparing advocates as a successful reconciliation of conservation and development—a model that others should adopt and to which Brazil should return. Missing from optimistic narratives of land sparing and ecological modernization is an understanding that while a peripheral region may shift from extraction to production and "develop," extraction cannot be eliminated from the capitalist system. Should the new Lula government or future Brazilian administrations return to "successful" land-sparing policies, deforestation in the Amazon may once again decline. Those declines will depend on displacement, however, just as they did in 2005–2015, when the land-sparing transition in the Brazilian Amazon drove deforestation across biomes and borders, into the Cerrado, the Bolivian lowlands, and beyond.

"Brasileros" on the Bolivian Frontier

The Vortex of Development

YRACRODRUON URUNDEUVA—KNOWN IN BRAZIL as *aroeira preta* and in Paraguay as *urundeymí*—is a slim hardwood tree found especially in South American tropical savannas and dry forests, such as the Brazilian Caatinga and Cerrado, and the Bolivian Chiquitania, where it is known as *cuchi*. Cuchi wood is extremely strong and resistant, but the trunks often branch low to the ground. These low-branching trees are less useful for some types of furniture or construction, but they are an ideal material for fence posts. As Brazilian cattle ranchers flooded into the South American interior beginning in the 1970s, boosted by infrastructure construction and government subsidies, they needed countless fence posts for their ever-expanding pastures.

Working with the Chiripá Indigenous people of eastern Paraguay in the early 1980s, anthropologist Richard K. Reed described the "second conquest" of industrial ranching and agriculture sweeping across the region. Traditional Chiripá agroforest livelihoods in Paraguay's Atlantic Forest biome centered on subsistence agriculture, hunting and fishing, and commercial extraction of forest products such as yerba mate and citrus oil. The expansion of ranching and agriculture in southern Brazil and eastern Paraguay in the 1970s created a new market for fence posts. Cuchi, or urundeymí, grew throughout Paraguay's Atlantic Forest, though with a distribution of just a few trees per hectare. From 1978 to 1982, agricultural

expansion in southern Brazil fueled a cuchi harvesting boom in eastern Paraguay. Young Chiripá men cutting by hand in teams of two
or three could each make five to seven fence posts a day. The posts
were sold to local intermediaries, who would sell them to Brazilian smugglers. Reed reported that "men could earn more money in
fence-post making than doing any other wage labor," and Chiripá
estimated that during the three years of the cuchi boom they cut
fifteen thousand posts per year. The 1983 devaluation of the Brazilian currency made Paraguayan posts more expensive relative to
Brazilian producers, ending the Paraguayan fence-post boom, but
by that time most of the cuchi trees near Chiripá communities had
already been harvested.[1]

Ranching expansion in southern Brazil, along with favorable
exchange rates and porous borders, led to the felling of tens of thousands of cuchi trees in eastern Paraguay at the turn of the 1980s.
Over the following two decades, Brazilian ranchers continued their
spread to the north and west, clearing thousands of square kilometers of rainforest and savanna every year and enclosing their
new pastures with a forest of fence posts. After 2004, land-sparing
policies slowed ranching expansion in the Brazilian Amazon, and
land-sparing proponents argued that increasing ranching productivity through intensive management practices like rotational grazing could decouple cattle production from deforestation.[2] Adopting
pasture rotations increases a rancher's need for fencing, however, so
even as the reduction in pasture expansion reduced fencing needs for
new pastures, ranching intensification multiplied demand for fence
posts. Amazonian deforestation declined, but the pillaging of cuchi
trees continued. Just as Brazilian demand spilled over the Paraguayan frontier at the turn of the 1980s, Brazilian demand spilled
over the Bolivian frontier at the turn of the 2010s. In 2018, in the
Bolivian border municipality of San Ignacio de Velasco, a forestry
association official told me cuchi had a very high demand in Brazil
for fence posts, saying that people would deforest just to harvest
cuchi to export to Brazil.[3] A 2021 anti-smuggling operation by Bolivian authorities gave another glimpse of this trade, intercepting an
illegal load of 257 cuchi posts on the Route 4 highway near Puerto
Suárez and the Brazilian border.[4]

The loss of cuchi trees from Paraguay to Bolivia has been a casualty of Brazil's growing cattle economy. While the land-sparing hypothesis claims that intensive ranching and cropping will reduce agricultural deforestation, these intensive production systems require substantial inputs, such as fertilizers, fossil fuels, irrigation, and fencing. Supply chains for these inputs can displace environmental impacts across borders and biomes. As Jason W. Moore observes, "The condition for a labor productivity revolution in one region is the expansion of 'accumulation by appropriation' on a much larger scale."[5] Demand for cuchi fence posts is just one of many pathways through which Brazilian agro-industrial development displaces deforestation. Likewise, deforestation frontiers emerge from complex combinations of causes. These chapters focus on San Ignacio de Velasco and the deforestation of the Bolivian Chiquitania to show the connections between productivist development in Brazil and extractive deforestation in the Bolivian lowlands.

In highlighting these connections, I aim to refute the land-sparing claim that deforestation reductions and agricultural intensification in the Brazilian Amazon after 2004 provide a global model for decoupling agro-industrial development from deforestation. To the contrary, Amazonian deforestation restrictions and agricultural intensification drove Brazilian ranchers, investors, and supply chains to other biomes, such as the Brazilian Cerrado and Bolivian Chiquitania, where they helped drive dramatic increases in forest clearing. I do not argue that Brazilians are primarily to blame for the destruction of the Chiquitano dry forest, nor do I identify direct displacement of ranchers or capital leaving the Brazilian Amazon for Bolivia. A hypothetical example of direct displacement would be a deforesting rancher in Mato Grosso or Pará who, in response to new land-sparing policies in the Brazilian Amazon, chose to buy and deforest land in Bolivia. In practice, deforestation frontiers are complex assemblages of actors, capital, technologies, and resources, and pathways of transnational displacement are largely indirect, materializing through shifting investment patterns, migration flows, and trade relations. For example, a rancher and land speculator in southern Brazil who is looking for cheap land, instead of buying and deforesting new land in the Amazon might now choose to buy and deforest new land in Bolivia. Other agro-industry actors—slaughterhouses and soy farmers, seed companies and financiers—begin to shift their investments as well, drawn to a new frontier of deforestation and profit.

These forms of indirect displacement or spillover are mostly invisible in the statistical modeling approaches often used to evaluate forest policy. In their statistical study of Brazil's Amazon Soy Moratorium, Robert Heilmayr and colleagues are candid that "distant and diffuse forms of leakage, such as accelerated deforestation in other countries ... operates through regional or global markets, [and] does not lend itself well for empirical estimation."[6] In Vietnam, forest conservation has occurred through substantial transnational displacement of deforestation via Vietnamese foreign investment and trade. Micah Ingalls and colleagues note the difficulty of distinguishing the independent displacement effect of Vietnamese conservation policies from other variables, and they argue that "a too-restrictive approach to biophysical accounting and causal attribution" focused only on direct, policy-driven leakage is likely to "substantially underestimate the impact footprints of displacement."[7] They focus instead on case studies of large-scale land concessions to Vietnamese companies in Cambodia and Laos to describe transboundary pathways of displaced deforestation.

While the causal pathways are often indirect, the effects of transnational displacement are very real. The Chiquitano forests of the Bolivian lowlands lie between the dry forests of the Chaco to the south and the humid forests of the Amazon to the north. In the seventeenth and eighteenth centuries, Jesuit missionaries gathered lowland Indigenous populations into mission towns, where a collective Chiquitano Indigenous ethnicity emerged. At the northern edge of the Chiquitania in the municipality of San Ignacio de Velasco (San Ignacio), where Chiquitano dry forests shade into the humid forests of the southwestern Amazon, the economy centered historically on extraction of forest products such as timber and rubber, subsistence agriculture, and some extensive ranching. San Ignacio covers an area of around 49,000 square kilometers, nearly twice the size of Vermont, and at the turn of the twenty-first century, 88 percent of the municipal territory was forested. Forest loss in the early 2000s was minimal, averaging 55 square kilometers per year between 2001 and 2004, and Bolivian NGO Fundación Amigos de la Naturaleza (FAN) (using data from the MapBiomas project) estimates total historical deforestation in San Ignacio up to 2005 at just 470 square kilometers.[8] After 2005, at the same time as deforestation in the Brazilian Amazon began to decline, deforestation in San Ignacio accelerated.

From 2005 to 2009, annual forest loss in San Ignacio nearly tripled to an average of 151 square kilometers per year. Rising deforestation in San Ignacio was driven by an influx of Brazilian ranchers and investors. As new policies restricted deforestation in the Brazilian Amazon, cheap land and lax regulations drew Brazilian actors and capital to the Bolivian lowlands. Land "sparing" in Brazil displaced deforestation to Bolivia and beyond, and this transboundary expansion of the Brazilian ranching economy consolidated a new deforestation frontier in San Ignacio, where over the course of a decade and a half (2005–2019) more than 3,800 square kilometers of forest were lost, an area larger than Long Island.

The following chapters explore the relations and flows through which this displacement has occurred. My argument is not an attempt at variable-based accounting, calculating "net" effects of Brazilian policy from x hectares of deforestation in Brazil and y hectares of leakage in Bolivia. Such an approach quite literally misses the forest for the trees. The mirage of Brazil's land-sparing success—and global myths of green agro-industrial modernization—are sustained by these accounting perspectives that remove "cases" from their contexts and apply variable-based models that miss indirect pathways of socioecological change. What might we learn if we instead approach the dialectical geography of displacement from the standpoint of San Ignacio de Velasco?

A central argument of this book is that capitalism develops through dialectics of extraction and production. Political institutions stabilize economic processes at specific territorial levels, giving rise to political-economic regimes that are primarily extractive or productivist. These regimes are sticky, but they are dynamic, and regions can transform from extractive peripheries to productivist cores. I have argued that land-sparing policies on tropical forest frontiers attempt to engineer such a transformation from extractive deforestation to productivist "green" agro-industry. From 2005 to 2015, land-sparing policies in Indonesia failed to transform entrenched extractive regimes, and deforestation accelerated. At the same time, land-sparing policies drove deforestation reductions and productivist intensification in the Brazilian Amazon, leading scholars and policymakers to tout Brazil as a model of green development.

In turning to Bolivia, my purpose is not to present a full characterization of the political-economic regimes governing the San Ignacio frontier. Like all capitalist political-economic regimes, those governing the Bolivian lowlands are hybrid. The rise of an industrial soy complex in Santa Cruz Department since the late 1980s has dramatically increased capital investment in the region, but Ben McKay emphasizes that "very little of the value-added components of the soy complex are absorbed in Bolivia; capital temporarily penetrates the countryside, circulates through the soil and is exported in its commodity form as a soybean to external markets where it is further processed and fed into the global grain–feed–meat complex." Consequently, he argues that "rather than a form of industrial agricultural development which implies value-added processing, sectoral linkages and employment generation, Bolivia's soy complex is better characterized as 'agrarian extractivism.'"[9] Similarly, new capital investments and industrial ranching techniques have transformed San Ignacio into "the promised land for ranching," in the words of Mercy Mayser, president of the San Ignacio Ranchers Association (AGASIV), and intensive practices such as scientific breeding and agriculture-ranching integration are increasing productivity.[10] At the same time, the ranching economy has grown through massive deforestation, devouring Chiquitano forest for cattle pastures.

My focus in this section is on Bolivian deforestation as *displacement*. Accordingly, rather than an in-depth analysis of Bolivian political-economic regimes, I aim to show the web of connections linking productivism in Brazil and extractive deforestation in Bolivia to make the more fundamental point that productivist capitalist development depends on expanded extraction and displaced destruction.

Displaced deforestation negates land-sparing arguments, yet perversely, new deforestation becomes an opportunity for new land sparing. Ignoring that Bolivia's rising deforestation is substantially a

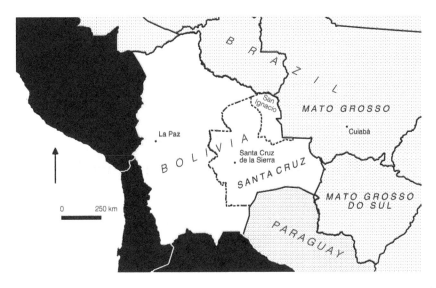

*Fig. 13. Map of Bolivia showing San Ignacio de Velasco
in Santa Cruz Department.*

displaced effect of land-sparing policies in Brazil, scholars and policymakers advocate land sparing to "green" Bolivia's agro-industrial
development. Today, rapid deforestation in San Ignacio brings
windfall profits to ranchers and investors. If tomorrow San Ignacio
becomes a center of zero-deforestation intensive agro-industry, it
will simply displace deforestation to new frontiers. The vortex of
"development" that forty years ago splintered Paraguay's cuchi trees
into fence posts is today bulldozing its way across lowland Bolivia.
The modernist promise to reconcile conservation with development
through land sparing is an illusion, belied by the lost forests of the
Bolivian Chiquitania.

CHAPTER EIGHT

"The Country Jumps the Fence"

T HE CITY OF SANTA CRUZ DE LA SIERRA lies just east of the Andean foothills near the banks of the Piraí River, in the upper reaches of the Amazon watershed. The city is the capital of Santa Cruz Department, which at over 370,000 square kilometers is the largest of Bolivia's nine departments and nearly as large as the neighboring country of Paraguay. This chapter describes Santa Cruz's transformation from a tropical backwater to Bolivia's agribusiness center, focusing on the role of Brazilian actors and investment in "developing" the Bolivian lowlands.

Bolivia's colonial economy centered on Andean mining—silver made Potosí one of the richest and most populous cities of the Spanish Empire, and after Bolivian independence in 1825, tin mining became the linchpin of the national political economy. The rubber boom at the turn of the twentieth century profoundly altered the socioecology of Bolivia's Amazonian lowlands, but because of the region's isolation, local rubber barons governed this early wave of lowland extraction with little influence from the Bolivian state.[1] Although initial oil discoveries in the Chaco region by U.S.-based Standard Oil played a role in the Chaco War of the 1930s, in which Bolivia lost a large portion of the Chaco to Paraguay, the tropical lowlands remained a poorly integrated hinterland of the Bolivian state until the mid-twentieth century.

During the 1940s, U.S. government officials identified resource-rich Bolivia as a strategic ally in the war against fascism. A 1941–1942 economic mission led by U.S. State Department official Merwin Bohan produced the so-called Bohan Plan, which advocated development of commercial agriculture in the Bolivian lowlands, to be supported by highway construction and migration of Andean peasants from the highlands. This vision crystallized after the Bolivian National Revolution of 1952 in the famous "March to the East." The Cochabamba–Santa Cruz highway was completed in 1954, connecting Santa Cruz to Bolivia's Andean heartland, and the new national government, supported by U.S. development aid, stimulated large-scale migration aimed at relieving poverty in the highlands and transforming the lowlands into a breadbasket of Green Revolution industrial agriculture for domestic consumption and export.[2] Over the following decades, Santa Cruz became the center of a commercial agricultural economy producing sugarcane, cotton, livestock, and rice, supported by cheap agricultural credit and (especially during the 1970s military dictatorship) large land grants to government cronies.

After 1985, structural adjustments and economic liberalization undermined peasant agriculture in the highlands with cheap imports while feeding the Santa Cruz agro-export frontier with migrant labor and capital investments. Annual agricultural deforestation in the "expansion zone" east of Santa Cruz de la Sierra increased from 68,000 hectares in 1986 to 225,000 in 1992, clearing land for wheat, cotton, sorghum, and especially soy production, which by 1992 accounted for nearly two-thirds of cropland in the expansion zone.[3] Additional support for the Santa Cruz soy sector came from the World Bank's Eastern Lowlands Project, which during the early 1990s invested $35 million focused on agricultural production, marketing, and infrastructure. While government and World Bank policies and investments encouraged agricultural expansion, the arrival of Brazilian soy producers launched Santa Cruz into the orbit of Brazilian agro-industry, supercharging soy production and driving massive deforestation.

Brazilian Frontiers in Bolivia

Brazilian economic reforms in the early 1990s squeezed the agricultural sector in the Brazilian South and expanded the export-oriented soy and ranching complex in the Brazilian Center-West.[4] Attracted by cheap land and inviting policies in Bolivia, several hundred Brazilian soy producers established themselves in Santa Cruz, marking the beginning of substantial spillover of Brazil's highly capitalized agribusiness sector into the Bolivian lowlands. "The country jumps the fence," proclaimed a special feature on emigration to neighboring countries published in 1995 in *Veja*, the leading Brazilian news magazine. "With rising national land prices and an agricultural sector greedy for new lands, it is only natural that so many producers have succumbed to the temptation to advance the Brazilian agricultural frontier on foreign soils," the article explained, remarking that the borderlands of neighboring countries were "sparsely populated corners, lacking in technology and investment, with almost everything still to be done." Noting the success of Brazilian agribusiness on earlier frontiers in countries like Uruguay and Paraguay, the article affirmed,

> It is numbers like these that lead Bolivia to send emissaries with a mission to captivate Brazilian producers with offers of cheap and fertile lands in the region of Santa Cruz de la Sierra. Two hundred large *fazendeiros* have already established themselves in the country in the last three years, with spectacular results. The virgin soil needs no fertilizer and they have managed to harvest 3500 kilos of soy per hectare, one third above the average in Mato Grosso.[5]

The fertility of "virgin" soils, of course, was a windfall of large-scale deforestation. The World Bank estimated that Santa Cruz lost nearly 1 million hectares of forest from 1989 to 1996.[6] In an interview with Brazilian scholar Heloisa Marques Gimenez, a former Bolivian official who oversaw agriculture and sustainable development reflected on the 1990s soy boom in Santa Cruz: "Basically, that boom is produced by Brazilians, who buy lands that weren't deforested, deforest, invest in improvements, and permit the development of all of the auxiliary industry to the agricultural sector: agricultural inputs improve, technology is incorporated, and, moreover, at first, they take advantage of the marketing channels that Brazil already had—Brazilian producers sold their production to Brazil, which was processed there, [then] exported or consumed by the Brazilian market."[7] Subsequently, soy processing capacity was also developed in Santa Cruz, through investments from Bolivian and transnational capital. U.S.-based Cargill and ADM, major buyers of soy in the Brazilian Amazon, have both operated in Bolivia since 1998.

In short, Brazilians were central to consolidating the soy sector in Santa Cruz through massive deforestation during the 1990s. (This early spillover was attributable to macroeconomic shifts and Bolivian policy incentives, rather than to forest conservation measures in Brazil, where deforestation in the 1990s was also on the rise.) Furthermore, the direct role of Brazilians in soy production was just one dimension of Brazilian involvement in the development of the Bolivian lowlands. Brazilian companies and government interests played a crucial role in constructing the logistical and political infrastructures for supporting and accelerating the agricultural frontier and expanding other extractive activities in the region. In the agro-industrial sector, Brazilian companies and investors consolidated control over large portions of the soy value chain, especially after Bolivia legalized transgenic soybean seeds in 2005. Brazilians own seed companies and warehouses in Santa Cruz, Brazilian barges transport Bolivian soy on the Paraguay River, and substantial proportions of the agricultural machinery and agro-chemicals used in Bolivian soy production are imported from Brazil.[8]

Beyond agribusiness, the fossil-fuel sector provides perhaps the clearest instance of Brazilian extraction from the Bolivian lowlands. Petrobras, the Brazilian parastatal oil company, entered Bolivia in 1996, where it has carried out oil and gas exploration and production across the Bolivian lowlands, including in protected areas such as Madidi National Park and the Isiboro Sécure Indigenous Territory and National Park (known as TIPNIS). In the late 1990s, Petrobras and the Brazilian National Development Bank (BNDES) helped finance the $2.15 billion Bolivia–Brazil gas pipeline operated by Shell and Enron, and a connecting pipeline from Santa Cruz to Cuiabá, Mato Grosso, was cut across the heart of the Chiquitania to provide gas to Brazil's "agribusiness capital."[9] By the time the Bolivian government under Evo Morales nationalized the fossil-fuel industry in 2006 (which involved cutting new deals with foreign companies), Petrobras had invested $1 billion in the Bolivian natural gas industry and accounted for around 20 percent of Bolivian GDP and nearly a quarter of Bolivian tax revenue, while Bolivia was the source for around half of Brazil's natural gas consumption.[10] Nationalization shifted some revenues, and Brazil has since developed more domestic gas sources, but the fundamental relations of extraction remain unchanged: Brazil extracts fossil fuels from the Bolivian periphery to fuel productivist infrastructures in the Brazilian core. In 2016, Petrobras and the Bolivian state-owned YPFB Chaco announced $1.2 billion in new investments to develop gas fields in the Bolivian Chaco.

Additionally, Brazil has aimed to support Brazilian energy and agribusiness investments in Bolivia, as well as export prospects for the Brazilian Center-West, by investing in Bolivia's transportation infrastructure. Infamously, BNDES was involved in 2008–2011 in a controversial $415-million project awarded to the Brazilian company OAS for construction of a road through Bolivia's TIPNIS reserve, where Petrobras also held exploration rights. While BNDES eventually withdrew financing in the face of protests and accusations of corruption, the TIPNIS project also revealed the formal, diplomatic support of the Brazilian state undergirding Brazilian investment in Bolivia. Brazilian president Lula traveled to Bolivia in 2009 to announce Brazilian support for the TIPNIS highway, allegedly pressuring OAS to take the contract, and as the project disintegrated in 2011 in the face of popular protests, Lula (by that time ex-president) traveled to Bolivia again to intercede with Morales in an attempt to save the project.[11] When the Bolivian government canceled the OAS contract in 2012, Brazilian president Dilma Rousseff reportedly reminded Morales that good relations between their countries "rely on the capacity of Brazilian companies to do business in Bolivia."[12]

Brazilian diplomatic support extends to the agribusiness sector in Santa Cruz as well. Miguel Urioste observes that "it is unlikely that there was any previous planning by the Brazilian state to promote migration and human settlement in Bolivia, but now that Brazilian nationals are established in Bolivia, the Brazilian state provides protection and support to these groups. Brazilian producers . . . know that they are backed and protected by both the Brazilian and Bolivian governments."[13] On my first visit to Santa Cruz in 2018, a Bolivian activist who has worked on land issues in the government and civil society sectors told me that around 2005, they expressed a concern at the government's land agency (Instituto Nacional de Reforma Agraria, INRA) that many of the best lands were in the hands of Brazilians, and the Brazilian Ministry of Foreign Affairs responded with formal notes calling their comment "xenophobic." When several years later the Bolivian land rights NGO Fundación TIERRA published a book by Miguel Urioste on land concentration and foreignization, the Brazilian ambassador asked for a meeting at the NGO's office, where he said he was concerned about the work and its "anti-Brazilian vision." "The Brazilian Government is protecting Brazilian investment, especially in agriculture," the activist concluded.[14]

In sum, through Brazilian migration and investment in the agribusiness sector, energy and infrastructure investments and financing from Brazilian companies and Brazilian state banks, and the diplomatic support of the Brazilian state, Brazilian actors and capital have driven the expansion of the agricultural and fossil-fuel frontiers in eastern Bolivia since the early 1990s, directly or indirectly clearing thousands of square kilometers of lowland forest. Brazilian agribusiness investments during the 1990s centered on soy production around Santa Cruz de la Sierra, but after 2004, as land-sparing policies pushed a productivist transition in the Brazilian Amazon, a new wave of Brazilian migration and investment swept across the Bolivian frontier, flowing this time into the ranching sector in the eastern borderlands. Over the course of the following decade, deforestation in the Brazilian Amazon declined to historic lows, while San Ignacio de Velasco transformed into the "pole of *cruceña* [Santa Cruz] ranching" and ground zero for Chiquitano forest destruction.[15]

CHAPTER NINE

San Ignacio de Velasco

From the Lost World to the Zebu Capital

W HEN IN 2018 I boarded a bus in Cuiabá, traveling west across the Cerrado to Cáceres and the Bolivian border, San Ignacio was a logical destination. Capital and largest municipality of Velasco Province, San Ignacio had over the past decade become a ranching boomtown and a deforestation hotspot. Reports that a new wave of Brazilian investors was playing a key role in this ranching frontier were enough to suggest San Ignacio as a place to explore transnational dynamics of agricultural deforestation. But there was an additional feature that drew me to San Ignacio, connecting this Bolivian borderland with the Brazilian and Indonesian frontiers I knew best: Noel Kempff Mercado National Park.

In the far north of San Ignacio, in the transition zone between Chiquitano dry forest, Cerrado savanna, and humid Amazonian forest, the Huanchaca Plateau rises over half a kilometer above the surrounding plains. British explorer Percy Fawcett's account of Huanchaca inspired Sir Arthur Conan Doyle's 1912 novel *The Lost World*, and the Bolivian government created Huanchaca National Park in 1979. In a 1986 expedition to the park, famed Bolivian biologist Noel Kempff Mercado was murdered by drug traffickers, and the park was renamed in 1988 in his honor. Noel Kempff Mercado

National Park was also, in the 1990s, the site of The Nature Conservancy's first REDD project. The park had a designated area of
750,000 hectares along the western bank of the Río Iténez, which
marks the Bolivian border with Brazil. Between the park and the
Río Paraguá to the west, a large area of intact tropical forest was occupied by logging concessions and Indigenous communities. TNC
partnered with Bolivian NGO FAN and the Bolivian government
in the Noel Kempff Mercado Climate Action Project, and with financing from American Electric Power Company, BP America, and
PacifiCorp, the project bought and retired three logging concessions between 1996 and 1997, adding another 830,000 hectares to
the park. In 2005, carbon reductions from the project underwent
third-party validation and verification, making Noel Kempff the
world's first third-party-verified REDD project.[1]

For over a decade, the Noel Kempff Climate Action Project
funded park management, ecotourism and community development initiatives, and carbon monitoring, but the inauguration of
Evo Morales in 2006 was the beginning of the end for the project. The Morales administration was opposed to carbon markets
and to co-management of a national park by private actors.[2] After
2009, "it became impossible to count on the participation of the
government," one of the project directors from FAN recalled.[3] Carbon credits from the project were never marketed, and by 2013 the
project was defunct. For TNC, Noel Kempff was a great success.
Responding to a 2009 Greenpeace report criticizing the project,
TNC affirmed,

> As the world's first project of its kind, the Noel Kempff Cli-
> mate Action Project was a pioneer project that tested and
> refined the science of forest carbon accounting and moni-
> toring.... The Noel Kempff project also serves as an exam-
> ple of how well-designed forest carbon projects can result
> in real, scientifically measurable and verifiable emissions re-
> ductions with important benefits for biodiversity and local
> communities.... The Nature Conservancy and other orga-
> nizations are now building on the experience and lessons
> learned in Noel Kempff to inform scientifically rigorous
> methods and standards for other forest carbon projects, and

> we are undertaking REDD projects that span entire political
> jurisdictions in Berau, Indonesia and Para, Brazil.[4]

In short, even as the Noel Kempff project began to unravel roughly
a third of the way through its thirty-year lifespan, TNC was scaling
up its Noel Kempff experience for jurisdictional REDD projects in
Berau and São Félix.

In 2019, over two decades after the project's inception, I sought
to visit Noel Kempff during a research trip to San Ignacio. It soon
became clear that touristic visits were no longer possible, even with
my rented 4x4. A company that formerly offered tours of Noel
Kempff responded to my inquiry: "Because we can no longer guarantee the quality of the tour to Noel Kempff N.P. (there is close to
zero maintenance in the park cabins) we have decided to no longer
offer trips to the park." They neglected to mention that the park
had also become unsafe. A former park director recounted that after 2005, NGO support diminished and pressures on the park increased. "Being a border zone brings dangerous situations of trafficking, drug trafficking," they explained. "SERNAP [the national
park service] decreased the budget for all protected areas. Tourist
infrastructure fell to ruin, and without tourism, the communities
feel the pinch. . . . The hotels were destroyed, enforcement activities were diminished, and crime increased," including illegal fishing, logging, hunting, and trafficking.[5] In 2021, Bolivian authorities
discovered two narcotics "megalaboratories" within the park, each
capable of producing half a ton of cocaine per day.[6]

Today, the forests around Noel Kempff National Park are beset by Andean settlers and Brazilian ranchers, driving land conflicts
with Indigenous communities and large-scale deforestation. At the
southern edge of the park, residents of the Indigenous community of
La Esperancita were reportedly expelled from their land by Brazilian ranchers, who accused them of stealing cattle and gave them an
ultimatum to leave; an Indigenous leader affirmed that no one dares
speak of the Brazilians out of fear.[7] Settlements by Andean colonists were promoted by Morales's Movimiento al Socialismo (MAS)
government to distribute patronage and assert political control over
Santa Cruz, the center of opposition to Morales. A 2015 law authorized forest clearing of up to twenty hectares on small properties,

turning settlements into a vehicle for legalized deforestation and fueling an economy of forest clearing and land trafficking.

These settlement policies have facilitated the expansion of Brazilian ranchers, even as they distract from the Brazilian presence in the region. The leader of San Ignacio's Indigenous association (Asociación de Cabildos Indígenas de San Ignacio de Velasco, ACISIV) alleges that an area west of Noel Kempff legally designated for settlers as Monte Alto community is in fact uninhabited and rented to Brazilians.[8] Collective outrage at settlement policies (which also threaten large properties with invasion and expropriation) has allowed large landowners and the municipal government in San Ignacio to paint themselves as allies of Indigenous communities. In February 2021, the municipal government created a new protected area (Bajo Paraguá Municipal Protected Area) of nearly 1 million hectares west of the national park, aiming to exert greater control over settlement and forest clearing in the region. Indigenous leaders, municipal officials, and the Santa Cruz press loudly denounced clearing by settlers in Bajo Paraguá, though initial areas deforested were on the order of sixty to eighty hectares.[9] Meanwhile, in 2020, two large properties near the Brazilian border deforested over 5,200 hectares, including 66 within Noel Kempff National Park itself.[10]

It is a cruel irony of "green" development, and of REDD policies in particular, that Noel Kempff was supposedly protected by a REDD project, and twenty years later the park is menaced, at least indirectly, by REDD's success. When we met in 2019 in FAN's offices on the outskirts of Santa Cruz, the organization's former Noel Kempff project director reflected, "In our experience, you can have great projects in sites like Noel Kempff, but it doesn't change the development dynamic. San Ignacio is still one of the municipalities with the greatest number of fires, with the most ranching deforestation. The territorial dynamic, the development dynamic has not changed, despite the fact that the municipal government is extremely proud of its protected area."[11] TNC took its lessons from Noel Kempff to Indonesia and Brazil, where they designed REDD programs centered on land sparing, attempting to engineer more fundamental transformations in regional development dynamics. While Indonesia's extractive regimes proved mostly resistant to their efforts, in Brazil TNC joined a political-economic coalition in São

Félix and beyond to launch a land-sparing transition. Although not always couched in the language of REDD, land-sparing "green" development policies succeeded for a decade in dramatically reducing deforestation and forest carbon emissions in the Brazilian Amazon region. Constraining and intensifying agriculture in the Brazilian Amazon displaced ranching expansion and deforestation elsewhere, however, including across the Bolivian border to the area around Noel Kempff, where agricultural clearing now threatens the park. "Twenty years ago, we were a long way from thinking about this [the agricultural frontier]," a former park director recalled, "but now it's right there nearby."[12] Brazil's role in rising deforestation in San Ignacio not only canceled out conservation "success" in the Brazilian Amazon but also undermined the earlier conservation "success" of Noel Kempff—a boomerang of "green" development and displaced destruction.

From Forestry to Ranching

Ranching expansion in San Ignacio was coupled with the collapse of the forestry sector. The long history of logging and woodworking in the municipality is attested by elaborately carved wooden columns that line the city's central square: towering men with spears in front of city hall, priests and musicians outside Hotel La Misión, monkeys and toucans at the Hotel San Ignacio, flowers and spirals on the columns of the cathedral and the Oriente Social Club. Businesses boast carved wooden signs, and winged wooden angels look down from walls and window frames. A San Ignacio native who has worked since the 1980s with MINGA, a community agricultural association, recounts, "This region generated its economy in the '70s and '80s and part of the '90s with timber, but everything is being exhausted. Timber gave life to the region. . . . Now timber has been replaced with ranching. The elite who manage the economy today are ranchers. . . . [They] deforest and plant pasture."[13] Paradoxically, it was the attempt to regulate illegal logging that plunged the forestry sector into full-blown crisis.

In 2009, following the promulgation of Bolivia's new constitution under Morales, a new forestry agency (Autoridad de Fiscalización y Control Social de Bosques y Tierra, ABT) was created to replace the Forestry and Agrarian Superintendency. ABT moved to clamp down on corruption and informality in the forestry sector at the same time as the timber extraction model was shifting from large concessions toward logging by community associations and private property owners. Imposing greater control over the forestry sector reduced the timber supply and increased production costs, raising prices for Bolivian timber.[14] An agronomist with the Velasco provincial government observed in 2018, "Timber is much more expensive than it was seven years ago. It used to be a gift, but now it's legal [*era regalo, pero hoy es legal*]."[15]

Rising domestic timber prices initially favored legalized logging operations, but higher prices also drove rising imports, and cheap furniture from Brazil and China flooded the Bolivian market, supported by the export-driven devaluation of the Brazilian and Chinese currencies. Furniture imports more than doubled in volume and tripled in value from 2009 to 2014, crashing the Bolivian furniture industry. Brazil was the primary source of Bolivian furniture imports, followed by China, with over 60 percent of wood product imports (principally cheap melamine-laminated fiberboard or plywood furniture) coming from Brazil.[16] The wave of cheap imports drove down prices and undermined the Bolivian forestry sector. In San Ignacio, where Brazilian ranchers had already begun to expand in the wake of deforestation controls in the Brazilian Amazon, the forestry crisis accelerated the economic shift to ranching. Describing this transition, a director at the Facultad Integral Chiquitana (FAICHI), the public agricultural college in San Ignacio, explained, "Here there was traditional ranching as a 'hobby,' but everyone made their living from timber. . . . With forestry restrictions, people turned to ranching as an alternative."[17] In sum, when Bolivia tried to rein in illegal logging, Brazilian and Chinese furniture imports overwhelmed the Bolivian forestry sector, transforming San Ignacio into a ranching platform from which Brazilian ranchers and investors export beef to China.

These macroeconomic drivers of ranching expansion were reinforced by Bolivian policies that systematically favored agriculture over forestry and progressively relaxed restrictions on deforestation while encouraging agricultural expansion. Yann le Polain de

Waroux and colleagues, in a 2016 study examining land-use policies and corporate agricultural investments in the Chiquitania and Gran Chaco through interviews with companies and statistical modeling, came to the straightforward conclusion that "companies that clear more forest invest where deforestation regulations are weak, and all companies seek out areas with low enforcement." Effectively describing the distinction between productivist and extractive economies, they write, "Whereas some [i.e., productivist] companies tend to produce in consolidated agricultural areas, relying on efficient agricultural systems based on outsourced services, others specialize in the colonization of forested areas, where they capture the transitory profits associated with resource frontiers. These deforestation-intensive [i.e., extractive] companies . . . are more sensitive to environmental regulations because their profitability depends on the integration of cheaper, forested land. They are usually involved in cattle ranching."[18] In the Bolivian lowlands, institutions favoring ranching over forestry include the tax regime and regulations related to properties' socioeconomic function. Bolivian agrarian reform laws require that properties fulfill an economic and social function (*función económico-social*, FES) or risk expropriation. After 2007, criteria required both legal possession and title for a property to meet the FES through forestry activities, while ranching and agriculture required only legal possession, and ranching activity could justify productive use at the very extensive rate of five hectares for every one head of cattle. Furthermore, forestry operations pay regular business and value-added taxes, while ranching and agriculture benefit from a special tax regime that charges ranching operations a flat rate of roughly 2 bolivianos ($0.29) for every hectare over 500 hectares.[19]

The "rapprochement" between the Morales government and lowland agribusiness elites after 2009, and especially from 2013, also resulted in policies facilitating deforestation.[20] The government's Agenda Patriótica Bolivia 2025, approved in 2013, enshrined agribusiness expansion as a national development goal, and Law 337, promulgated that same year, effectively amnestied agricultural deforestation that had taken place from 1996 to 2011. Meanwhile, precise data about settlements for Andean colonists issued by the government land agency (INRA) have been impossible to obtain, even for the mayors of the lowland municipalities where the settlements are located. Reports suggest that between 2014 and 2018, INRA turned over 1.2 million hectares of state lands in Santa Cruz.[21] TIERRA, the Bolivian land rights NGO, estimates 1,400 new settlements in the Chiquitania since 2014, and the leader of ACISIV reports 250 settlements in San Ignacio.[22] Law 741, passed in 2015, raised the area of deforestation permitted on small properties from five to twenty hectares, so a settlement with thirty lots implies six hundred hectares of legal deforestation. "They arrive with an axe on their shoulder and a match in their hand," exclaimed an environment official with the San Ignacio government.[23] The MAS government's settlement policy is publicly reviled in Santa Cruz, but as a report in the Bolivian magazine *Nómadas* observes, these colonists are the spearhead of deforestation because they have the political and economic power to invade lands, and deforested settlement lands are then often trafficked for agriculture and ranching. "Behind the peasant, there is a businessman," remarked an ABT official in San Ignacio.[24]

While government policies legalized extensive deforestation, they also failed to deter illegal deforestation. "It's easier to pay a fine than to obtain a permit," the FAICHI director complained, adding, "Those who don't respect the law progress and get ahead, while those who respect the law have no opportunity."[25] "People prefer to deforest first [and deal with bureaucracy later]," an ABT official in San Ignacio told me, acknowledging that the majority of deforestation was illegal. "The ranching sector wants to deforest right away to make its pastures, and bureaucratic approval can take time."[26] When in 2011 ABT publicized a list of the worst repeat offenders of forest regulations, the Brazilian rancher Osias Wagner Greve had the third-highest number of infractions of any person in Bolivia.[27] In addition to owning land in San Ignacio, Greve was the general manager of Frigorífico Chiquitano, San Ignacio's largest slaughterhouse. With five counts of illegal deforestation and four counts of illegal burning, Greve was just two spots ahead of Luis Fernando Saavedra Bruno (three deforestation and four burning infractions), one of the wealthiest Bolivian ranchers. Saavedra Bruno, who owns large areas in San Ignacio, became one of the most important cattle breeders in the Bolivian lowlands after importing Nelore cows from Brazil in the 1980s.[28] Clearly, large ranchers in San Ignacio have little compunction about illegal forest clearing.

In sum, from around 2009 onward, the collapse of the forestry sector and a suite of policies facilitating agribusiness expansion and deforestation combined to accelerate the conversion of the Chiquitano forest into pastures. The Chiquitano landscape today is a complex mosaic of dry forests and cattle pastures, mission towns and Mennonite colonies, lowland Chiquitano communities and migrant settlers from highland Indigenous groups. A full explanation for ranching expansion in San Ignacio would include everything from government settlement policies to infrastructure construction to the drug economy. Paving of the highway connecting San Ignacio with Santa Cruz via San Ramón (a northern route) was completed in 2017, and in 2019 a Chinese state company began work on paving the road to San José de Chiquitos (a southern route) with financing from the World Bank. Soon, cattle from San Ignacio belonging to Brazilian ranchers may be slaughtered in a facility built by Brazilian capital and exported to China over a road paved by a Chinese company. Already in 2019, "the effect of paving the [northern] highway has been keenly felt," a San Ignacio official told me, observing that "principally the highway has driven ranching development," but it would also support the growth of soy cultivation in the municipality.[29] "The highway has given a strong push to ranching," Mercy Mayser, president of the San Ignacio Ranchers Association (AGASIV) confirmed, "and with the San José highway it will be another way out."[30] Construction of an airport in San Ignacio at the end of the 2010s was also expected to fortify the ranching economy, and at the same time touched off a land rush, with reports of over 4,400 hectares deforested near the airport between 2020 and mid-2021.[31] Meanwhile, the cocaine trade across the Bolivia-Brazil border not only uses cattle ranches as transit points but likely fuels investments in ranching as a form of money laundering.[32]

In this chapter, my purpose is not to give a complete account of the San Ignacio ranching frontier, however, but rather to highlight specifically the role of Brazilian actors and capital in ranching expansion and deforestation in order to make two central points:

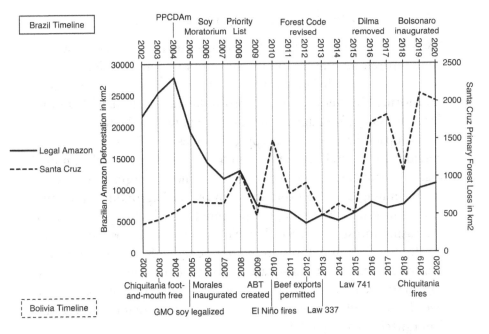

Fig. 14. Deforestation in the Brazilian Amazon and Santa Cruz, Bolivia. Brazilian data are PRODES Legal Amazon deforestation statistics, which guide official policies. Bolivian data are humid primary forest loss in Santa Cruz Department detected by Global Forest Watch. Timelines highlight key policies and events. In Bolivia, Law 337 amnestied past deforestation, and Law 741 raised deforestation limits on small properties.

1. The Brazilian influx to San Ignacio came after 2004 and especially after 2007, coinciding with the ratcheting up of land-sparing policies and declining deforestation in the Brazilian Amazon.
2. Brazilian ranchers were drawn to San Ignacio by cheap land and the ability to deforest, and Brazilian investment accelerated ranching expansion at the expense of forests.

These facts underlie my argument that increasing deforestation in Bolivia was driven in part by displacement from Brazil. The land-sparing claim is that agro-industrial development in the Brazilian Amazon after 2004 saved forests, but land sparing in Brazil was coupled with massive forest destruction in the Chiquitania (fig. 14). The land-sparing claim was a fallacy.

Brazilian Ranching in San Ignacio

"Brasil ya no tiene bosque"—"Brazil has no more forest"—was a common refrain among my interlocutors in San Ignacio.[33] Looking across the Bolivian border to the east, they saw a landscape transformed by Mato Grosso's agro-industrial juggernaut. "On the Brazilian side, it's all agriculture and ranching," said a former Noel Kempff park director. "Corn, soy, trangenics. . . . There's just a small corridor [of natural vegetation] along the riverbank, which is nothing."[34] Meanwhile, in San Ignacio, "It's almost a virgin zone, just at the beginning of being exploited," a provincial agronomist told me. "Many investors are seeing the potential."[35] A FAN report showed increasing forest loss in San Ignacio in the early 2000s but marked a definitive leap in deforestation after 2004, with annual deforestation rates rising from 59 square kilometers per year in 2000–2004 to 149 square kilometers per year in 2005–2014. In that 2005–2014 decade of Brazil's land-sparing success, the total deforested area in San Ignacio quadrupled.[36]

Ranching expansion was the primary driver of accelerating deforestation, and the growth of the ranching economy was fueled by foreign investment. The Chiquitania was certified free of foot-and-mouth disease in 2003, and foreign investors from across the region began to enter the San Ignacio ranching sector. "The 'zebu capital' doubles its herd with foreign investment," declared a 2019 feature story in the Santa Cruz newspaper *El Deber*. "Argentinians, Brazilians, Uruguayans, Irish, and Paraguayans join the ranchers of San Ignacio de Velasco and drive ranching development. Agribusiness, miners and bankers also invest."[37]

Brazilians are far from the only foreign investors in San Ignacio, in other words, yet Brazilians are without doubt the most substantial foreign presence. Concrete statistics on Brazilian landownership in San Ignacio are not public, and foreign ownership is in any case often obscured through the use of Bolivian front companies known as *palos blancos*. Urioste in 2011 offered a rough estimate that Brazilian ranchers owned around 700,000 hectares in three Santa Cruz border provinces.[38] The dearth of public statistics on the Brazilian presence is in part by design, as Brazilians and their Bolivian counterparts in government and agribusiness seek to avoid nationalist backlash.[39] Nonetheless, the Brazilian influence in San Ignacio is universally recognized and easily visible, from Brazilian barbecue restaurants in the town center to the Brazilian-built slaughterhouse on a hill across the reservoir.

Brazilians call themselves *brasileiros*, and in common with many of Brazil's Spanish-speaking neighbors, San Ignacio residents adapt the Portuguese term, often calling Brazilians "brasileros" rather than the more formal Spanish *brasileños*. I focus here on the role of "brasileros" on the San Ignacio ranching frontier. Other scholars have noted, often in passing, the Brazilian role in the ranching sector. Anne Cristina de la Vega-Leinert and Christoph Huber affirm that accelerated deforestation in the Bolivian lowlands is being driven partly by "increasing land concentration in the hands of foreign investors, farmers and cattle ranchers, a process closely associated with land conversion and use across the border in neighboring Brazil," though they do not detail the concrete mechanisms through which this cross-border "leakage" materializes.[40] Similarly, Robert Müller, Pablo Pacheco, and Juan Carlos Montero observe,

> Accumulation of private capital in Brazil, due to the economic boom in this country, is especially relevant for Bolivia. . . . Much of private capital in Brazil is generated by agribusinesses. At the same time, the development of Bolivia's agricultural sector lies behind Brazil's and lands are much cheaper. In addition, deforestation control has increased considerably in recent years in Brazil. Consequently, there are huge flows of international investment capital, especially from Brazil, being directed to agribusinesses in Bolivia, thus promoting mechanized agriculture and cattle ranching. In the areas of San Ignacio de Velasco or southern Guayaramerín, for example, it is reported that a large part of cattle ranching is done with Brazilian capital and there is a strong informal cross-border livestock trade with Brazil.[41]

Their study does not provide further detail on these Brazilian connections, however. I offer here a deeper understanding of what the Brazilian influx looks like and how it works.

"When I was ten years old, there weren't Brazilians here in San Ignacio," a young municipal environment official told me in 2019 as we drove together to a project visit in the Indigenous community of San Juancito. "It must be about fifteen years that the Brazilian presence has emerged," they reflected, dating the Brazilian influx to roughly 2004.[42] An activist in Santa Cruz described Brazilian expansion as first "flowing over the natural dam of the frontier [*rebalse natural através de las fronteras*]." "Land is cheaper in Bolivia," they observed. "Individuals come to invest." In a second stage, they saw an expansion of Brazilian corporations with Brazilian capital "accumulating links in the production chain."[43] "Brazilian geopolitics is expansionary," a municipal conservation official in San Ignacio affirmed. "They view the Chiquitania as a zone of expansion."[44] I describe the "spillover" or expansion of Brazilians and accelerating deforestation in the San Ignacio ranching sector along several dimensions. First, the most direct Brazilian role in ranching deforestation comprises land control and forest clearing by Brazilian ranchers. Next, I discuss more indirect pathways through which Brazilian actors and capital drive ranching deforestation, including flows of knowledge and technology (especially cattle genetics) and investments in infrastructure—namely, the Frigorífico Chiquitano slaughterhouse.

In 2004, the Brazilian government launched PPCDAm, its new policy framework for combating Amazonian deforestation. The 2006 Amazon Soy Moratorium steered Amazonian soy expansion in Brazil to existing pasture areas, and in 2008 the Brazilian government cracked down further on illegal deforestation with the announcement of its "priority list" of municipalities for deforestation monitoring and enforcement. Deforestation in the Brazilian Amazon declined, land values rose, and ranchers seeking cheap forestland for new pastures began to look elsewhere. Sleepy San Ignacio was suddenly in the crosshairs.

My interviewees in San Ignacio universally reported that Brazilian presence in the municipality began to increase in the 2005–2010 period. In June 2019, I interviewed an official in San Ignacio's municipal Directorate of Environment and Water who had just spent the weekend in a workshop with environmental activists and local communities discussing Brazilian agricultural expansion and water scarcity. "Sometimes you have such a great pressure from a gigantic country," they began, trailing off. "For a Brazilian to buy land here, it's a bargain. . . . I have been in San Ignacio for nineteen years, and the Brazilian presence has been most notable in the past ten years. There have been more Brazilian ranches and more deforestation. They have come because it's cheap to buy land here, labor is cheap, fuel is cheap."[45] "It was something drastic," the FAICHI director recalled when discussing land purchases and forest clearing by Brazilians in the early 2010s. "They deforested illegally, paid the fines, and everything's good [*no pasa nada*]."[46] The avidity with which Brazilian ranchers sought land and cleared forests was commonly remarked upon: "Private properties have enormous areas. They deforest areas and go and pay someone," a community forestry association official explained in 2018. Of the Brazilian ranchers who had been coming to San Ignacio for "around ten years," they affirmed, "land is very cheap. They buy one thousand hectares and in two months deforest eight hundred hectares."[47] As mentioned above, the Brazilian rancher Osias Wagner Greve was third on ABT's list of worst repeat offenders in 2011, while recent reports allege that Brazilians are involved in land trafficking in Bajo Paraguá and have chased the Indigenous community of La Esperancita off its land.

The young municipal environment official described additional cases of transboundary land invasions by Brazilians near Laguna Marfil, a municipal protected area on the Brazilian border, fifty kilometers south of Noel Kempff, and to the east near the border communities of San Vicente and Santa Catarina, where "Brazilian businessmen have cut down a ton. Brazilian businessmen come with everything ready and they settle." The official said their department and NGO partners were trying to work with Indigenous communities to prevent "agroindustrial invasions."[48] An ABT official in San Ignacio was forthright about the role of Brazilian ranchers in deforestation: "Communities do not have the capacity to deforest large areas," the official explained. "Large clearings are done by the larger private properties. Large ranchers are foreigners, and Brazilians are the largest ranchers here."[49] In short, interviews, news stories, and ABT data confirm that Brazilian ranchers have taken advantage of cheaper land and weak regulations in Bolivia to engage in large-scale deforestation in San Ignacio after 2004 and especially since the end of the 2000s.

Moreover, the Brazilian role in accelerating ranching deforestation in San Ignacio reaches beyond direct land control and forest clearing. The intensive, productivist ranching economy in Brazil has pumped industrial ranching knowledge and technologies into the Chiquitania, as well as supporting a cross-border trade in cattle and "genetic material" (primarily embryos and semen) that has stimulated the growth and profitability of the Bolivian ranching sector. In the absence of effective forest protections, increasing profits in Bolivian ranching drive new investments and new deforestation.

An informal, cross-border cattle trade reportedly exists between ranchers in San Ignacio and their counterparts in Brazil, though details of these exchanges are difficult to uncover.[50] A veterinarian with the regional ranching association in Santa Cruz (FEGASACRUZ) observed, "There is no official protocol for transport of cattle over the border, but with a dry border of so many kilometers. . . . For producers that are there, there are exchanges. Cattle don't know where the frontier is, and there is informal trade. If the price is good, people will do it."[51] More important to the growth of San Ignacio's ranching economy, however, was the transfer of knowledge and technology from the Brazilian ranching sector. The agricultural technician for the provincial government recalled that as recently as the late 2000s, Bolivian ranchers in San Ignacio "had a very rustic, old-school mentality. With the arrival of Brazilian and Argentinian ranchers, they have brought new technologies, and they [Bolivians] learn and copy. Before, the rancher would say just 'pasture is pasture,' and they wouldn't cultivate. They would send cattle to the bush to live their lives."[52] Knowledge and technology transfers take a variety of forms in addition to the practices diffused by Brazilian migrants. In 2008–2009, for example, Embrapa (the Brazilian government's agricultural research corporation) and CIAT (Centro de Investigación Agrícola Tropical, the agricultural research agency of Santa Cruz Department) strengthened their ties by signing a technical cooperation agreement and holding a joint workshop in the border city of Corumbá, Brazil. Since 2010, Brazilian ranchers and Embrapa researchers have shared their experiences in ranching "best practices" with Bolivian ranchers, students, and officials in a series of events in Santa Cruz supported by the environmental NGO WWF-Bolivia.[53]

One of the most prominent areas of cross-border exchange and Brazilian technological influence in the Bolivian ranching sector is in cattle breeding, especially through "genetic" or artificial breeding practices such as artificial insemination and embryo transfer. The FAICHI director reflected that in San Ignacio's traditional ranching economy in the early 2000s, "There was no genetic improvement of the herd. Reproduction was left to God."[54] With the shift toward more productivist, industrial ranching practices, Bolivian ranchers began to focus on "genetic improvement," seeking cattle that gain weight quickly, with good "carcass quality" for slaughter, and cows that produce more cattle efficiently. Mercy Mayser, president of the San Ignacio Ranchers Association, says that cattle weight in the municipality has doubled thanks to genetic improvements, and cattle can now weigh up to 1,000 kilos (while prize bulls can weigh over 1,300 kilos).[55] These genetic improvements, which increase the profitability of Bolivian ranching, have been realized primarily through linkages with the Brazilian ranching economy and involve Bolivian ranchers of all sizes. As in Brazil, the boom in large-scale ranching in San Ignacio has drawn Indigenous and settler communities into the cattle economy, and in 2016 the Bolivian government imported 9,000 cattle from Brazil "to repopulate the [smallholder] cattle herd with Brazilian genetics," delivering 1,039 Brazilian heifers to San Ignacio and another 424 to the neighboring municipality of San Rafael.[56]

Among large ranchers in Santa Cruz, the uncontested leader in cattle genetics is Luis Fernando Saavedra Bruno. With a background in banking and real estate development—"I consider myself an entrepreneur down to my marrow," he once said—Saavedra Bruno's ranching holdings include Hacienda El Carmen, an extensive complex of five ranches in San Ignacio.[57] In the mid-1980s, Saavedra Bruno imported Nelore cows from two Brazilian ranches, turning his Hacienda Nelorí property north of Santa Cruz de la Sierra into a breeding center. While Saavedra Bruno's initiative was an early factor in transferring "improved genetics" from Brazil to Bolivia, Brazilian ranchers also worked to develop Bolivia as a market for "genetic exports." "The sale of live animals and genetic material (semen and embryos) from the Brazilian cattle herd to Bolivian ranchers can be intensified as early as this year," proclaimed a 2003 report in a Mato Grosso newspaper on a mission by the Brazilian Zebu Breeders Association (Associação Brasileira dos Criadores de Zebu) to the Santa Cruz ranching expo. "To expand business with Bolivia, which has been chosen as the first target of the [genetic exports] campaign, Brazil is investing in marketing zebu ranching," the story continued, reporting the opinion of a Brazilian representative that "Bolivian ranching has enormous potential to expand, due to the quantity and quality of potential agricultural land and the ideal climate for ranching."[58]

As artificial breeding technologies developed and spread in the Brazilian ranching sector during the 2000s, Saavedra Bruno continued to import Brazilian cattle genetics to Bolivia, buying embryos from a Brazilian breeder around 2010.[59] In 2016, Brazil and Bolivia signed sanitary protocols permitting a bilateral trade in embryos and cloning of Bolivian cattle in Brazilian labs for reexport to Bolivia.[60] The first Bolivian ranch to export cells to Brazil was Saavedra Bruno's Hacienda Nelorí, which in 2017 sent genetic material from ten cows for cloning in an Embrapa-affiliated lab.[61] This trade in cattle genetics spread beyond Saavedra Bruno's ranches, especially as artificial insemination in beef cattle became increasingly common during the late 2010s. By 2021, Bolivia had grown into the largest market for Brazilian bull semen exports for beef breeds. Of the 467,964 doses of beef breed semen exported by Brazil that year, over a third (157,834 doses) were imported by Bolivia.[62] The genetics trade has begun to flow in both directions as well, as Bolivian breeders export semen and embryos to Brazil (albeit in much smaller quantities).[63]

Saavedra Bruno's three decades of leadership in Bolivian cattle breeding have won him numerous recognitions in both Bolivia and Brazil, including the Golden Zebu (Cebú de Oro) in 2003 from the Bolivian Zebu Breeders Association and an "Oscar for Ranching" in 2012 from the Brazilian Nelore Breeders Association. He was also recognized by ABT in 2011 for three illegal deforestation offenses and four illegal burning offenses from 2003 to 2011, making him one of the worst repeat offenders of forest regulations in Bolivia.[64] In other words, after 2004, the Brazilian ranching sector was less able to profit from deforestation in the Brazilian Amazon, but through the trade in cattle "genetics," Brazilian ranchers and companies opened new frontiers of profit linked to ranching expansion and deforestation in Bolivia, and the genetics trade formed another coupling between the Bolivian lowlands and Brazil's massive ranching economy.

Moving through the ranching supply chain in San Ignacio, Brazilian influence extends from Brazilian genetic "inputs" to land control and deforestation by Brazilian ranchers, and that influence continues beyond the farm gate when cattle are sold for slaughter. While the Chiquitania was certified free of foot-and-mouth disease in 2003, Bolivia was not certified disease-free until 2014, and from 2008 to 2012 Bolivian government regulations prohibited beef exports, meaning that beef production in San Ignacio during the initial period of ranching expansion after 2005 went entirely to the Bolivian domestic market. Two small abattoirs served the local market, while large ranchers would generally sell their cattle to fattening operations near Santa Cruz, where large slaughterhouses are located.

Early in the ranching boom, Brazilian rancher Osias Wagner Greve saw the opportunity for an industrial slaughterhouse in San Ignacio and brought together a group of Brazilian and Bolivian investors (including AGASIV, the San Ignacio Ranchers Association) to build a $5 million facility on 41 hectares just north of the San Ignacio town center.[65] Their new Frigorífico Chiquitano slaughterhouse, with an initial processing capacity of three hundred animals per day, operated in a "test period" from its construction in 2006 until 2012, when Bolivia's beef export ban was lifted and the company began to seek access to export markets. Frigorífico Chiquitano succeeded in exporting beef to Peru, and in 2015 it accounted for 1.3 percent of Bolivia's total beef production, but by 2016 the slaughterhouse was shuttered.[66] Reasons for the company's failure are murky. One informant described the company as "closed off," while another noted that they were slow to pay ranchers for their cattle.[67] It seems likely, however, that the closure of the slaughterhouse had at least something to do with the legal troubles of its Brazilian owners.

Greve, who became the Frigorífico Chiquitano general manager, was third nationally on ABT's 2011 list of repeat offenders,
with numerous infractions for illegal deforestation and burning in
2003–2011. In 2012, he boasted that cattle slaughtered at the Frigorífico Chiquitano could be marketed as "green" (*"animal verde"*)
because they were raised entirely on pasture without confinement.
Of course, pasture expansion, as Greve knew from experience, relied
on deforestation. Not only was Greve a repeat offender of forest
regulations, his consortium behind Frigorífico Chiquitano included
a cast of notoriously corrupt Brazilian ranchers and politicians from
Mato Grosso. The major investor, with a quarter of the shares in the
company, was reportedly Bento Ferraz Pacheco, a Brazilian rancher
with property in the Pontes e Lacerda region of Mato Grosso near
the border with San Ignacio.[68] In 2003, five workers were liber-
ated from slave-labor conditions on a ranch owned by Pacheco
in the border municipality of Vila Bela, Greve's hometown.[69] In
2010, Pacheco was accused by the Mato Grosso Public Ministry of
heading a criminal organization of thirty people involved in smuggling illegal products through ranches in the border region.[70] After
Pacheco's death in 2012, his daughter accused Greve and Brazilian
businessman Elvis Antonio Klauk of conspiring to dispossess her of
her shares in Frigorífico Chiquitano.[71] Another partner in the company was José Geraldo Riva Jr., son of the famously corrupt president of the Mato Grosso Legislative Assembly, José Geraldo Riva,
who embezzled millions of dollars in public funds while in office.[72]
In short, the Frigorífico Chiquitano slaughterhouse was an investment in the San Ignacio ranching economy by extractive Brazilian
capital linked to Mato Grosso.

Whatever role the slaughterhouse may have played in its owners'
shady financial networks, the construction of a multimillion-dollar
export-standard processing plant bolstered economic prospects for
ranching in San Ignacio. After Frigorífico Chiquitano collapsed in
2016, the slaughterhouse facility was sold in 2018 to the meat processing company BFC. BFC invested around $3 million in the plant
and began full operations in October 2019. The press quoted Mercy
Mayser, president of AGASIV, predicting that the reopening of the
slaughterhouse would support the production and growth of the
cattle herd in San Ignacio, while the FEGASACRUZ veterinarian

told me that BFC's arrival had raised the interest of some ranchers in the region in raising animals to slaughter, rather than selling their cattle to feedlot operations near Santa Cruz.[73] By early 2020, BFC was slaughtering an average of 330 cattle per day in San Ignacio, with plans to expand their capacity to 1,000 cattle per day. Beef from San Ignacio was exported to China, Vietnam, Paraguay, and Democratic Republic of Congo, and BFC aimed to export nearly 80 percent of its meat production in 2020–2022, eyeing new markets in Russia, Chile, and Brazil.[74] BFC's purchase and expansion of the Frigorífico Chiquitano facility thus created new export-oriented demand for the San Ignacio ranching sector, giving additional impetus to ranching expansion and coinciding with rising deforestation and land conflicts in the municipality.

At first blush, BFC's slaughterhouse does not appear to be an instance of displaced deforestation by Brazilian actors, beyond the legacy of Brazilian investment in the original physical plant. Bolivian press reports refer to BFC as a Paraguayan company, or a Bolivian company with Paraguayan investors, since BFC corporation is a 51-percent-owned Bolivian subsidiary of the Paraguayan Frigorífico Concepción, which from 2010 to 2017 was Paraguay's largest beef exporter.[75] Frigorífico Concepción, however, is owned by Brazilian businessman Jair de Lima, and BFC's remaining shares are owned by another of Lima's companies and by Brazilian businessman Pedro Pascutti, who is vice president of Frigorífico Concepción and one of Lima's longtime business partners.

In June 2019, I drove up to the barbed-wire fence surrounding the BFC complex in San Ignacio. To the right of the gate, a sign with the Bolivian and Chinese flags read "Welcome" in Spanish, Chinese, and English—a relic from the recent visit of the Chinese inspection mission that approved the slaughterhouse for export to their country. To the left of the gate, a plaque given by the San Ignacio Municipal Government in 2011 recognized Frigorífico Chiquitano "for its contribution to the productive development of the region and to job creation."

After checking in at the guardhouse, I was shown to the front office building. The slaughterhouse was not operating at the time, since BFC was working on an expansion of the facility, and the complex was quiet. In the bare foyer, a set of shelves displayed the packaging for BFC's "Beef Club" brand. Down a narrow hallway, I arrived in the office of one of the plant managers. When I asked my first question in Spanish, he responded almost entirely in Portuguese. A Brazilian from Mato Grosso do Sul, he had just moved to Bolivia after working with Frigorífico Concepción in Paraguay. He said that Bolivia was like Paraguay used to be for the beef industry—in the late 1990s, no one knew about Paraguay as a meat exporter, but now it was a major player.[76] If Bolivia was the new Paraguay for beef exports, as the BFC manager affirmed, it was also the new Paraguay for Brazilian capital, and more specifically for Jair de Lima.

From his beginnings as a butcher in the early 1980s, Lima and his original business partner, Waldir Cândido Torelli, entered the meatpacking industry. From 1987 through the 1990s, Lima and Torelli rode Brazil's ranching boom, building their Grupo Torlim into a conglomerate of slaughterhouses, ranches, and related agribusiness companies across São Paulo, Paraná, Santa Catarina, Mato Grosso do Sul, and Mato Grosso States. In 1997, they opened Frigorífico Concepción in Paraguay, and in 2000 they opened a slaughterhouse in Paranatinga, next door to Nova Ubiratã at the edge of the Amazon biome. Legal troubles for Lima and Torelli began to pile up in the early 2000s during Lula's first presidential term. In 2003, an investigation into tax evasion and cattle smuggling began at the Grupo Torlim slaughterhouse in Ponta Porã, Mato Grosso do Sul, on the Paraguayan border. Investigators discovered that Grupo Torlim had committed social security fraud worth 70 million reais, and in 2004 the courts seized ranches and other company property worth over 23 million reais.[77] That same year, FUNAI (Brazil's Indigenous peoples agency) determined that a ranch owned by Lima and Torelli in Paranhos, Mato Grosso do Sul, was located in the Arroio-Korá Indigenous Territory, lying just across the border from Mbaracayú, where twenty years earlier Richard Reed had documented the effects of Brazilian ranching expansion for the Chiripá. Torelli left Grupo Torlim around 2008 and was later implicated in an illegal logging ring in northern Mato Grosso. With the breakup of Grupo Torlim, Jair de Lima took over full control of Frigorífico Concepción. (Torelli alleges that Lima fraudulently appropriated his shares in the company.) Since 2010, Lima "dedicates himself exclusively to Frigorífico Concepción."[78]

In Paraguay, Lima made Frigorífico Concepción the cornerstone of a conglomerate of ranching, transport, and retail companies. Frigorífico Concepción became one of Paraguay's leading beef
exporters, and by 2020 the company was responsible for over one-
fifth of Paraguay's beef processing volume and had gross revenues
of over $300 million.[79] Lima's time in Paraguay has not been un-
eventful. In 2018, the Paraguayan authorities suspended Frigorífico
Concepción's export permits for illegally importing beef from Brazil
into Paraguay. The export restrictions were subsequently lifted in a
move that attracted allegations of bribery and influence-peddling.[80]
That same year, Lima and Pascutti used Frigorífico Concepción to
purchase the Frigorífico Chiquitano slaughterhouse built by their
Brazilian compatriots in San Ignacio, Bolivia. The creation of BFC
and purchase of a slaughterhouse in Bolivia placed Frigorífico Concepción and its Brazilian owners in a position to profit from the rapidly expanding ranching frontier in San Ignacio, at the same time as it
added geographical diversity to Frigorífico Concepción's operations
and gave the company access to the Chinese market (which is closed
to Paraguayan exports). BFC began full operations in October 2019,
and just three months later Lima used BFC to guarantee a $100 mil-
lion bond issue by Frigorífico Concepción on the New York Stock
Exchange. Over the course of 2020, Frigorífico Concepción issued
$161 million in bonds guaranteed by BFC, and in 2021 the company
refinanced with a new $300 million bond issue, again guaranteed by
BFC. Frigorífico Concepción planned to invest $15 million in pro-
ceeds from their bond issues to more than double BFC production
capacity to process a thousand cattle per day. The company planned
to hire a Bolivian contractor for construction, but $6.6 million in
expenses for the San Ignacio slaughterhouse expansion would go to
Brazilian companies for machinery and equipment related to refrig-
eration, fattening, deboning, and corrals.[81] New York–based law firm
Cleary Gottlieb advised Frigorífico Concepción on their $300 mil-
lion bond issue, BofA Securities (Bank of America's investment
banking arm) served as book-runner and manager for the issue, and
the securities were rated by international rating agencies.[82]

With the BFC slaughterhouse in San Ignacio, Brazilian capital
that had moved to Paraguay now expanded into Bolivia, mirroring
the decadal displacement of deforestation by the Brazilian ranching

Fig. 15. Cattle pasture and Chiquitano forest in Velasco Province, July 2018.
(Author's photo)

sector from the Paraguayan Atlantic Forest to the Bolivian Chiquitania. Legal crackdowns in Brazil in the mid-2000s pushed Jair
de Lima into Paraguay, and from Paraguay he expanded into Bolivia, a frontier specialist pushing the peripheries of Brazil's ranching economy. In San Ignacio de Velasco, cattle owned by Brazilians
are inseminated with semen from Brazilian bulls and slaughtered in
a processing plant owned by Brazilian investors. When the Brazilian government cracked down on deforestation after 2004, scholars, NGOs, and policymakers claimed that increasing agricultural
production and decreasing deforestation in the Brazilian Amazon
meant that forests were being "spared" and Brazilian agribusiness
was becoming "green." At the very same time, Brazilian ranchers and
companies, backed by Brazilian government investment and diplomatic support, poured into the Bolivian lowlands, driving a ranching boom and large-scale forest destruction. Ranching expansion
in Bolivia was not just a source of profit for frontier actors; it also
bolstered the agro-industrial economy in Brazil: Bolivia provided

a new market for value-added Brazilian inputs, such as "genetics" and slaughterhouse machinery, and profits realized on the Bolivian frontier were often repatriated or reinvested in Brazil. While there are other domestic and transnational connections driving Bolivian frontier expansion, the Brazilian influence is preponderant. The Brazilian agro-industrial economy, meanwhile, is not autonomous but rather a component of the global capitalist system. International investors finance Brazilian businessmen in Paraguay to export Bolivian beef to China. Bank of America, Cleary Gottlieb, and Standard & Poors all get a cut. Production depends on extraction, and while land-sparing advocates celebrated a productivist transition in the Brazilian Amazon, the Chiquitania went up in flames.

Feedbacks and False Solutions

T HE 2019 SOUTH AMERICAN wildfires drew international attention, as ranchers in Pará torched the forest in their Day of Fire and the skies of São Paulo went dark with smoke. The fires that blackened the skies of Brazil's largest city were not those in the Brazilian Amazon, however, but rather the wildfires burning across Brazil's borders in Paraguay and Bolivia.[1] For a moment, a combination of winds from the west blocked by an oceanic cold front provided a visible link between the wealth of São Paulo and the ecological destruction on which it depends. Fire and wind overwhelmed the fiction that "sustainability" could be defined by national borders. "As Amazon Burns, Fires in Next-Door Bolivia Also Wreak Havoc," reported the *New York Times* in August 2019.[2] In Santa Cruz Department, over fifteen thousand square kilometers of forest burned in the 2019 fire season, an area larger than the U.S. state of Connecticut. Residents took to the streets of Santa Cruz and La Paz to protest the Morales government's handling of the fire crisis, and in San Ignacio, where forest fires burned 3,610 square kilometers, a group of Indigenous protesters launched a weekslong march to Santa Cruz de la Sierra to demand that Morales declare a national disaster and accept foreign aid.[3]

The catastrophic 2019 fires in the Chiquitania, for all their devastation, were a tragedy foretold. Natural fire is rare in the Chiquitano dry forest, although agricultural clearing with fire is a traditional practice of Indigenous farmers. Government colonization policies and ranching expansion after the mid-2000s, however, brought a series of feedbacks that resulted in increasingly large and uncontrolled wildfires in the region. Already in 2010, El Niño–linked drought set the stage for epic wildfires that burned around twenty thousand square kilometers of forest in Santa Cruz, and Bolivia that year lost the third-largest area of tropical primary forest of any country, surpassed only by Brazil and Indonesia. Global climate change processes are raising temperatures and reducing rainfall in the Bolivian lowlands, which increases fire risk.[4] Ranchers and colonists use fire to clear land, and that deforestation leads to even higher temperatures and lower precipitation. In San Ignacio, annual precipitation in 2001–2018 was 17 percent lower than in 1981–2000, and in the dry season months rainfall diminished by nearly 50 percent while average temperatures increased by 0.6 degrees Celsius. In deforested areas, moreover, heat islands can increase temperatures up to 8 degrees Celsius relative to areas under forest cover, accelerating evaporation and water stress.[5] The ecocidal expansion of large-scale ranching is turning the Chiquitania into a tinderbox, undermining its own productivity. According to Bolivia's business chamber, the country's 2019 fires left about 300,000 cows without pasture.[6]

In a conversation in 2018 at MINGA, the San Ignacio community agriculture cooperative, an agricultural technician told me that forty years before, the climate was humid enough for Chiquitano communities to grow rice. "Something is reducing the rains," they observed. "Why is this happening? Is it because of deforestation here? Or in neighboring countries? There is no subterranean water. If they put everything into ranching, and in ten, fifteen, or twenty years there's no more water, what are the cows going to eat? And the boom is over. People who foresee profit don't think of their descendants."[7] Brazilian ranchers and investors flocked to San Ignacio for cheap land and lax forest regulations, but amid heat, drought, and fires, the windfall profits of this new agricultural frontier may be short-lived.

The Land-Sparing Treadmill

After 2004, land-sparing policies reduced deforestation in the Brazilian Amazon, but the displacement of deforestation to the Bolivian

Chiquitania belies eco-modernist narratives of agricultural industrialization as green development. Face to face with the ecological
destruction of the planet's best-preserved tropical dry forest, however, many environmentalists and policymakers hew stubbornly to a
partial, variable-based perspective. They see Bolivian deforestation
as a problem of extensive ranching practices that can be solved with
intensification, rather than an effect of systemic capitalist relations
where production depends always on expanding extraction.

As far back as the 1990s, when the World Bank's Eastern
Lowlands Project sought to transform Santa Cruz into a hub of
export-oriented agribusiness, the project included a study "to examine the development potential of Santa Cruz's livestock industry, and explore ways of increasing production without significant
deforestation." Yet even as the bank "explored" land sparing, the
Eastern Lowlands Project helped drive nearly 1 million hectares of
deforestation, almost 40 times the 25,000 hectares of new clearing
the project plan had predicted.[8] Two decades later and after over a
million more hectares of primary deforestation, Victor Yucra, director of forest and land management at ABT, told a reporter, "Our
concern is in ensuring that intensive agricultural production takes
place within a framework that also provides for sustainable forestry
and protection for standing forests."[9]

Environmental cooperation and NGO programs have similarly
replicated land-sparing arguments on the Bolivian frontier. At a presentation in San Ignacio in July 2018, GIZ's PROBOSQUE project
proposed intensification with feed supplements and pasture rotations as a strategy for reducing the environmental impacts of ranching development. A June 2018 brief from the project noted, however, "In the short term, intensification can avoid the necessity of
expanding pasture areas to increase cattle production. Nonetheless,
it is unlikely that it helps to protect forest in the long term so long
as agricultural expansion remains a national policy."[10] Meanwhile,
WWF has since 2010 brought Brazilian ranchers and Embrapa researchers to Bolivia to promote ranching "best practices." At a pair
of events in 2010 in the capital of Santa Cruz and the border town of
San Matías, WWF reported that "the Brazilian ranchers, as well as
WWF technicians, explained the application of ranching best practices . . . emphasizing the Brazilian experience in the search to avoid

environmental impacts and improve ranching production."[11] According to a Bolivian agronomy student at a 2017 seminar in Santa Cruz supported by WWF and attended by Embrapa scientists, "The most interesting topic was ranching best practices. We saw statistically how those practices can improve our activity without, necessarily, having to buy more land. . . . [With pasture rotations,] we can have more cattle in a smaller space with a large production and good return. What's more, we care for the environment this way as well, without having to deforest more to produce."[12] Thus, land-sparing policies and ranching intensification supported by NGOs and the Brazilian government in the Brazilian Amazon drove Brazilian actors and capital to invest in ranching deforestation in Bolivia, where an NGO then brought Brazilian ranchers and Brazilian government scientists to instruct Bolivians in "land-sparing" intensive ranching to solve their environmental problems. During WWF's decade of efforts to promote sustainable ranching in Santa Cruz, ranching deforestation skyrocketed, and in 2021 the Santa Cruz Ranchers Federation (FEGASACRUZ) awarded WWF-Bolivia its Medal of Ranching Merit in recognition of the organization's "collaborative work" with the ranching sector.[13]

To paraphrase Eduardo Gudynas, land sparing, like other forms of capitalist development, is a zombie concept.[14] The "solution" to extraction is always intensification, even though intensification drives new extraction—new deforestation calls for more land sparing, underdevelopment calls for more development. To break away from this treadmill of land-sparing and modernization thinking requires understanding capitalist development and ecology not as the discrete, reified properties of particular territories (viewing Indonesian deforestation separately from Japanese timber imports and European biofuels policy, or Bolivian deforestation separately from Brazilian forest governance and agro-industry). Rather, capitalist development and ecology are the products of relations among places. From a relational perspective, we can recognize *displacement* as a fundamental spatial dynamic in the capitalist dialectic of extraction and production. This dialectical understanding moves beyond the concept of a "shadow ecology" (the idea that a country's economy has environmental impacts beyond that country's borders) to a recognition that all capitalist development depends on extraction, and the interactions of extractive and productivist political-economic regimes facilitate the geographical displacement of environmental destruction.[15] Immanuel Wallerstein, in his analysis of the Industrial Revolution, writes, "The creation of vast new areas as the periphery of the expanded world-economy made possible a shift in the role of some other areas."[16] While he was describing how the integration of Asia and Africa into the capitalist periphery enabled the United States and Germany to develop into core powers, he could just as easily have been describing how the expansion of agricultural frontiers in Paraguay and Bolivia made possible agricultural industrialization in the Brazilian Amazon, or how at an earlier time expansion into the Amazon made possible agricultural industrialization in the Brazilian South and Southeast. Expansion of the extractive periphery is a necessary condition for capitalist development.

I have described in these chapters how a land-sparing approach to "green" development in the Brazilian Amazon displaced extractive deforestation to the Bolivian Chiquitania, but the Bolivian lowlands are far from the only periphery where ecological destruction feeds Brazil's "green" agro-industry. Declines in Brazil's Amazonian deforestation also coincided with dramatic increases in Brazilian agricultural expansion and deforestation in the Paraguayan Chaco and the eastern "Matopiba" region of the Brazilian Cerrado.[17] Policymakers, corporations, environmentalists, and academics claimed Brazil's Amazonian "deforestation success story" as a model for reconciling development and conservation through land sparing, but land sparing is an illusion that depends on displacement, and capitalist development is metastasizing extraction—an engine of ecocide.

Alibis of Ecocide

DURING MY RESEARCH IN Brazil in 2013, I was affili-
ated with the Center for Sustainable Development at
the University of Brasília. The center was located in a
half-finished building with a dirt parking lot in the middle of campus. One day as I walked toward the building, a professor
called me over to a spindly sapling planted in the red Cerrado earth
outside the center. "Do you know what this is?" the professor asked
me, running his hands over the feathery leaves. "This is a *pau-brasil*."

I was looking at a ghost.

The brazilwood tree (*Paubrasilia echinata*), known in Portuguese as *pau-brasil*, is native to Brazil's Atlantic Forest, which once
stretched over three thousand kilometers along the eastern coast
of South America. Called *ibirapitanga*—red tree—by the Indigenous
Tupi, the tree's orange-red wood yields a red-violet dye that was
used by the Tupi to color feathers and cotton fiber. The first Portuguese expeditions to South America in the early 1500s brought back
samples of the wood to Europe, where the growing textile industry
relied on sappanwood from India and Southeast Asia for red dyes
that were then in fashion. Pau-brasil offered an abundant and accessible alternative to sappanwood, and brazilwood extraction quickly
became the cornerstone of Portugal's South American trade—so
much so that the land Pedro Cabral had christened "Vera Cruz"
soon became known as Brazil, after its prized red wood.[1]

Europeans obtained brazilwood from the Tupi, who would fell trees and cut them into logs weighing twenty to thirty kilograms, which they would carry to the coast to trade with European ships. In the early 1500s, Portuguese merchants imported around 1,200 tonnes of brazilwood per year, and French traders soon began to frequent the Brazilian coast as well. The French ship *La Pèlerine*, famously captured by the Portuguese in 1532 on her return from Pernambuco, reportedly carried 3,000 jaguar skins, 300 monkeys, 600 parrots, cotton, and 5,000 quintals of brazilwood—over 290 tonnes.[2] Warren Dean estimates average brazilwood extraction during the sixteenth century at 8,000 tonnes per year, requiring the logging of nearly 2 million trees during just the first century of European trade and likely affecting up to 6,000 square kilometers of Atlantic Forest.[3]

By 1605, the Portuguese crown became concerned that rapacious extraction might exhaust brazilwood stocks, and it attempted to impose new regulations to limit the trade. With the extirpation of coastal brazilwood populations, seventeenth-century Portuguese colonists moved inland, using African slaves imported for coastal sugar plantations to harvest the remaining upriver brazilwood stands.[4] Europeans exploited brazilwood nearly to extinction, and colonial agriculture (especially sugar and coffee production) decimated the tree's Atlantic Forest habitat. Pau-brasil was declared the national tree of Brazil in 1978, but by 1992 it was listed by IBAMA as endangered. Today it is planted in cities across Brazil as an ornamental and patriotic tree, including at the Center for Sustainable Development in Brasília, far outside its native range, but brazilwood has significantly reduced reproductive success in these urban ecosystems, where it encounters fewer native pollinators.[5]

By 1990, centuries of colonial extraction, agricultural clearing, and settlement had reduced Brazil's Atlantic Forest, brazilwood's native habitat, to just 8 percent of its original size. Yet agro-industrial intensification, urbanization, and conservation policies appeared finally, at the end of the twentieth century, to "spare" land for a forest transition, and the Atlantic Forest recovered by 2005 to around 11 percent of its original area. This recovery of the Brazilian Atlantic Forest hardly meant that Brazilian development had become green, however. After its almost complete destruction over five hundred years of capitalist "development," the Atlantic Forest's slow recovery was achieved only through the displacement of deforestation to the Brazilian Amazon.[6] Amazonian deforestation fueled apparent land sparing, green development, and ecological modernization in the Brazilian Southeast, just as after 2005 deforestation in the Bolivian Chiquitania fueled apparent land sparing in the Brazilian Amazon.

The word *brasileiro* originally referred not to Portuguese New World settlers but to those logging and trading in brazilwood, pau-brasil. As the Portuguese territories became identified with their dyewood as the "land of Brazil," their inhabitants became known as *brasileiros*. Dean observes lyrically that "hence all Brazilians, upon reflection, appear to be engaged in the office, or trade, of dyewood logging, a peculiar and poignant designation now that dyewoods have long disappeared from commerce and the tree itself has become quite rare in its native habitat."[7] Yet from the ruins of the Atlantic Forest, brasileiros took their trade to other frontiers, devouring the Amazon before setting their sights on the Chiquitania. Today, when a Bolivian in San Ignacio speaks of the "brasilero" ranchers and land grabbers in their municipality, they are speaking of Brazilians, but it does not take much imagination to see in these brasileiros the spirit of their dyewood-logging predecessors—agents of extraction stretching across the centuries.

In 2005, a group of Cambridge scientists coined the term "land sparing" to argue that intensive agriculture could meet food production and conservation goals more effectively than less intensive, "wildlife-friendly farming." Their land-sparing concept crystallized an argument for the environmental benefits of industrial agriculture that had circulated in scientific literature since the 1980s, notably associated with Nobel laureate Norman Borlaug, who claimed that increasing agricultural yields saved land for other uses.[8] Since 2005, this land-sparing hypothesis has reverberated globally in the discourses of scientists, environmental NGOs, agribusiness corporations, and governments, all claiming that agricultural intensification can save natural lands while "feeding the world" and stimulating economic growth. Focusing on tropical forest loss as a major driver of climate change, environmentalists, researchers, and policymakers promote land sparing to address agricultural deforestation in

Indonesia and Brazil, the global leaders in rainforest destruction. They aim to transform Borneo and the Amazon into centers of "green" agricultural development: with land sparing, they promise, "everybody wins."

Brazil appeared to prove them right. From 2005 to 2015, under a suite of land-sparing policies, deforestation in the Brazilian Amazon declined to historic lows and agricultural production increased. Advocates declared land sparing a success. Yet at the same time as Brazil gave "proof" of the land-sparing hypothesis, land-sparing initiatives in Indonesia failed to control accelerating deforestation. The contrast between Indonesia and Brazil during this period underscores two of this book's main arguments. First, the limitations and frustrations of land-sparing efforts in Indonesia contradict the idea of land sparing as a universal policy framework and the Brazilian experience as a "model" that might be effectively transferred elsewhere. Second, the complex, contested implementation of land-sparing policies in both Indonesia and Brazil forces us to understand land sparing not simply as a question of conservation and agricultural policy but rather as the emblem for a much broader set of political-economic transformations.

Land sparing is a prescription for ecological modernization: an attempt both to catalyze development through agricultural industrialization and to decouple that development from the clearing of forests and other "natural" lands. The first section of the book adopts a historical and transnational perspective to show how land sparing in Indonesia was frustrated by extractive political-economic institutions across multiple territorial levels, underlining the long-term persistence of extraction as the foundation of global capitalist "development" and the centrality of land use for capitalist value production. The Indonesian experience is not a national anomaly of poor policy and wasted resources but rather a typical example of extractive regimes in the capitalist periphery.

Extraction of energy and materials from one place enables concentration of energy and materials in another. Understanding how extraction from Indonesia has underwritten capitalist "development" from the Netherlands to Japan, we are prepared to look at land-sparing development in Brazil from the other side of the glass: what are the shifting geographies of extraction on which productivist development in the Brazilian Amazon depends? The second section of the book examines the logics of Brazilian land-sparing policies and their contested and uneven effects on the Amazonian frontier. Productivist, agro-industrial growth in the Brazilian Amazon dispossessed small farmers and Indigenous people and sucked in materials, energy, and profits from new extractive frontiers. Brazilian land sparing "succeeded" by shifting the geographies of extraction, linking productivist development in the Brazilian Amazon with expanded extraction elsewhere. The third section of the book demonstrates those linkages empirically, showing how Brazil's land-sparing transition displaced extractive deforestation to lowland Bolivia.

Land-sparing policies in Indonesia failed to overcome entrenched extraction. Land-sparing policies in Brazil appeared to succeed by displacing extraction to Bolivia and beyond. Land sparing is not a simple formula for green development that can be prescribed across the Global South, and intensive industrial agriculture does not spare land for nature. Land sparing relies on displacement to create the illusion of conservation within ever-expanding webs of destruction. In short, it is an alibi of ecocide.

The Other End of the Rainbow

The land-sparing hypothesis took its present form within the broader discourse of ecological modernization that has emerged since the 1970s, centered on the principle that capitalism's ecological contradictions can be resolved internally to achieve "green" development. Under this eco-modernist umbrella, land sparing is joined by environmental Kuznets curves, forest transition theory, and other narratives of environment and development "win-wins." These are arguments rooted in modernization thinking, viewing industrial growth as the necessary pathway to a prosperous and sustainable future.

Irish folklore holds that there is a pot of gold at the end of the rainbow. Capitalist ideology holds much the same thing. Modernization narratives promise a "pot of gold" at the end of the development rainbow for countries in the Global South. Aside from the fact that the rainbow's "developed," golden end will be always out of reach for most, these narratives fail to mention that the *other* end of the rainbow is the toxic pit where the gold was mined. Displacement renders ecological modernization a hypocrisy.

It is nothing new to observe that the wealth of some depends on the exploitation of others, or that environmental health in one place may be gained by displacing environmental destruction someplace else. In Western social theory, these insights crystallize in ecological world systems analysis and ideas of environmental load displacement and ecologically unequal exchange. Paul Trawick and Alf Hornborg, for example, noting the reliance of human economies on finite stocks of raw materials, refute capitalist narratives of unlimited wealth creation, explaining that "in the physical world, and in the 'real economy,' the creation of wealth is an illusion, because to produce it, to accumulate it, and to consume it is fundamentally to degrade and to destroy."[9] The illusion that production and modernization are somehow separate from extraction and destruction is maintained through displacement (which separates production and extraction geographically) and expansion (which counteracts degradation by bringing new resources into the system). These relations are captured in Jason W. Moore's aphorism that "the condition for a labor productivity revolution in one region is the expansion of 'accumulation by appropriation' on a much larger scale." A growing core requires an expanding periphery. This is, as Richard Walker and Jason Moore put it, "the vortex of accumulation."[10]

The myth of ecological modernization rests on a partial, linear, variable-based understanding of capitalist development. It extends the observation that some places become "developed" into the fallacy that over time, everywhere can become developed and there will be no more extraction. In the case of forests, modernization theories of land sparing and forest transitions replicate this error, extending the observation that in some places agricultural intensification has coincided with declining deforestation to the fallacy that forest conservation and agro-industrial development are globally compatible. The land sparing argument writ large—that there will be less extraction globally if there is more intensified production globally—is only logically feasible if production somehow dematerialized, effectively producing more with less at a global level. In historical and contemporary capitalism, dematerialization has not occurred; to the contrary, from 1970 to 2010 global extraction of primary materials increased in both absolute and per capita terms, and from 2000 to 2010 global material intensity also *increased*, requiring more material inputs for every unit of GDP.[11] The problem, as this book has shown, is that production depends on extraction, and capitalist development is not a linear process of productive growth in specific places but rather a dialectic through which productivism in some places feeds on extraction in others.[12] The myth of modernization ignores the other end of the rainbow.

At the global level, capitalist development is destruction. The spatial unevenness of that destruction—the geography of capitalism as colonialism—is the condition that allows global destruction to continue. Whereas classical world systems analysis and dependency theory may have imagined a more rigid, national-level division of Northern cores and Southern peripheries, post-structuralist scholarship has emphasized hybrid and fractal interactions of production and extraction "at all possible scales."[13] I have sought in this book to take a middle ground, based on the observation that "zones of accumulation" and "spaces of dispossession" are in practice stabilized and reproduced at specific territorial levels by productivist or extractive *political-economic regimes*.[14] Because political-economic processes are institutionalized at particular territorial levels, the distinction between extractive and productivist political-economic regimes is an effective heuristic for multilevel analyses of global capitalism. This approach helps to explain, for example, how land-sparing policies work in frontier municipalities, and why during the decade after 2004 land sparing appeared successful in Brazil but not in Indonesia.

In one sense, extractive territories are *always* zones of displacement. The productivist centers that suck energy and materials from extractive peripheries concentrate wealth while displacing the social and ecological costs of their consumption. Not all extraction is displaced—exploitative and environmentally destructive processes continue in productivist economies—but the declining rate of profit in a closed system guarantees that productivist centers will rely on additional extraction elsewhere. Displacement is a fundamental feature of capitalist geography. The "illusion of wealth"—that capitalist production is creative rather than destructive—relies on this general form of displacement.

The "illusion of modernization" is not just that capitalism creates wealth but also that capitalist production can resolve its contradictions internally, becoming more equitable and more sustainable. This illusion of modernization—that capitalist development makes things better for people and planet—relies on more specific, political processes of displacement. The land-sparing displacement described in this book is one example in which land-sparing policies deliver "green" development in one place by displacing deforestation elsewhere. "Modernizing displacement" is both social and ecological—labor protections and environmental regulations in core regions displace dangerous, low-wage, and polluting industries to more peripheral zones.[15]

Modernization measures to improve environmental quality and social welfare generally respond not to economic imperatives of capitalist production but rather to social and political imperatives. As ecological economist Giorgos Kallis explains, "There is no [growth] imperative in the abstract, but only in the concrete sense that capitalism becomes politically and socially unstable if it fails to produce growth and good conditions of accumulation," and, we can add, improved social and ecological living conditions for key political constituencies.[16] Similarly, discussing the importance of the "semiperiphery" as a middle stratum of the capitalist world system, Wallerstein writes that "the world-economy as an economy would function every bit as well without a semiperiphery. But it would be far less *politically* stable, for it would mean a polarized world-system."[17] Concretely, with regard to land sparing, there is no immediate economic imperative for capitalists to reduce deforestation in the Brazilian Amazon or Indonesian Borneo. The industrial soy complex in the Amazon can coexist with large-scale forest clearing, as resurgent deforestation under the Bolsonaro administration made clear. Similarly, palm oil industrialization in Kalimantan could coexist with continued plantation-driven deforestation. Costs from ecological feedbacks like fires, haze, or drought are often borne by governments and society, with little impact on agribusiness profits. Rather, land-sparing and other "green development" agendas are largely political projects that respond to social pressures (whether domestic or transnational) for improved environmental and welfare outcomes.

The tragic irony of land sparing and other ecological modernization efforts is that even as they seek to curb the ecological ills of capitalist development—to save forests, clean waterways, and clear the air—their reliance on industrial growth means they end up pushing environmental costs onto others. They are saving a rainforest and losing the world. Modernizing displacement is thus a political project that relies fundamentally not just on the displacement of environmental and social costs but also on the deferral of political responsibility.[18] Capitalism sacrifices life for profit, and those who profit evade responsibility through displacement. Modernization offers illusions of "synergies" and "win-wins," but by failing to reckon with the destruction and exploitation underlying consumption and wealth, and by failing to confront powerful actors who profit at the expense of others, eco-modernist "solutions" are denialist fantasies hastening planetary collapse.

This tragedy of modernization is doubly ironic in that even the winners receive only fool's gold. Development has costs, modernization narratives acknowledge, but they argue that the end goal is worth it—healthy environments and good quality of life. Yet even the fruits of development are poisons. Diets based on industrial soy and palm oil are not just unhealthy for the environment, they are unhealthy for human consumers. The rise of the corporate food regime since World War II, based on the spread of "modern" diets high in processed foods (made with cheap soy and palm oils) and meat consumption (bolstered by tropical cattle ranching and soy-meal animal feed), "solved" problems of food scarcity by destroying food sovereignty and igniting a global obesity epidemic.[19] Thanks to a modern abundance of high-calorie, nutrient-poor foods, the proportion of the Brazilian population with obesity increased from 7 percent in 1980 to 18 percent in 2015. In some neighborhoods in São Paulo, center of Brazil's industrial modernization, 30 percent of children are obese and another 30 percent are malnourished.[20] Modernist forest "recovery," meanwhile, is too often little more than the green desert of a eucalyptus plantation.[21] These toxic outcomes have a simple explanation: capitalism maximizes profit, not welfare. In the end, five centuries of displacement cannot hide a single global reality: capitalist development is ecocide.

Ecocide is the systematic destruction of the living world.[22] It is a crime, but who is to blame? At one level, ecocide is "structural violence" that emerges from the political economy of global capitalism. To the degree that ecocide is systemic, we are all complicit.[23] Yet some are clearly more responsible than others for ecological destruction. People and organizations who use positions of power to profit from extraction deserve special blame, from Bob Hasan to Bank of America. In 2021, Indigenous leaders and activists requested the International Criminal Court to investigate Jair Bolsonaro for ecocide as a crime against humanity.[24] He should be held responsible for his actions.

But what of the eco-modernists? What of the NGOs, policymakers, academics, and agribusinesses who claim that more cattle and more oil palm can save forests, even as they abet or ignore displaced destruction? Some perhaps are cynical and know the falsehood of their claims.[25] Many others are likely sincere but fall victim to modernization narratives and their self-fulfilling prophecies. "Is halting deforestation in the Amazon, an area nearly the size of the continental United States, feasible?" asked TNC chief scientist Peter Kareiva and co-authors in a famous 2012 essay. "Is it even necessary? . . . Just as the United States was dammed, logged, and crisscrossed by roads, it is likely that much of the Amazon will be as well."[26] For the "pragmatic" eco-modernist, not damming and not logging is, apparently, not an option.[27] Regardless of their logics or goals, these environmentalists' faith in ecological modernization is misplaced. The claim that capitalist development can save the planet is the primary alibi for global ecocide.

Replanting

Capitalism is, quite literally, a dead end. The analytic of displacement can alert us to flaws in proposals for addressing poverty and environmental degradation, and it can help us slip free from capitalism's ecocidal embrace. When "solutions" promise increased profit at reduced social and environmental cost, we need only trace the spillovers to find where costs are being displaced. Capitalism survives through the incessant manipulation of geographical scales—

developing Japan by degrading Borneo; greening Brazil by deforesting Bolivia. The way beyond ecocide is to reject these "scalar fixes."[28]
The scale of economic processes, and the scale of political decision
making, must be local. When the economy of pau-brasil was limited
to the Indigenous Tupi who shared its forest, the trees survived and
thrived. When the pau-brasil economy became a vector of capitalist
extraction for European markets, the trees were logged almost to
extinction.

Localization does not mean environmental damage will never
occur, but it ensures that the benefits and costs of environmental
change accrue to the community responsible for those decisions.
This principle is the core of bioregionalism, an orientation common to many of the people and movements building alternatives to
capitalism. Bioregionalism holds that economics and politics should
be scaled to the needs and values of a particular "life place."[29] As biologist Raymond Dasmann observed in the 1970s, capitalist society
consists of "biosphere people":

> Biosphere people are those who can draw on the resources
> of many ecosystems, or the entire biosphere, through net-
> works of trade and communication. Their dependence on
> any one ecosystem is partial, since they can rely on others
> if any one fails. Drawing as they do on planetary resources
> they can bring great amounts of energy and materials to
> bear on any one ecosystem—they can devastate it, degrade
> it, totally destroy it and then move on.[30]

The bioregional perspective calls for humans to live more as "ecosystem people . . . who depend almost entirely upon a local ecosystem, or a few closely related ecosystems."[31] Living bioregionally, as
"ecosystem people," refuses the displacement and deferral of responsibility that characterize biosphere people and capitalist geographies. Bioregional economies presently still suffer from capitalist displacement, through processes like global climate change and
transboundary pollution, but the more bioregions delink from the
capitalist system, the more its engines of externalization will slow
and stall, and the capitalist vortex will be forced to either transform
or implode.

Potawatomi scholar Robin Wall Kimmerer writes, "For all of us, becoming indigenous to a place means living as if your children's future mattered, to take care of the land as if our lives, both material and spiritual, depended on it."[32] The move away from capitalism begins by replanting ourselves in our life place. Capitalist development is ecocide, but from the brazilwood trees on the streets of São Paulo to the castanheiras in Amazonian cattle fields, from the Moluccan clove trees that survived extirpation to the Bolivian cuchi trees not yet felled for fence posts, more abundant worlds struggle every day to take root and to grow. We must renounce displacement, delink from ecocide, and begin to replant ourselves and our worlds. By delinking and replanting, we can find life beyond this mass extinction, but only if we accept the responsibility of belonging to a place.

Appendix

Deforestation Rates in Indonesia, Brazil, and Bolivia

The following figures show annual primary deforestation for key regions. Data for the Brazilian Legal Amazon and Brazilian states and municipalities are from PRODES, the Brazilian government's satellite-based monitoring system, and report deforestation as clear-cutting of primary forest. I report PRODES data because they are transparent, publicly available, and form the basis for Brazilian government policy.

Data for all other regions are satellite-based estimates from the Global Forest Watch (GFW) data platform and report deforestation as loss of humid primary forest with greater than 30 percent canopy cover. The "Global Tropics" figure shows total humid primary forest loss for the pantropical region as reported by GFW. The figure for East Kalimantan reflects the current boundaries of the province and excludes the territory of present-day North Kalimantan from all calculations.

Indonesia and Bolivia lack long-term official annual deforestation data that are publicly available and spatially explicit. I report GFW data outside of Brazil because they provide globally consistent, remote sensing–based annual primary forest loss estimates from 2001 onward. PRODES and GFW are not directly comparable, but both accurately represent primary deforestation trends.[1]

Improvements in available satellite data and adjustments to the GFW algorithm have led to better detection of small-scale clearing in GFW forest loss data over time, especially after 2015. In Indonesia, large-scale clearing predominates, and overall forest loss was captured effectively by the initial algorithm.[2] In Bolivia, while part of the jump in forest loss reported by GFW after 2015 may be attributable to better detection of small-scale clearing, this increase is consistent with multiple sources reporting accelerated forest loss due to government settlement policies, the 2015 increase in legal deforestation limits (Law 741), agribusiness clearing, and fires. Remote sensing–based data from the MapBiomas project corroborate the 2016 spike in Bolivian forest loss detected by GFW.

The Global Tropics

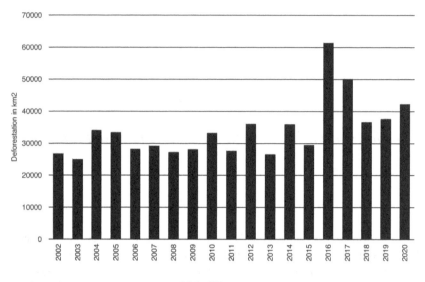

Global Tropics

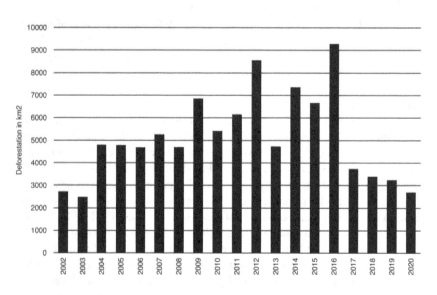

Indonesia

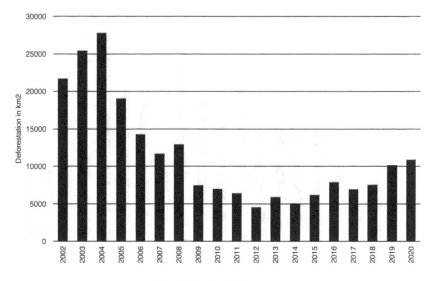

Brazilian Legal Amazon

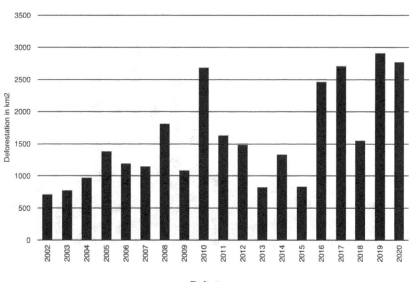

Bolivia

Indonesia

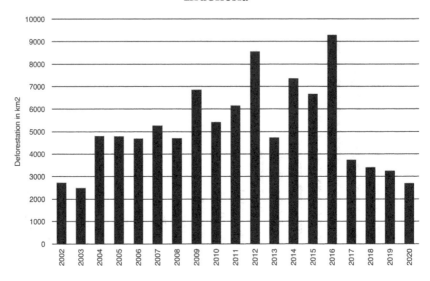

Indonesia

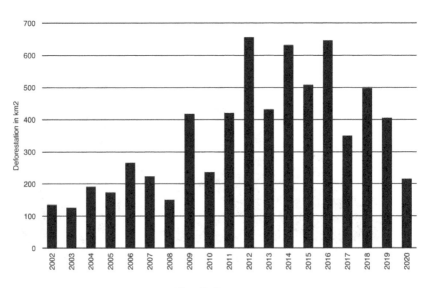

East Kalimantan

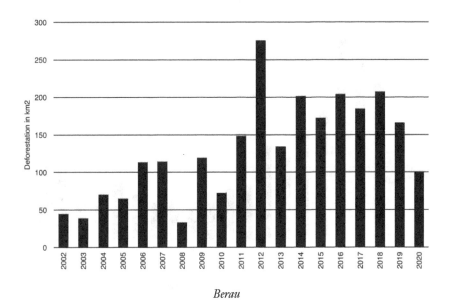

Berau

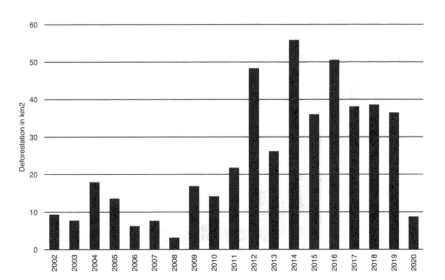

Kutai Timur

Brazil

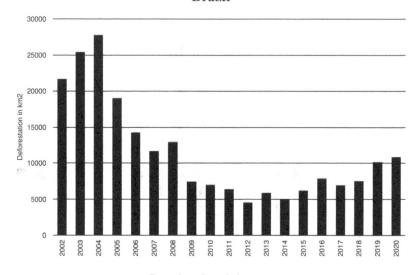

Brazilian Legal Amazon

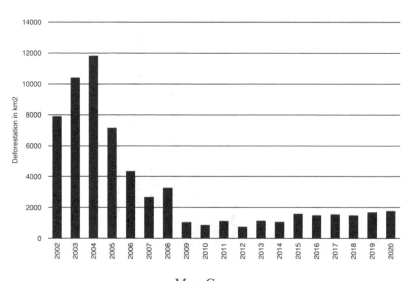

Mato Grosso

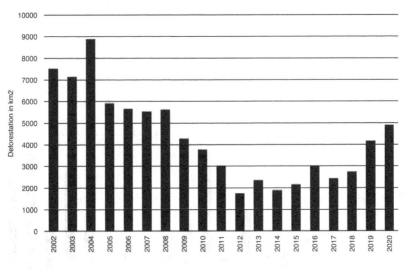

Pará

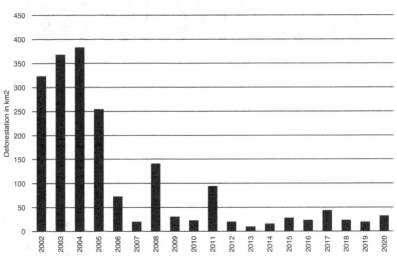

Ubiratã

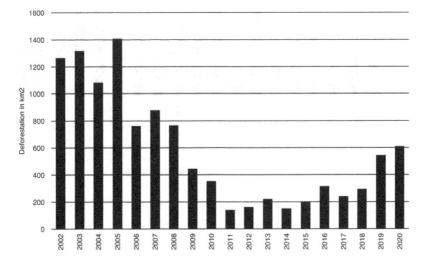

São Félix do Xingu

Bolivia

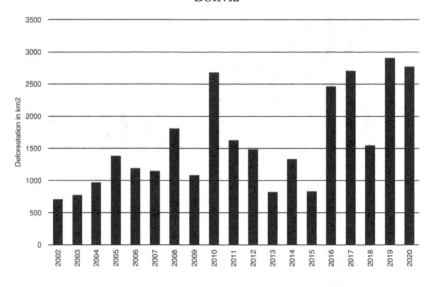

Bolivia

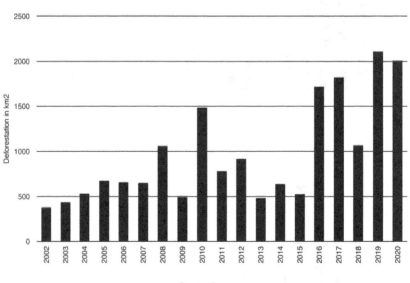

Santa Cruz

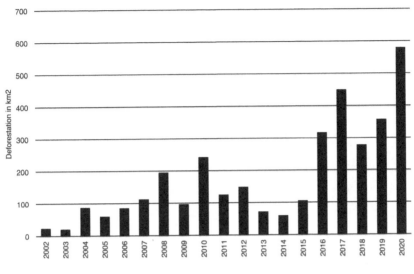

San Ignacio de Velasco

Notes

Introduction

1. José Almeida, "Do Extrativismo à Domesticação: As Possibilidades da Castanha-do-'Pará" (PhD diss., Universidade de São Paulo, 2015).
2. Richard Grove, *Green Imperialism: Colonial Expansion, Tropical Island Edens, and the Origins of Environmentalism, 1600–1860* (New York: Cambridge University Press, 1995).
3. Michael R. Dove cogently critiques this "rain-forest crunch" thesis: Dove, "A Revisionist View of Tropical Deforestation and Development," *Environmental Conservation* 20, no. 1 (1993): 17–56.
4. Calculated from Global Forest Watch, https://gfw.global/3q68CFg. Defining "forest" and measuring forest cover and deforestation is a complex political and scientific problem. Francis Putz and Kent Redford emphasize that "there is a clear need for widely accepted definitions of forest, deforestation, forest degradation, and forest restoration that are politically expedient but culturally sensitive, ecologically reasonable, and technologically feasible. The danger of overly simple definitions is that they can obscure substantial losses in what most people value as forest." Recognizing that forest inherently "will remain something of a social construct," they propose a classification system focused on ecosystem structure and composition based on "old growth forest" as a reference state, which is characterized by old trees and associated structural characteristics and has not been substantially modified in composition (through silviculture) or in structure (through degradation processes such as uncontrolled harvesting, pollution, species invasion, or fire). Putz and Redford, "The Importance of Defining 'Forest': Tropical Forest Degradation, Deforestation, Long-Term Phase Shifts, and Further Transitions," *Biotropica* 42, no. 1 (2010): 12. That definition coincides with the category of tropical "primary forest," which on the Global Forest Watch data platform is defined following Svetlana Turubanova and colleagues as "mature natural humid tropical

forest cover that has not been completely cleared and regrown in recent history." Svetlana Turubanova et al., "Ongoing Primary Forest Loss in Brazil, Democratic Republic of the Congo, and Indonesia," *Environmental Research Letters* 13 (2018): 1. Primary forests capture many of the values people care about in relation to deforestation and are the focus of most tropical forest conservation policy. My research examines these policies and their effects, so I use data focused on "primary forests" in my analysis, but I endeavor to situate these policies and data within the complex dynamics of agricultural and forest land uses and ecological succession in tropical landscapes. The appendix provides deforestation rates for key regions examined in this book and further discussion of deforestation data.

5. Paul Waggoner, "How Much Land Can Ten Billion People Spare for Nature? Does Technology Make a Difference?" *Technology in Society* 17, no. 1 (1995): 17–34; Norman E. Borlaug, "Feeding a World of 10 Billion People: The Miracle Ahead," *In Vitro Cellular and Developmental Biology— Plant* 38, no. 2 (2002): 221–28; David Lee, Paul Ferraro, and Christopher Barrett, "Introduction: Changing Perspectives on Agricultural Intensification, Economic Development and the Environment," in *Tradeoffs or Synergies? Agricultural Intensification, Economic Development and the Environment*, ed. David Lee and Christopher Barrett (Wallingford, U.K.: CABI, 2001), 1–16.

6. Rhys Green et al., "Farming and the Fate of Wild Nature," *Science* 307, no. 5709 (2005): 550–55.

7. Anne Rosenbarger et al., "How to Change Legal Land Use Classifications to Support More Sustainable Palm Oil in Indonesia," World Resources Institute, 2013, https://www.wri.org/research/how-change-legal-land-use-classifications-support-more-sustainable-palm-oil-production.

8. Gregory M. Thaler, "The Land Sparing Complex: Environmental Governance, Agricultural Intensification, and State Building in the Brazilian Amazon," *Annals of the American Association of Geographers* 107, no. 6 (2017): 1424–43.

9. Belinda Arunarwati Margono et al., "Primary Forest Cover Loss in Indonesia over 2000–2012," *Nature Climate Change* 4, no. 8 (2014): 730–35.

10. Erica Simmons and Nicholas Rush Smith, "Comparison with an Ethnographic Sensibility," *PS: Political Science and Politics* 50, no. 1 (2017): 127.

11. Gillian Hart, "Relational Comparison Revisited: Marxist Postcolonial Geographies in Practice," *Progress in Human Geography* 42, no. 3 (2018): 371–94.

12. Robert Heilmayr et al., "Brazil's Amazon Soy Moratorium Reduced Deforestation," *Nature Food* 1 (2020): 801–10, https://doi.org/10.1038/s43016-020-00194-5.

13. S. Cuéllar et al., "Mapa de Deforestación de Las Tierras Bajas y Yungas de Bolivia, 2000–2005–2010" (Santa Cruz de la Sierra, Bolivia: Fundación Amigos de la Naturaleza [FAN], 2012), http://www.fan-bo.org/mapa

-de-deforestacion-de-las-tierras-bajas-y-yungas-de-bolivia-2000–2005–2010/; Global Forest Watch.

14. Robert Müller, Pablo Pacheco, and Juan Carlos Montero, "The Context of Deforestation and Forest Degradation in Bolivia: Drivers, Agents and Institutions" (Bogor, Indonesia: Center for International Forestry Research, 2014).

15. SCZ07 190618. Citations of author interviews are given using a unique identifying code for each interviewee, comprising a combination of letters and numbers, followed by the date on which the interview took place, written in yymmdd format.

16. Mighty, "Mighty Field Investigation—September 2016," 2016, https://www.dropbox.com/s/eqnaoyk7aphea9n/Brazil and Bolivia Case Studies.docx?dl=0.

17. Daniel Redo, Andrew C. Millington, and Derrick Hindery, "Deforestation Dynamics and Policy Changes in Bolivia's Post-Neoliberal Era," *Land Use Policy* 28, no. 1 (2011): 227–41; Miguel Urioste, "Concentration and 'Foreignisation' of Land in Bolivia," *Canadian Journal of Development Studies / Revue Canadienne d'Études du Développement* 33, no. 4 (2012): 439–57.

18. See, e.g., Urioste, "Concentration and 'Foreignisation' of Land in Bolivia."

19. Florence Pendrill et al., "Agricultural and Forestry Trade Drives Large Share of Tropical Deforestation Emissions," *Global Environmental Change* 56 (2019): 1–10.

20. Adam Smith, *An Inquiry into the Nature and Causes of the Wealth of Nations* (1776), book 3, chapter 1.

21. W. W. Rostow, *The Stages of Economic Growth: A Non-Communist Manifesto* (New York: Cambridge University Press, 1960). While Rostow touted his theory as "non-communist," narratives of industrial modernization were central to post–World War II state-communist development policy as well.

22. Douglass C. North, *Structure and Change in Economic History* (New York: Norton, 1981); Daron Acemoglu, Simon Johnson, and James A. Robinson, "The Colonial Origins of Comparative Development: An Empirical Investigation," *American Economic Review* 91, no. 5 (2001): 1369–1401; Peter Evans, *Embedded Autonomy: States and Industrial Transformation* (Princeton, NJ: Princeton University Press, 1995); Atul Kohli, *State-Directed Development: Political Power and Industrialization in the Global Periphery* (New York: Cambridge University Press, 2004).

23. Acemoglu, Johnson, and Robinson, "Colonial Origins of Comparative Development"; Evans, *Embedded Autonomy*.

24. John Bellamy Foster and Hannah Holleman, "The Theory of Unequal Ecological Exchange: A Marx-Odum Dialectic," *Journal of Peasant Studies* 41, no. 2 (2014): 199–233; Immanuel Wallerstein, *The Capitalist World-Economy* (New York: Cambridge University Press, 1979); Fernando Henrique Cardoso and Enzo Faletto, *Dependency and Development in Latin America* (Berkeley: University of California Press, 1979).

25. Stephen Bunker, *Underdeveloping the Amazon: Extraction, Unequal Exchange, and the Failure of the Modern State* (Urbana: University of Illinois Press, 1985); Alf Hornborg, "Towards an Ecological Theory of Unequal Exchange: Articulating World System Theory and Ecological Economics," *Ecological Economics* 25, no. 1 (1998): 127–36; Jason W. Moore, *Capitalism in the Web of Life: Ecology and the Accumulation of Capital* (New York: Verso, 2015).

26. Alain de Janvry explores the relationship between articulated and disarticulated economies in his classic *The Agrarian Question and Reformism in Latin America* (Baltimore: Johns Hopkins University Press, 1981). Stephen Bunker summarizes de Janvry's contribution: "Socially articulated economies produce goods for internal consumption. The resulting acceleration of social and economic activity through linkages between wages, consumption capacity, and markets enhances return to capital and expands production of goods. This partially resolves the contradictions between wage costs and profits, making wage increases systemically rational. The disarticulated economy, in contrast, depends on external markets and therefore lacks any internal consumption-driven accelerator to rationalize high wages." Bunker argues that the dialectic between extraction and production runs deeper than de Janvry's analysis, however: "The articulation and acceleration of the productive economy, then, does not only depend on nor is it adequately described by a wage-consumption-profit-production treadmill calculated in exchange values. It also requires the concentration and coordination of human and non-human energy flows and their embodiment in both complex social organization and durable infrastructure. This it achieves at the cost of the extractive economy and extracted environment." Bunker, *Underdeveloping the Amazon*, 32, 34.

27. Cardoso and Faletto, *Dependency and Development in Latin America*, xxiii.

28. Bunker, *Underdeveloping the Amazon*, 30–31.

29. Amy Trauger and Jennifer Fluri, "Zones of Accumulation Make Spaces of Dispossession: A New Spatial Vocabulary for Human Geography," *ACME: An International Journal for Critical Geographies* 20, no. 1 (2021): 1–16.

30. I use "ideal types" in the Weberian sense—"ideal" meaning "theoretical," not "desirable." The multiple uses of terms such as "extraction" and "production" pose a challenge for choosing an appropriate terminology for these regimes. I describe an "extractive" regime following the usage of the term for "extractive industries," and more specifically Paul K. Gellert's existing description of an "extractive regime." Gellert, "Extractive Regimes: Toward a Better Understanding of Indonesian Development," *Rural Sociology* 75, no. 1 (2010): 28–57. I do not use the term "extractivism" or an "extractivist" regime because extractivism, especially in Amazonian scholarship, may refer to livelihoods centered on harvesting of non-timber forest products such as rubber, although there is also scholarly discussion

of extractivism with regard to unsustainable natural resource extraction. Eduardo Gudynas, "Extracciones, Extractivismos, y Extrahecciones: Un Marco Conceptual Sobre la Apropiación de Recursos Naturales," *Observatorio Del Desarrollo* 18 (2013): 1–18. On the other hand, where "mode of production" is used to distinguish an extractive economy from a productive economy, the terms "production" and "productive" appear ambiguous, so I refer to a "productivist" regime corresponding to a particular, intensive mode of production. This usage harkens to discussions of "productivism" as an intensifying, modernizing "regime" in agriculture, as well as a more general discursive and material configuration of capitalist development and modernization. Geoff A. Wilson, "From Productivism to Post-Productivism and Back Again? Exploring the (Un)Changed Natural and Mental Landscapes of European Agriculture," *Transactions of the Institute of British Geographers* 26, no. 1 (2001): 77–102; cf. Jason W. Moore, "Cheap Food and Bad Climate: From Surplus Value to Negative Value in the Capitalist World-Ecology," *Critical Historical Studies*, Spring (2015): 1–43. On "technomass," see Alf Hornborg, *The Power of the Machine: Global Inequalities of Economy, Technology, and Environment* (New York: Altamira Press, 2001).

31. M. Kearney, "The Local and the Global: The Anthropology of Globalization and Transnationalism," *Annual Review of Anthropology* 24 (1995): 547–65; Arjun Appadurai, *Modernity at Large: Cultural Dimensions of Globalization* (Minneapolis: University of Minnesota Press, 1996).

32. Note that governmental hierarchies operate within and beyond conventional, historically specific understandings of the nation-state. Cf. Neil Brenner, "Beyond State-Centrism? Space, Territoriality, and Geographical Scale in Globalization Studies," *Theory and Society* 28 (1999): 39–78, and William I. Robinson, "Social Theory and Globalisation: The Rise of a Transnational State," *Theory and Society* 30, no. 2 (2001): 157–200.

33. Stephen Perz provides a review of ecological modernization theories and research, including environmental Kuznets curves (which claim that capitalism resolves its environmental problems through the development process) and forest transition theory (an environmental Kuznets curve for forests, claiming that regions shift from deforestation to reforestation as they develop). Perz, "Reformulating Modernization-Based Environmental Social Theories: Challenges on the Road to an Interdisciplinary Environmental Science," *Society and Natural Resources* 20, no. 5 (2007): 415–30.

34. Marcia Macedo et al., "Decoupling of Deforestation and Soy Production in the Southern Amazon During the Late 2000s," *Proceedings of the National Academy of Sciences* 109, no. 4 (2012): 1341–46.

35. "Position Case of H. Suwarna Abdul Fatah," Integrated Law Enforcement Approach, Center for International Forestry Research (CIFOR), 2010, https://www2.cifor.org/ilea/_pf/1/_ref/indicators/cases/decision/suwarna_AF.html.

36. KALTIM03 150307.

37. BAPPEDA01 150324.

38. Humid primary forest loss in oil palm concessions (2009–2017) in East Kalimantan, calculated using Global Forest Watch. Awang served as governor from December 2008 to September 2018. North Kalimantan Province was excised from East Kalimantan Province in 2012. Figures for present-day North Kalimantan are included for 2009–2011 only, when the territory was part of East Kalimantan Province and under Awang's governorship.

39. On the plantation system in Kalimantan, see Julia and Ben White, "Gendered Experiences of Dispossession: Oil Palm Expansion in a Dayak Hibun Community in West Kalimantan," *Journal of Peasant Studies* 39, nos. 3–4 (2012): 995–1016, and Tania Li, "After the Land Grab: Infrastructural Violence and the 'Mafia System' in Indonesia's Oil Palm Plantation Zones," *Geoforum* 96 (2018): 328–37. On the palm oil supply chain for one East Kalimantan district, see Tiza Mafira, Randy Rakhmadi, and Cherika Novianti, "Towards a More Sustainable and Efficient Palm Oil Supply Chain in Berau, East Kalimantan," Climate Policy Initiative, July 2018, https://climatepolicyinitiative.org/wp-content/uploads/2018/07/Towards-a-more-sustainable-and-efficient-palm-oil-supply-chain-in-Berau-East-Kalimantan-Full-publication.pdf.

40. Doug Boucher et al., "Deforestation Success Stories: Tropical Nations Where Forest Protection and Reforestation Policies Have Worked" (Cambridge, MA: Union of Concerned Scientists, 2014), https://www.ucsusa.org/resources/deforestation-success-stories; Jeff Tollefson, "Battle for the Amazon," *Nature* 520 (2015): 20–23: "Environmentalists are also transferring their experience in Brazil to Indonesia. . . . 'There are seeds of what we saw in Brazil ten years ago in Indonesia today,' [environmental scientist Daniel] Nepstad says" (23).

41. Unless otherwise noted, Brazilian Amazon deforestation figures in this book are from the Brazilian National Institute for Space Research (INPE). Since 1988, INPE's PRODES program has used Landsat satellite imagery to annually report deforestation of areas over 6.25 hectares in the Amazon. INPE defines deforestation as clear-cutting of primary forest with a forest baseline from the mid-1970s. Forest degradation that stops short of full conversion to an alternative land cover is not reported, and once an area has been clear-cut, it is considered permanently deforested. For PRODES data, see "PRODES—Amazônia," INPE, n.d., http://www.obt.inpe.br/OBT/assuntos/programas/amazonia/prodes, and for methodology, see "Metodologia Utilizada nos Projetos PRODES e DETER," INPE, 2019, http://www.obt.inpe.br/OBT/assuntos/programas/amazonia/prodes/pdfs/Metodologia_Prodes_Deter_revisada.pdf. For examples of calls for a return to "successful" land sparing, see Philip Fearnside, "Business as

Usual: A Resurgence of Deforestation in the Brazilian Amazon," *Yale Environment 360*, April 18, 2017, https://e360.yale.edu/features/business-as -usual-a-resurgence-of-deforestation-in-the-brazilian-amazon,   which calls for establishing new protected areas, and John Cannon, "Brazil Hits Emissions Target Early, but Rising Deforestation Risks Reversal," *Mongabay*, August 23, 2018, https://news.mongabay.com/2018/08/brazil-hits -emissions-target-early-but-rising-deforestation-risks-reversal/,   which quotes Brazilian scientist Carlos Souza, of the environmental NGO Imazon, saying, "The government is dismantling the environmental gains from the past decade and there is less funding to command and control illegal deforestation." See also the account of Amazonian ranching intensification as sustainability strategy in Erasmus K. H. J. zu Ermgassen et al., "Results from On-the-Ground Efforts to Promote Sustainable Cattle Ranching in the Brazilian Amazon," *Sustainability* 10 (2018): 1301, https://doi.org/10.3390/su10041301.

42. Unless otherwise noted, Indonesia and Bolivia deforestation figures in this book are from Global Forest Watch, a data platform that includes satellite-based annual forest loss estimates at a resolution of 30 meters since 2000, where forest denotes vegetation higher than 5 meters with greater than 30 percent canopy cover, and forest loss is stand-replacement disturbance from forest to non-forest. Global Forest Watch combines forest loss data with data on the location of primary forests to calculate primary forest loss. See Global Forest Watch, https://globalforestwatch.org/.

43. Brad Plumer, "Tropical Forests Suffered Near-Record Tree Losses in 2017," *New York Times*, June 27, 2018, https://www.nytimes.com/2018/06/27/climate/tropical-trees-deforestation.html; Mikaela Weisse and Liz Goldman, "We Lost a Football Pitch of Primary Rainforest Every 6 Seconds in 2019," Global Forest Watch, 2020, https://blog.globalforestwatch .org/data-and-research/global-tree-cover-loss-data-2019.

44. Rebecca L. Lewison et al., "Accounting for Unintended Consequences of Resource Policy: Connecting Research That Addresses Displacement of Environmental Impacts," *Conservation Letters* 12 (2019): e12628, https://doi.org/10.1111/conl.12628.

45. Sven Wunder, "How Do We Deal with Leakage?" in *Moving Ahead with REDD: Issues, Options and Implications*, ed. Arild Angelsen (Bogor, Indonesia: CIFOR, 2008), 74.

46. Cf. John Agnew, "The Territorial Trap: The Geographical Assumptions of International Relations Theory," *Review of International Political Economy* 1, no. 1 (1994): 53–80.

47. Pendrill et al., "Agricultural and Forestry Trade Drives Large Share of Tropical Deforestation Emissions"; Neus Escobar et al., "Spatially-Explicit Footprints of Agricultural Commodities: Mapping Carbon Emissions Embodied in Brazil's Soy Exports," *Global Environmental Change* 62 (2020): 102067.

48. Patrick Meyfroidt and Eric Lambin, "Forest Transition in Vietnam and Displacement of Deforestation Abroad," *Proceedings of the National Academy of Sciences* 106, no. 38 (2009): 16142.

49. Peter Richards, Robert T. Walker, and Eugenio Y. Arima, "Spatially Complex Land Change: The Indirect Effect of Brazil's Agricultural Sector on Land Use in Amazonia," *Global Environmental Change* 29 (2014): 1–9.

50. Fanny Moffette and Holly Gibbs, "Agricultural Displacement and Deforestation Leakage in the Brazilian Legal Amazon," *Land Economics* 97, no. 1 (2021): 155–79.

51. Heilmayr et al., "Brazil's Amazon Soy Moratorium Reduced Deforestation."

52. Heilmayr et al., "Brazil's Amazon Soy Moratorium Reduced Deforestation," 808, 806.

53. Micah Ingalls et al., "The Transboundary Displacement of Deforestation Under REDD+: Problematic Intersections Between the Trade of Forest-Risk Commodities and Land Grabbing in the Mekong Region," *Global Environmental Change* 50 (2018): 255.

54. Cf. Putz and Redford, "The Importance of Defining 'Forest.'"

55. Cf. Nguyen Tien Hoang and Keiichiro Kanemoto, "Mapping the Deforestation Footprint of Nations Reveals Growing Threat to Tropical Forests," *Nature Ecology and Evolution* 5 (2021): 845–53.

56. Yann le Polain de Waroux et al., "Land-Use Policies and Corporate Investments in Agriculture in the Gran Chaco and Chiquitano," *Proceedings of the National Academy of Sciences* 113, no. 15 (2016): 4024.

57. Gustavo Oliveira and Susanna Hecht, "Sacred Groves, Sacrifice Zones and Soy Production: Globalization, Intensification and Neo-Nature in South America," *Journal of Peasant Studies* 43, no. 2 (2016): 270.

58. Philip McMichael, "Incorporating Comparison Within a World-Historical Perspective: An Alternative Comparative Method," *American Sociological Review* 55, no. 3 (1990): 386.

59. Hart, "Relational Comparison Revisited."

60. Municipalities (*municípios*) and districts (*kabupaten*) are the secondary jurisdictional levels in Brazil and Indonesia, respectively, below states (Brazil) or provinces (Indonesia). Municipalities (*municípios*) in Bolivia are the tertiary jurisdictional level below departments and provinces but constitute the primary unit of local governance, analogous to Brazilian municipalities and Indonesian districts. I refer to these three units collectively as "municipalities." Fieldwork comprised 11 months in Brazil in 2013–2014, 8 months in Indonesia in 2014–2015, 2.5 months in Brazil in 2018, 2 weeks in Bolivia in 2018, and 1 month in Bolivia in 2019.

61. Another part of my research examines The Nature Conservancy's (TNC) tropical forest conservation programs as a window into the role of NGOs in global environmental governance. I discuss that work elsewhere, not in this book. See Gregory M. Thaler, "Ethnography of Environmental Governance: Towards an Organizational Approach," *Geoforum* 120 (2021): 122–31.

62. All translations in this book from Indonesian, Portuguese, and Spanish are my own unless otherwise noted.

63. Hugh Gusterson, "Studying Up Revisited," *Political and Legal Anthropology Review* 20, no. 1 (1997): 116.

64. Allison Loconto et al., "The Land Sparing–Land Sharing Controversy: Tracing the Politics of Knowledge," *Land Use Policy* 96 (2020): 103610.

65. Jason W. Moore, "The Capitalocene, Part I: On the Nature and Origins of Our Ecological Crisis," *Journal of Peasant Studies* 44, no. 3 (2017): 594–630.

Overview: Extractive Regimes

1. DISBUN01 150310.

2. David Gaveau et al., "Rapid Conversions and Avoided Deforestation: Examining Four Decades of Industrial Plantation Expansion in Borneo," *Scientific Reports* 6 (2016): 32017.

3. Lisa Curran et al., "Lowland Forest Loss in Protected Areas of Indonesian Borneo," *Science* 303, no. 5660 (2004): 1000–1003; Peter Dauvergne, *Shadows in the Forest: Japan and the Politics of Timber in Southeast Asia* (Cambridge, MA: MIT Press, 1997).

4. Indonesia's average annual deforestation rate in the 1990s was substantially higher than in the early 2000s due especially to massive forest loss from the 1997–1998 El Niño–linked drought and fires that far exceeded the background rate of direct anthropogenic clearing. See D. O. Fuller, T. C. Jessup, and A. Salim, "Loss of Forest Cover in Kalimantan, Indonesia, Since the 1997–1998 El Niño," *Conservation Biology* 18, no. 1 (2004): 249–54, and D. O. Fuller and M. Fulk, "Burned Area in Kalimantan, Indonesia Mapped with NOAA-AVHRR and Landsat TM Imagery," *International Journal of Remote Sensing* 22, no. 4 (2001): 691–97. The availability of burned land for agricultural expansion momentarily lessened the impetus for new forest clearing, while the political-economic turmoil of the Asian financial crisis and fall of the Suharto regime negatively affected the investment climate for plantation expansion, translating into below-average deforestation rates at the turn of the century. Nonetheless, Matthew Hansen et al. describe a "near-monotonic increase" in forest clearing from 2000 to 2005, and this acceleration continued for a decade until 2015. Hansen et al., "Quantifying Changes in the Rates of Forest Clearing in Indonesia from 1990 to 2005 Using Remotely Sensed Data Sets," *Environmental Research Letters* 4, no. 3 (2009): 034001.

5. Gaveau et al., "Rapid Conversions and Avoided Deforestation."

6. These figures are clearly very bad, and they are also worse than most people initially realize, for the simple reason that deforestation is cumulative. With each year's clearing, less primary forest remains, meaning that every hectare cleared next year represents a greater proportion of remaining

forest than a hectare cleared this year. From the perspective of forest conservation, if annual forest loss is stable, deforestation is getting
worse. When annual loss is accelerating, we are on a steep slope toward
extinction.

7. Erik Meijaard, "Erik Meijaard: Going Beyond Environmental Pacifiers in Indonesian Conservation," *Jakarta Globe*, November 10, 2015,
   http://jakartaglobe.beritasatu.com/opinion/erik-meijaard-going-beyond
   -environmental-pacifiers-indonesian-conservation/.

8. Heinz Schandl et al., "Global Material Flows and Resource Productivity:
   Assessment Report for the UNEP International Resource Panel" (Paris:
   UNEP, 2016).

9. On "policy failure," see William Ascher, "Understanding Why Governments in Developing Countries Waste Natural Resources," *Environment:
   Science and Policy for Sustainable Development* 42, no. 2 (2000): 8–18; and for
   a critique of market failure arguments, see Dove, "A Revisionist View of
   Tropical Deforestation and Development."

10. Todd Gitlin, "Occupy's Predicament: The Moment and the Prospects for
    the Movement," *British Journal of Sociology* 64, no. 1 (2013): 3–25, notes
    the use of this slogan by the Occupy movement.

11. Paul K. Gellert, "A Brief History and Analysis of Indonesia's Forest Fire
    Crisis," *Indonesia* 66 (1998): 85.

12. I am engaging in this section with Gellert's primary statement of the "ex-
    tractive regime" concept: Gellert, "Extractive Regimes."

13. This argument brings basic insights of dependency theory into a socio-
    ecological framework. Jason W. Moore similarly elaborates a key dis-
    tinction between *exploitation* of labor-power and *appropriation* of unpaid
    work and energy. In an extractive regime, even commodified labor-
    power is strongly characterized by what Joan Acker calls "corporate non-
    responsibility for reproduction"—sweatshop labor is profitable thanks to
    the appropriation of unpaid reproductive labor that sustains its workforce.
    Extractive regimes appropriate the unpaid work and energy of humans
    and the rest of nature and export those materials and energy to core econ-
    omies, where they feed productivist circuits of resource transformation,
    consumption, and capital accumulation. See Moore, "The Capitalocene,
    Part II: Accumulation by Appropriation and the Centrality of Unpaid
    Work/Energy," *Journal of Peasant Studies* 45, no. 2 (2018): 237–79, and
    Acker, "Gender, Capitalism and Globalization," *Critical Sociology* 30, no. 1
    (2004): 17–41.

14. I am using "mode of production" in the broad sense adopted by Stephen
    Bunker, who deploys "the more inclusive definitions of mode of produc-
    tion, which relate multiple aspects of social, legal, political, and commer-
    cial activities within unified frames of analysis," where distinct modes of
    production are integrated through the capitalist world system. In Bunker's
    analysis as in mine, modes of production may be characterized as extrac-

tive or productivist (in Bunker's terminology, "productive"). See Bunker, *Underdeveloping the Amazon*, 23.

15. Cf. Dorothy Smith, "Institutional Ethnography," in *Qualitative Research in Action: An International Guide to Issues in Practice*, ed. Tim May (London: Sage, 2002), 150–61.

16. David Gaveau et al., "Four Decades of Forest Persistence, Clearance and Logging on Borneo," *PLoS ONE* 9, no. 7 (2014): e101654.

17. N. Adri, "Fish in Mahakam River Delta Contaminated by Heavy Metals," *Jakarta Post*, April 13, 2015, http://www.thejakartapost.com/news/2015/04/13/fish-mahakam-river-delta-contaminated-heavy-metals.html; Anne-Sophie Pellier et al., "Through the Eyes of Children: Perceptions of Environmental Change in Tropical Forests," *PLoS ONE* 9, no. 8 (2014): e103005.

Chapter 1. Four Hundred Years of Extraction

1. Pieter C. Emmer and Jos J. L. Gommans, *The Dutch Overseas Empire, 1600–1800* (New York: Cambridge University Press, 2020), 276.

2. M. C. Ricklefs, *A History of Modern Indonesia Since c. 1200*, 3rd ed. (New York: Palgrave Macmillan, 2001), 75.

3. D. W. Davies, *A Primer of Dutch Seventeenth Century Overseas Trade* (The Hague: Martinus Nijhoff, 1961), 55–56.

4. Ricklefs, *A History of Modern Indonesia*; Emmer and Gommans, *The Dutch Overseas Empire*.

5. Ricklefs, *A History of Modern Indonesia*, 155.

6. Ricklefs, *A History of Modern Indonesia*, 157.

7. Lisa Tilley, "Extractive Investibility in Historical Colonial Perspective: The Emerging Market and Its Antecedents in Indonesia," *Review of International Political Economy* 28, no. 5 (2021): 1099–118.

8. Ricklefs, *A History of Modern Indonesia*, 160; Tilley, "Extractive Investibility in Historical Colonial Perspective." Perhaps more so now than in its own time, when the Cultivation System was widely considered oppressive and immoral, it is not difficult to find an ideologue of capitalist modernization willing to argue that extraction benefits its victims. Melissa Dell and Benjamin A. Olken, economists from Harvard and MIT, argue that areas where the Dutch built sugar factories "are today more industrialized, have better infrastructure, are more educated, and are richer than nearby counterfactual locations. . . . The results suggest that the economic structures implemented by colonizers to facilitate production can continue to promote economic activity in the long run." Dell and Olken, "The Development Effects of the Extractive Colonial Economy: The Dutch Cultivation System in Java," *Review of Economic Studies* 87, no. 1 (2020): 164–203. The Javanese must surely be grateful.

9. Ann Laura Stoler, *Capitalism and Confrontation in Sumatra's Plantation Belt, 1870–1979*, 2nd ed. (Ann Arbor: University of Michigan Press, 1995), 17.

10. "Plantations in Indonesia," Global Forest Watch, www.globalforestwatch
    .org.

11. Stoler, *Capitalism and Confrontation*, 14–15.

12. J. Thomas Lindblad, *Between Dayak and Dutch: The Economic History of
    Southeast Kalimantan 1880–1942* (Providence, RI: Foris, 1988); Nancy
    Peluso and Peter Vandergeest, "Genealogies of the Political Forest and
    Customary Rights in Indonesia, Malaysia, and Thailand," *Journal of Asian
    Studies* 60, no. 3 (2001): 761–812.

13. Peluso and Vandergeest, "Genealogies of the Political Forest."

14. Michael R. Dove, "Transition from Native Forest Rubbers to Hevea
    Brasiliensis (Euphorbiaceae) Among Tribal Smallholders in Borneo," *Eco-
    nomic Botany* 48, no. 4 (1994): 382–96.

15. Helen Godfrey, *Submarine Telegraphy and the Hunt for Gutta Percha: Chal-
    lenge and Opportunity in a Global Trade* (Boston: Brill, 2018), 4.

16. Dove, "A Revisionist View of Tropical Deforestation and Develop-
    ment," 20.

17. Tilley, "Extractive Investibility in Historical Colonial Perspective," 1105.

18. Stoler, *Capitalism and Confrontation*, 126.

19. Jaechun Kim, "U.S. Covert Action in Indonesia in the 1960s: Assessing
    the Motives and Consequences," *Journal of International and Area Studies*
    9, no. 2 (2002): 63–85.

20. Kai M. Thaler, "US Action and Inaction in the Massacre of Communists
    and Alleged Communists in Indonesia (1965–1966)," in *Dirty Hands and
    Vicious Deeds: The US Government's Complicity in Crimes Against Humanity
    and Genocide*, ed. Samuel Totten (Toronto: University of Toronto Press,
    2018), 23–69.

21. David Easter, "'Keep the Indonesian Pot Boiling': Western Covert In-
    tervention in Indonesia, October 1965–March 1966," *Cold War History* 5,
    no. 1 (2005): 52–70.

22. Ascher, "Understanding Why Governments in Developing Countries
    Waste Natural Resources."

23. H. Gyde Lund, "When Is a Forest Not a Forest?" *Journal of Forestry* 100,
    no. 8 (2002): 21.

24. Within the forest estate, areas are classified according to permitted land
    uses, which under the Consensus Forest Land Use Plan (*Tata Guna Hu-
    tan Kesepakatan*), created in the early 1980s, comprise nature reserve or
    conservation areas, protection forests, limited production forests, nor-
    mal production forests, and conversion forests. Conservation and re-
    serve forests are geared to the protection of biodiversity and ecosystem
    function, protection forests are intended to protect soil and hydrological
    functions, limited production forests are open to low-intensity selective
    logging, normal production forests are open to more intensive logging,
    and conversion forests may be fully logged and converted to agricultural
    or other land uses, at which point they are excised from the forest estate

and reclassified as "other use areas" (*Areal Penggunaan Lain*, APL). These classifications are ostensibly based on topographic and climatic characteristics, including slope, soil type, and rainfall intensity, but they were decided without regard for local land uses or existing land cover, and it is not uncommon for land within the forest estate to be highly degraded or occupied by settlements or agricultural land uses. Nancy Peluso, "Whose Woods Are These? Counter-Mapping Forest Territories in Kalimantan, Indonesia," *Antipode* 27, no. 4 (1995): 383–406. The Directorate General of Forestry was made a ministry in 1964, downgraded to a directorate in 1967, and restored to ministerial status in 1983. In late 2014, the Ministry of Forestry merged with the Ministry of Environment to form the new Ministry of Environment and Forestry.

25. Ahmad Dhiaulhaq and Ward Berenschot, "A 150-Year-Old Obstacle to Land Rights," *Inside Indonesia* 141 (July–September 2020), https://www.insideindonesia.org/a-150-year-old-obstacle-to-land-rights.

26. Christopher Barr, "Bob Hasan, the Rise of Apkindo, and the Shifting Dynamics of Control in Indonesia's Timber Sector," *Indonesia* 65 (1998): 1–36.

27. Charles Victor Barber and Kirk Talbott, "The Chainsaw and the Gun: The Role of the Military in Deforesting Indonesia," *Journal of Sustainable Forestry* 16, no. 3 (2003): 131–60.

28. Barr, "Bob Hasan," 7.

29. Paul K. Gellert, "The Shifting Natures of 'Development': Growth, Crisis, and Recovery in Indonesia's Forests," *World Development* 33, no. 8 (2005): 1345–64.

30. Barr, "Bob Hasan"; Dauvergne, *Shadows in the Forest.*

31. Christopher Barr et al., "Financial Governance and Indonesia's Reforestation Fund During the Soeharto and Post-Soeharto Periods, 1989–2009: A Political Economic Analysis of Lessons for REDD+" (Bogor, Indonesia: CIFOR, 2010).

32. Peter Vandergeest and Nancy Peluso, "Empires of Forestry: Professional Forestry and State Power in Southeast Asia, Part 2," *Environment and History* 12, no. 4 (2006): 52–53.

33. David Gaveau et al., "Evaluating Whether Protected Areas Reduce Tropical Deforestation in Sumatra," *Journal of Biogeography* 36, no. 11 (2009): 2165–75; Curran et al., "Lowland Forest Loss in Protected Areas of Indonesian Borneo."

34. Vedi Hadiz and Richard Robison, "Neo-Liberal Reforms and Illiberal Consolidations: The Indonesian Paradox," *Journal of Development Studies* 41, no. 2 (2005): 231.

35. Gellert, "The Shifting Natures of 'Development,'" 1351.

36. Krystof Obidzinski, A. Andrianto, and C. Wijaya, "Cross-Border Timber Trade in Indonesia: Critical or Overstated Problem? Forest Governance Lessons from Kalimantan," *International Forestry Review* 9, no. 1 (June 2007): 532.

37. Harriet Friedmann and Philip McMichael, "Agriculture and the State System," *Sociologia Ruralis* 29, no. 2 (1989): 93–117.

38. Kimberly Carlson et al., "Carbon Emissions from Forest Conversion by Kalimantan Oil Palm Plantations," *Nature Climate Change* 2, no. 10 (2012): 1–5; cf. John F. McCarthy, "Processes of Inclusion and Adverse Incorporation: Oil Palm and Agrarian Change in Sumatra, Indonesia," *Journal of Peasant Studies* 37, no. 4 (2010): 821–50.

39. Figures for bribes are reported in Eko N. Setiawan et al., "Opposing Interests in the Legalization of Non-Procedural Forest Conversion to Oil Palm in Central Kalimantan, Indonesia," *Land Use Policy* 58 (2016): 472–81.

40. Li, "After the Land Grab."

41. Lotte Woittiez et al., "Yield Gaps in Oil Palm: A Quantitative Review of Contributing Factors," *European Journal of Agronomy* 83 (2017): 57–77; Nelson B. Villoria et al., "Will Yield Improvements on the Forest Frontier Reduce Greenhouse Gas Emissions? A Global Analysis of Oil Palm," *American Journal of Agricultural Economics* 95, no. 5 (2013): 1301–8.

42. Li, "After the Land Grab."

43. Arthur Neslen, "Leaked Figures Show Spike in Palm Oil Use for Biodiesel in Europe," *The Guardian* (London), June 1, 2016, http://www.theguardian.com/environment/2016/jun/01/leaked-figures-show-spike-in-palm-oil-use-for-biodiesel-in-europe; Oliver Pye, "The Biofuel Connection—Transnational Activism and the Palm Oil Boom," *Journal of Peasant Studies* 37, no. 4 (2010): 851–74.

44. Nancy Peluso, Suraya Afiff, and Noer Fauzi Rachman, "Claiming the Grounds for Reform: Agrarian and Environmental Movements in Indonesia," *Journal of Agrarian Change* 8, nos. 2–3 (April 2008): 382.

45. Joan Martínez-Alier, *The Environmentalism of the Poor: A Study of Ecological Conflicts and Valuation* (Northampton, MA: Edward Elgar, 2002).

46. Helena Manhartsberger, "One Mountain—One Struggle: A Story About Zombies, Dragons, Punks, and Farmers in Their Fight Against Giants," *ASEAS—Austrian Journal of South-East Asian Studies* 6, no. 1 (2013): 202–16; Edwin Jurriens, "Art, Image and Environment: Revisualizing Bali in the Plastiliticum," *Continuum* 33, no. 1 (2019): 119–36.

47. Tessa Toumbourou et al., "Political Ecologies of the Post-Mining Landscape: Activism, Resistance, and Legal Struggles over Kalimantan's Coal Mines," *Energy Research and Social Science* 65 (2020): 101476.

48. "Forestry Ministry Reluctant to Relinquish Control over Forests," *Down to Earth Newsletter*, March 2014, http://www.downtoearth-indonesia.org/id/node/1105; Cory Rogers, "Indonesia's Indigenous Wage Two-Pronged Battle for Legal Recognition," *Mongabay*, April 27, 2016, https://news.mongabay.com/2016/04/perda-push/; Steve Rhee, "The Fight for Indonesia's Forests," Ford Foundation, August 5, 2020, https://www.fordfoundation.org/news-and-stories/stories/the-fight-for-indonesias-forests/.

49. Anne Casson, Yohanes I Ketut Deddy Muliastra, and Krystof Obidzinski, "Land-Based Investment and Green Development in Indonesia: Lessons from Berau District, East Kalimantan" (Bogor, Indonesia: CIFOR, 2015), ix, http://www.cifor.org/publications/pdf_files/WPapers/WP180Obidzinski.pdf.

50. Rosenbarger et al., "How to Change Legal Land Use Classifications," 2.

51. Anggi M. Lubis, "Gapki Says 'No' to Moratorium Extension," *Jakarta Post*, April 24, 2013, http://www.thejakartapost.com/news/2013/04/24/gapki-says-no-moratorium-extension.html.

52. Zachary R. Anderson et al., "Green Growth Rhetoric Versus Reality: Insights from Indonesia," *Global Environmental Change* 38 (2016): 30–40; Jonathan Vit, "Under Gov't Pressure, Palm Oil Giants Disband Green Pledge," *Mongabay*, July 1, 2016, https://news.mongabay.com/2016/07/under-government-pressure-palm-oil-giants-disband-green-pledge/.

Chapter 2. Deforesting the "Green Province"

1. Chris P. A. Bennett et al., "East Kalimantan Program (Indonesia) Program Review Report," TNC, 2004.

2. Erik Meijaard, "No More Fires in Indonesia?" *Mongabay*, June 20, 2016, https://news.mongabay.com/2016/06/no-more-fires-in-indonesia/; Shannon N. Koplitz et al., "Public Health Impacts of the Severe Haze in Equatorial Asia in September–October 2015: Demonstration of a New Framework for Informing Fire Management Strategies to Reduce Downwind Smoke Exposure," *Environmental Research Letters* 11, no. 9 (2016): 094023.

3. Edward Aspinall, "A Nation in Fragments," *Critical Asian Studies* 45, no. 1 (2013): 39.

4. Rona A. Dennis and Carol P. Colfer, "Impacts of Land Use and Fire on the Loss and Degradation of Lowland Forest in 1983–2000 in East Kutai District, East Kalimantan, Indonesia," *Singapore Journal of Tropical Geography* 27, no. 1 (2006): 30–48; Florian Siegert and Anja Hoffmann, "The 1998 Forest Fires in East Kalimantan (Indonesia)—A Quantitative Evaluation Using High Resolution, Multitemporal ERS-2 SAR Images and NOAA-AVHRR Hotspot Data," *Remote Sensing of Environment* 72, no. 1 (2000): 64–77.

5. Robert Field, Guido Van Der Werf, and Samuel Shen, "Human Amplification of Drought-Induced Biomass Burning in Indonesia Since 1960," *Nature Geoscience* 2, no. 3 (2009): 185–88.

6. Peter Dauvergne, "The Political Economy of Indonesia's 1997 Forest Fires," *Australian Journal of International Affairs* 52, no. 1 (1998): 13.

7. KUTIM03 150520.

8. KUTIM05 150522.

9. Krystof Obidzinski and Agus Andrianto, "Illegal Forestry Activities in Berau and East Kutai Districts, East Kalimantan: Impacts on Economy, Environment and Society" (Bogor, Indonesia: CIFOR, 2005); "Luas Tanaman Perkebunan Menurut Jenis Tanaman dan Kabupaten/Kota (Ha), Tahun 2015," BPS Provinsi Kalimantan Timur, 2017, https://kaltim.bps.go.id/linkTabelStatis/view/id/27.

10. Andrew Vayda and Ahmad Sahur, "Bugis Settlers in East Kalimantan's Kutai National Park" (Jakarta: CIFOR, 1996).

11. Moira Moeliono and Edy Purwanto, "A Park in Crisis: Local Governance and National Policy," in 12th Biennial IASC Conference, Cheltenham, U.K., 2008, https://dlc.dlib.indiana.edu/dlc/bitstream/handle/10535/2127/Moeliono_106401.pdf?sequence=1.

12. G. Limberg et al., "Incentives to Conserve or Convert? Can Conservation Compete with Coal in Kutai National Park, Indonesia?" *International Journal of Biodiversity Science, Ecosystem Services and Management* 5, no. 4 (2009): 192.

13. Moeliono and Purwanto, "A Park in Crisis." In East Kalimantan, hunter-gatherer groups have historically been ethnic Punan. Indigenous upland agriculturalist groups in Borneo are generically known as "Dayak," though settled Punan may also refer to themselves as "Dayak Punan." I refer to all settled, upland, predominantly Christian or animist Indigenous groups as "Dayak." These groups are distinct from the Muslim Kutai and other Malay populations that live primarily along the coasts.

14. Moeliono and Purwanto, "A Park in Crisis"; UNMUL03 150309; KALTIM05 140311.

15. Akiko Morishita, "Contesting Power in Indonesia's Resource-Rich Regions in the Era of Decentralization: New Strategy for Central Control Over the Regions," *Indonesia* 86 (October 2008): 81–107; "Position Case of H. Suwarna Abdul Fatah," CIFOR.

16. Kholish Chered, "Kemungkinan Besar Enclave Taman Nasional Kutai 7.800 Hektare," *Tribun Kaltim*, March 13, 2014, http://kaltim.tribunnews.com/2014/03/13/kemungkinan-besar-enclave-taman-nasional-kutai-7800-hektare.

17. Quoted in Hendar, "Taman Nasional Kutai: Solusi Konflik Lamban, Taman Nasional Pelan-Pelan Terjual (Bagian II-Habis)," *Mongabay Indonesia*, October 27, 2013, http://www.mongabay.co.id/2013/10/27/taman-nasional-kutai-solusi-konflik-lamban-taman-nasional-pelan-pelan-terjual-bagian-ii-habis/.

18. "Pemkab Kutim Akan Gusur Lahan Sawit di Dekat Bandar Sangkima," *Warta Kutim*, April 2, 2017, http://wartakutim.com/2017/04/02/pemkab-kutim-gusur-lahan-sawit-dekat-bandar-sangkima/.

19. "Derap Langkah Kurangi Pemanasan Global—Anggota Tetap GCF vs Permata Merah Delima," Dr. H. Awang Faroek Ishak (blog), http://awangfaroekishak.info/post-18-track-record-afi-lanjutan—habis.htm.

20. TNC35 150321. Awang's esteem for Schwarzenegger was enduring. East Kalimantan served as chair of GCF in 2017, and Awang made known that he intended to invite Schwarzenegger to the GCF Annual Meeting in Balikpapan, although Schwarzenegger was no longer governor of California. According to a 2017 report in the Indonesian national media: "'Arnold Schwarzenegger has promised me that he will come if GCF is held in East Kalimantan in order to enliven the event,' Awang Faroek said in Samarinda on Sunday, Feb. 12. The East Kalimantan governor said Arnold Schwarzenegger will be invited since he was one of the cofounders of the GCF. 'Arnold Schwarzenegger and I [among others] had co-founded the GCF,' Awang Faroek said. According to Awang Faroek, Arnold Schwarzenegger's presence will make East Kalimantan proud and would be an honor for The Terminator actor. 'We will invite him as an individual not [as part of an] institution. I hope he will be willing [to come] and I still have his personal number. We expect Arnold to give a speech on environmental conservation, particularly to anticipate global warming,' Awang Faroek explained." "E. Kalimantan to Invite Arnold Schwarzenegger to GCF 2017," *Tempo*, February 13, 2017, https://en.tempo.co/read/news/2017/02/13/055845877/E-Kalimantan-to-Invite-Arnold-Schwarzenegger-to-GCF-2017. No doubt to Awang's disappointment, Schwarzenegger did not come to Balikpapan for the event.

21. "Deklarasi Kalimantan Timur Hijau," Kamar Dagang dan Industri Kalimantan Timur, 2010, http://www.kadinkaltim.com/?p=781.

22. *Kalimantan Timur*, the Indonesian name for East Kalimantan, is frequently abbreviated to *Kaltim*.

23. KALTIM04 150310.

24. BAPPEDA01 150324.

25. KALTIM04 150310.

26. M. Ghofar, "Gubernur Kaltim Terbitkan Pergub Perkuat Kebijakan Moratorium," *Antara Kaltim*, February 20, 2015, http://www.antarakaltim.com/berita/24083/gubernur-kaltim-terbitkan-pergub-perkuat-kebijakan-moratorium; KALTIM03 150307; KALTIM04 150310.

27. Bronson Griscom and R. C. Goodman, "Reframing the Sharing vs Sparing Debate for Tropical Forestry Landscapes," *Journal of Tropical Forest Science* 27, no. 2 (2015): 145–47; Bronson Griscom et al., "Carbon and Biodiversity Impacts of Intensive Versus Extensive Tropical Forestry," *Conservation Letters* 11, no. 1 (2018): e12362.

28. "East Kalimantan's Sector Strategies Towards Low Carbon Economy," DNPI Indonesia, DNPI Green Review on REDD+, 2011, 79.

29. GIZ02 150303.

30. Governor's Message to "Seminar Implikasi Undang-Undang Nomor 23 tahun 2014 tentang Pemerintahan Daerah dalam Tata Kelola Sumberdaya Alam di Provinsi Kalimantan Timur," 23 March 2015, Governor's Office, Samarinda, East Kalimantan, from author field notes.

31. Hadi Daryanto, "Optimizing Land Use Management in East Kaliman-tan," East Kalimantan Government/DNPI, 2011, 14, 12, 16.

32. Saturnino Borras and Jennifer Franco, "From Threat to Opportunity? Problems with the Idea of a 'Code of Conduct' for Land-Grabbing," *Yale Human Rights and Development Law Journal* 13, no. 2 (2010): 507–23.

33. "From Dutch Colonialism to Date," *Jakarta Post*, June 5, 2010, http://www.thejakartapost.com/news/2010/06/05/letter-from-dutch-colonialism-date.html.

34. TNC31 150205; DISHUT02 150310.

35. East Kalimantan Government, "Gubernur: Hentikan Penerbitan Ijinan di 10 Kabupaten dan Samarinda," Balitbangda Kaltim, 2013, http://litbang.kaltimprov.go.id/berita-298-gubernur-hentikan-penerbitan-ijinan-di-10-kabupaten-dan-samarinda-.html.

36. KALTIM08 150513.

37. A. S. Subkhan, "Bupati Kutai Timur Tolak Moratorium Tambang di Kaltim," *Tambang*, March 21, 2013, http://www.m.tambang.co.id/detail_berita.php?category=18&newsnr=7103.

38. BAPPEDA01 150324.

39. KALTIM05 140311.

40. Y Samuel Laurens, "Melihat Maloy Setelah 8 Tahun Diresmikan," *Nomor Satu Kaltim*, January 23, 2021, https://nomorsatukaltim.com/kek-maloy-setelah-8-tahun/.

41. Ahmad Agus Arifin, "Akses KIPI Maloy Diperbaiki Tahun 2021," *Nomor Satu Kaltim*, November 5, 2020, https://nomorsatukaltim.com/akses-kipi-maloy-diperbaiki/; Benny Oktariyanto, "Tambah Dua Perusahaan, Total Sudah 19 Investor Siap Benamkan Modal di KEK Maloy," *Nomor Satu Kaltim*, September 17, 2020, https://nomorsatukaltim.com/tambah-dua-perusahaan-total-sudah-19-investor-siap-benamkan-modal-di-kek-maloy/.

42. KALTIM09 150324.

43. In October 2012, the four northernmost districts of East Kalimantan split to become the new province of North Kalimantan (Kalimantan Utara). These four districts were for the most part heavily forested, and the cre-ation of North Kalimantan substantially reduced the total area of pri-mary forest in East Kalimantan. Nonetheless, large areas of primary for-est remained in the north (Berau) and interior of East Kalimantan's new boundaries.

44. GIZ05 150427.

Chapter 3. Losing the Forest, Sparing the Trees

1. Krystof Obidzinski and Christopher Barr, "The Effects of Decentraliza-tion on Forests and Forest Industries in Berau District, East Kalimantan" (Bogor, Indonesia: CIFOR, 2003).

2. Obidzinski and Barr, "The Effects of Decentralization on Forests and Forest Industries in Berau District, East Kalimantan"; Casson, Muliastra, and Obidzinski, "Land-Based Investment and Green Development in Indonesia."

3. Obidzinski and Barr, "The Effects of Decentralization on Forests and Forest Industries in Berau District, East Kalimantan"; Obidzinski and Andrianto, "Illegal Forestry Activities in Berau and East Kutai Districts, East Kalimantan."

4. Obidzinski and Barr, "The Effects of Decentralization on Forests and Forest Industries in Berau District, East Kalimantan"; "Produk Domestik Regional Bruto," BPS Kabupaten Berau, 2017, https://beraukab.bps.go .id/linkTableDinamis/view/id/8.

5. Bronson Griscom et al., "Synthesizing Global and Local Datasets to Estimate Jurisdictional Forest Carbon Fluxes in Berau, Indonesia," *PLoS ONE* 11, no. 1 (2016): e0146357; Laura J. Sonter et al., "Mining Drives Extensive Deforestation in the Brazilian Amazon," *Nature Communications* 8 (2017), https://doi.org/10.1038/s41467-017-00557-w.

6. "Luas Tanaman Perkebunan Menurut Jenis Tanaman dan Kabupaten/ Kota (Ha), Tahun 2015."

7. Author field notes, April 21, 2015.

8. Sulistyo A. Siran, "The Importance of STREK Plots in Contributing Sustainable Forest Management in Indonesia," in *Permanent Sample Plots: More Than Just Forest Data—Proceedings of International Workshop on Promoting Permanent Sample Plots in Asia and the Pacific Region*, ed. Hari Priyadi, Petrus Gunarso, and Markku Kanninen (Bogor, Indonesia: CIFOR/ ITTO, 2005), 99–107, http://www.cifor.org/publications/pdf_files/Books/ BPriyadi0601.pdf; Obidzinski and Andrianto, "Illegal Forestry Activities in Berau and East Kutai Districts, East Kalimantan."

9. Stephan Mantel, "Berau Model Forest Area Environmental Datasets and Maps: Land Systems Inventory," Berau Forest Management Project, 2001, http://www.dephut.go.id/Halaman/PDF/prd17.pdf; André Oosterman, "Carbon Trading for Sustainable Forest Management: The Case of the Berau Model Forest" (Jakarta: Berau Forest Management Project, 2000).

10. GIZ03 150330.

11. TNC35 150321.

12. TNC35 150321.

13. TNC41 150611.

14. TNC42 150709.

15. TNC29 141223; TNC41 150611.

16. Berau REDD+ Working Group, "Berau Forest Carbon Program, 2011– 2015: Berau's Contribution to the World" (Tanjung Redeb, Indonesia: Berau REDD+ Working Group, 2011), iv, 14, http://tfcakalimantan.org/ wp-content/uploads/2012/12/BFCP-English_Compile-Done.pdf.

17. TNC34 150316.

18. SIGAP-REDD+ is an acronym for *Aksi Inspiratif Warga untuk Perubahan dalam REDD+*, or Inspirational Popular Action for Change Within REDD+; see Herlina Hartanto, Tomy S. Yulianto, and Taufiq Hidayat, *SIGAP-REDD+: Aksi Inspiratif Warga Untuk Perubahan Dalam REDD+* (Jakarta: TNC, 2014).

19. GIZ05 150427.

20. GIZ03 150330.

21. TNC50 150813.

22. Berau village names are pseudonyms. Cf. Gregory M. Thaler, "Equifinality in the Smallholder Slot: Cash Crop Development in the Brazilian Amazon and Indonesian Borneo," *Comparative Politics* 53, no. 4 (2021): 687–722; Gregory M. Thaler and Cut Augusta Mindry Anandi, "Shifting Cultivation, Contentious Land Change and Forest Governance: The Politics of Swidden in East Kalimantan," *Journal of Peasant Studies* 44, no. 5 (2017): 1066–87; and Robert Fletcher et al., "Natural Capital Must Be Defended: Green Growth as Neoliberal Biopolitics," *Journal of Peasant Studies* 46, no. 5 (2019): 1068–95.

23. Descriptions of swidden systems in eastern Indonesian Borneo include Makoto Inoue and Abubakar M. Lahjie, "Dynamics of Swidden Agriculture in East Kalimantan," *Agroforestry Systems* 12, no. 3 (1990): 269–84; Timothy C. Jessup, "Persistence and Change in the Practice of Shifting Cultivation in the Apo Kayan, East Kalimantan, Indonesia," *Indo-Pacific Prehistory Association Bulletin* 10 (1991): 218–25; Carol J. Pierce Colfer and Richard Dudley, "Shifting Cultivators of Indonesia: Managers or Marauders of the Forest? Rice Production and Forest Use among the Uma' Jalan of East Kalimantan" (Rome: Food and Agriculture Organization, 1993); and Carol J. Pierce Colfer, *The Longhouse of the Tarsier: Changing Landscapes, Gender and Well Being in Borneo* (Phillips, ME: Borneo Research Council, 2008).

24. TNC-Indonesia, "TNC Conditional Payment Agreement with [Gunung Madu] Village," November 13, 2013.

25. Pirard and Lapeyre, "Building a Rapid Assessment Tool to Help Design Community Incentive Agreements in the Context of the Berau Forest Carbon Program: The Example of 2 Model Villages," Institut pour le Développement Durable et les Relations Internationales/TNC, August 9, 2013.

26. "TFCA [Tropical Forest Conservation Act] Kalimantan Implementation Plan 2013–2017" (USAID/MOF/WWF/TNC, n.d.), 23.

27. James C. Scott, *The Art of Not Being Governed: An Anarchist History of Upland Southeast Asia* (New Haven, CT: Yale University Press, 2009).

28. Nancy Peluso, "Plantations and Mines: Resource Frontiers and the Politics of the Smallholder Slot," *Journal of Peasant Studies* 44, no. 4 (2017): 968.

29. GIZ04 150416; BER04 150408.

30. BER13 150415; BER04 150408.

31. TNC42 150709; also TNC32 150302.

32. BLI (Research, Development, and Innovation Agency)/P3SEKPI (Research and Development Center for Socio-Economics, Policy, and Climate Change), "Emission Reductions Program Idea Note (ERPIN): Towards a Greener and Developed East Kalimantan: A Provincial Emission Reductions Program in Indonesia" (Bogor, Indonesia: Forest Carbon Partnership Facility, 2016), https://www.forestcarbonpartnership .org/system/files/documents/Indonesian%20ER-PIN%2020160429 %20Final.pdf.

33. TNC34 150501.

34. TNC31 150205.

35. For a more detailed account of this episode, see Thaler and Anandi, "Shifting Cultivation, Contentious Land Change and Forest Governance."

36. There have been some changes over time to the methods behind the Global Forest Watch (GFW) data from which these statistics are calculated, making the data potentially more sensitive to small-scale clearing, especially after 2015. GFW notes, however, that in Indonesia, where large-scale clearing predominates, loss was already well captured by the initial algorithm. A conservative inference is that average annual primary forest loss roughly doubled from 2005–2009 to 2010–2014, and the rate in 2015–2019 was at least as high as 2010–2014, if not higher.

37. TNC41 150611.

38. TNC30 150128.

39. GIZ06 150427.

40. GIZ06 150427.

41. TNC32 150302; TNC30 150128.

42. TNC32 150302.

43. Interviewee codes withheld for participant security.

44. TNC42 150709; BER19 150418.

45. Josephine Moulds, "Bumi Reveals $200m Black Hole in Financial Results," *The Guardian*, May 31, 2013, http://www.theguardian.com/business/2013/ may/31/bumi-reveals-200m-black-hole-results; Jeremy Kahn and William Mellor, "Nat Rothschild Rues 'Terrible Mistake' in Deal Gone Sour," Bloomberg, May 8, 2013, http://www.bloomberg.com/news/articles/ 2013-05-07/nat-rothschild-rues-terrible-mistake-in-deal-gone-sour.

46. Merrill Lynch was acquired by Bank of America in 2009, and the 2010 donation was made by Bank of America Merrill Lynch. "Merrill Places $325 Million for Berau Coal," *Finance Asia*, December 11, 2006, https:// www.financeasia.com/article/merrill-places-325-million-for-berau-coal/ 69961; Katherine Demopoulosin, "Stake in Indonesia's Berau Coal Sold," *Financial Times*, November 30, 2009, https://www.ft.com/content/ 078be912-ddea-11de-b8e2-00144feabdco; "Roger Suyama," LinkedIn, https://sg.linkedin.com/in/rogersuyama; Bank of America, "Bank of

America Merrill Lynch Supports The Nature Conservancy's Innovative Forest Project on Kalimantan" (Jakarta, 2010), http://newsroom .bankofamerica.com/press-release/environment/bank-america-merrill -lynch-supports-nature-conservancys-innovative-forest-.

47. Meijaard, "Erik Meijaard: Going Beyond Environmental Pacifiers in Indonesian Conservation."

Reflection: Green at Last?

1. Mikaela Weisse and Elizabeth Goldman, "Primary Rainforest Destruction Increased 12% from 2019 to 2020," *Global Forest Review: Forest Pulse*, 2021, https://research.wri.org/gfr/forest-pulse.
2. "This Is What the Jokowi Administration Has Done to Support Indonesia's Palm Oil Industry," *Jakarta Globe*, November 2, 2018, https:// jakartaglobe.id/business/this-is-what-the-jokowi-administration -has-done-to-support-indonesias-palm-oil-industry/. See also "Jokowi Calls for Increase in Palm Oil Production," *Tempo*, October 30, 2018, https://en.tempo.co/read/922974/jokowi-calls-for-increase-in-palm-oil -production.
3. "This Is What the Jokowi Administration Has Done to Support Indonesia's Palm Oil Industry."
4. Karlis Salna, Rieka Rahadiana, and Yoga Rusmana, "Jokowi Wants Indonesia to Be More Than a Raw Materials Giant," Bloomberg, October 2, 2019, https://www.bloomberg.com/news/articles/2019-10-02/ jokowi-wants-indonesia-to-be-more-than-just-a-raw-material-giant.
5. Hans Nicholas Jong, "Indonesia's Biofuel Bid Threatens More Deforestation for Oil Palm Plantations," *Mongabay*, December 21, 2020, https:// news.mongabay.com/2020/12/indonesia-biofuel-deforestation-oil-palm -plantation-b30/.
6. Koya Jibiki and Erwida Maulia, "Palm Oil Biodiesel Makes Volatile Bet for Indonesia's Pertamina," *Nikkei Asia*, February 16, 2021, https://asia .nikkei.com/Business/Energy/Palm-oil-biodiesel-makes-volatile-bet-for -Indonesia-s-Pertamina.
7. Jong, "Indonesia's Biofuel Bid Threatens More Deforestation for Oil Palm Plantations."
8. Gecko Project, "New Player Starts Clearing Rainforest in World's Biggest Oil Palm Project," *Mongabay*, March 24, 2020, https://news.mongabay .com/2020/03/new-player-starts-clearing-rainforest-in-worlds-biggest -oil-palm-project/.
9. Hoong Chen Teo et al., "Environmental Impacts of Planned Capitals and Lessons for Indonesia's New Capital," *Land* 9, no. 11 (2020): 438.
10. Gellert, "Extractive Regimes," 31.
11. Li, "After the Land Grab," 336.
12. Stoler, *Capitalism and Confrontation*, 141.

13. "US Bans Malaysian Palm Oil Producer over Forced Labour," BBC, October 1, 2020, https://www.bbc.com/news/business-54366607.

14. Zaidi Isham Ismail, "FGV Scouts for Land in Asean, Africa (HL)," *New Straits Times* (Kuala Lumpur), August 14, 2013, 1.

15. "Felda Unable to Proceed with Brazil Plan for Now," *New Straits Times*, November 4, 2009, 2.

16. Zaidi Isham Ismail, "Felda Shifts Focus To Africa For Expansion," *New Straits Times*, December 21, 2009, 2.

17. Jeremy Campbell, *Conjuring Property: Speculation and Environmental Futures in the Brazilian Amazon* (Seattle: University of Washington Press, 2015), 198.

Overview: An Amazonian Success Story

1. Field notes from event "Amazon Fund, the World's Biggest Conservation Experiment?" December 6, 2015, Global Landscapes Forum, Paris.

2. Heilmayr et al., "Brazil's Amazon Soy Moratorium Reduced Deforestation," 801; Boucher et al., "Deforestation Success Stories."

3. Tollefson, "Battle for the Amazon," 20.

Chapter 4. The Amazonian Extractive Economy

1. Susanna Hecht and Alexander Cockburn, *The Fate of the Forest: Developers, Destroyers, and Defenders of the Amazon*, updated ed. (Chicago: University of Chicago Press, 2010), 63.

2. Marianne Schmink and Charles Wood, *Contested Frontiers in Amazonia* (New York: Columbia University Press, 1992).

3. Hecht and Cockburn, *The Fate of the Forest*, 71–72.

4. Barbara Weinstein, *The Amazon Rubber Boom, 1850–1920* (Stanford, CA: Stanford University Press, 1983).

5. Larry Rohter, "Of Rubber and Blood in Brazilian Amazon," *New York Times*, November 23, 2006, http://www.nytimes.com/2006/11/23/world/americas/23brazil.html.

6. Weinstein, *The Amazon Rubber Boom*, 267–68.

7. James Grogan et al., "Over-Harvesting Driven by Consumer Demand Leads to Population Decline: Big-Leaf Mahogany in South America," *Conservation Letters* 3, no. 1 (2010): 12–20.

8. With the establishment of SPVEA, the Brazilian government defined the area of the "Legal Amazon" as a target of regional policy. The Legal Amazon currently includes the present-day states of Acre, Amapá, Amazonas, Mato Grosso, Pará, Rondônia, Roraima, Tocantins, and the western part of the state of Maranhão. The Amazon biome of humid tropical forest, as designated by the Brazilian Institute for Geography and Statistics (IBGE), covers the majority of the Legal Amazon, though substantial portions of

the states of Mato Grosso, Tocantins, and Maranhão are designated as falling within the Cerrado (savanna) biome.

9. Almeida, "Do Extrativismo à Domesticação."

10. Weinstein, *The Amazon Rubber Boom*, 42.

11. Hecht and Cockburn, *The Fate of the Forest*, 64–65.

12. General Golbery do Couto e Silva, quoted in Hecht and Cockburn, *The Fate of the Forest*, 116.

13. Giorgio de Antoni, "O Programa Piloto Para Proteçao das Florestas Tropicais do Brasil (PPG-7) e a Globalização da Amazônia," *Ambiente e Sociedade* 13, no. 2 (2010): 299–313; "The Biggest Iron Ore Exporter in the World," in *Vale—Our History* (Rio de Janeiro: Vale, 2012), 136–75, http://www.vale.com/EN/aboutvale/book-our-history/Pages/default .aspx.

14. Gold mining, meanwhile, will forever be remembered for the gold rush at Serra Pelada, also in the Carajás region, where at its peak in the early 1980s an estimated 100,000 men swarmed a giant open pit, seeking their fortunes in metal clawed from the earth.

15. Schmink and Wood, *Contested Frontiers in Amazonia*, 61.

16. Cynthia Simmons et al., "The Amazon Land War in the South of Pará," *Annals of the Association of American Geographers* 97, no. 3 (2007): 567–92.

17. Ronaldo Brasiliense, "Escândalo da Sudam: Todos Ricos, Todos Soltos!" *Congresso Em Foco*, December 16, 2005, http://congressoemfoco.uol.com .br/noticias/escandalo-da-sudam-todos-ricos-todos-soltos/; "Fraude em Fundos de Sudene e Sudam Pode Chegar a R$16,6 Bilhões, Diz Ministério," *O Globo*, April 11, 2010, http://oglobo.globo.com/economia/ fraude-em-fundos-de-sudene-sudam-pode-chegar-r-166-bilhoes-diz -ministerio-3025590.

18. Barbalho's legal troubles have continued, however. The federal police allege that he received kickbacks for his 2010 Senate campaign from the consortium behind the construction of the Belo Monte hydroelectric dam on the Xingu River in Pará. In 2021, meanwhile, the Brazilian Public Ministry, a body of independent government prosecutors, requested Barbalho's disqualification from public office after his media company engaged in illegal electoral propaganda in 2018 to secure the election of Jader Barbalho's son, Helder Barbalho, as governor of Pará. Helder Barbalho has not fallen far from his father's tree. Not only has the Public Ministry requested his removal from office for crimes related to his 2018 election campaign, but he has also been investigated for illegal corporate donations to his unsuccessful campaign for governor in 2014, and as governor his administration has been marked by a corruption scandal over the purchase of faulty respirators at inflated prices during the COVID-19 pandemic. At the time of writing, both father and son remain in office.

19. David Skole and Compton Tucker, "Tropical Deforestation and Habitat Fragmentation in the Amazon: Satellite Data from 1978 to 1988," *Science*

260 (1993): 1905–10. See also "Avaliação da Floresta Amazônica" (São José dos Campos, Brazil: INPE, 1989), http://www.obt.inpe.br/prodes/Prodes1989.pdf.

20. Sergio Margulis, "Causes of Deforestation in the Brazilian Amazon" (Washington, DC: World Bank, 2004); "Levantamento de Informações de Uso e Cobertura Da Terra Na Amazônia," Embrapa, September 2011, https://ainfo.cnptia.embrapa.br/digital/bitstream/item/84434/1/relatorio-final-Terraclass.pdf; V. De Sy et al., "Land Use Patterns and Related Carbon Losses Following Deforestation in South America," *Environmental Research Letters* 10, no. 12 (2015): 124004.

21. Susanna Hecht, "Environment, Development and Politics: Capital Accumulation and the Livestock Sector in Eastern Amazonia," *World Development* 13, no. 6 (1985): 663–84; Maria Bowman et al., "Persistence of Cattle Ranching in the Brazilian Amazon: A Spatial Analysis of the Rationale for Beef Production," *Land Use Policy* 29, no. 3 (2012): 558–68.

22. E. Bradford Burns, *A History of Brazil*, 3rd ed. (New York: Columbia University Press, 1993), 71–75.

23. Cf. Michael Hechter, *Internal Colonialism: The Celtic Fringe in British National Development, 1536–1966* (London: Routledge and Kegan Paul, 1975).

24. A. Simoes and C. Hidalgo, "The Economic Complexity Observatory: An Analytical Tool for Understanding the Dynamics of Economic Development," workshop at the Twenty-Fifth AAAI Conference on Artificial Intelligence, 2011, http://atlas.media.mit.edu/s63xbq; "World Development Indicators," World Bank, 2017, http://data.worldbank.org.

25. The military government replaced the 1934 Forest Code in 1965. The 1965 Forest Code remained in effect until a revised Forest Code was passed in 2012.

26. Hecht and Cockburn, *The Fate of the Forest*.

27. A. Veríssimo et al., *Áreas Protegidas na Amazônia Brasileira: Avanços e Desafios* (Belém/São Paulo: Imazon/ISA, 2011). I use the term "protected areas" hereafter in relation to Brazil to refer generically to strictly protected and sustainable-use conservation areas and Indigenous territories.

28. *Reserva Extrativista* is usually translated as "Extractive Reserve," but to distinguish between extractivism (which refers here to traditional natural-resource-based livelihoods) and my broader analysis of capitalist extraction, I translate the term literally as "Extractivist Reserve."

29. Margaret Keck and Kathryn Sikkink, *Activists Beyond Borders: Advocacy Networks in International Politics* (Ithaca, NY: Cornell University Press, 1998).

30. Margaret Keck, "Social Equity and Environmental Politics in Brazil: Lessons from the Rubber Tappers of Acre," *Comparative Politics* 27, no. 4 (1995): 409–24.

31. Veríssimo et al., *Áreas Protegidas na Amazônia Brasileira*.

32. Antoni, "O Programa Piloto Para Proteçao das Florestas Tropicais do Brasil"; Carlos Valério Aguiar Gomes et al., "Extractive Reserves in the Brazilian Amazon Thirty Years After Chico Mendes: Social Movement Achievements, Territorial Expansion and Continuing Struggles," *Desenvolvimento e Meio Ambiente* 48 (2018): 74–98.

Chapter 5. The Logic of Brazilian Land Sparing

1. On supply-chain sustainability, see Daniel Nepstad et al., "Slowing Amazon Deforestation Through Public Policy and Interventions in Beef and Soy Supply Chains," *Science* 344, no. 6188 (2014): 1118–23; Holly Gibbs et al., "Did Ranchers and Slaughterhouses Respond to Zero-Deforestation Agreements in the Brazilian Amazon?" *Conservation Letters* 9, no. 1 (2016): 32–42; and Heilmayr et al., "Brazil's Amazon Soy Moratorium Reduced Deforestation." On protected areas, see Daniel Nepstad et al., "Inhibition of Amazon Deforestation and Fire by Parks and Indigenous Lands," *Conservation Biology* 20, no. 1 (2006): 65–73, and Britaldo Soares-Filho et al., "Role of Brazilian Amazon Protected Areas in Climate Change Mitigation," *Proceedings of the National Academy of Sciences* 107, no. 24 (2010): 10821–26. On compliance with environmental regulations, see Juliano Assunção, Clarissa Gandour, and Rudi Rocha, "Deforestation Slowdown in the Legal Amazon: Prices or Policies?" (Rio de Janeiro: Climate Policy Initiative, 2012), and Eugenio Y. Arima et al., "Public Policies Can Reduce Tropical Deforestation: Lessons and Challenges from Brazil," *Land Use Policy* 41 (2014): 465–73.

2. Nepstad et al., "Slowing Amazon Deforestation Through Public Policy and Interventions in Beef and Soy Supply Chains," Supplementary Materials, S18.

3. "Rendering technical" is a move that defines and depoliticizes social problems to make them amenable to governance interventions. See Tania Li, *The Will to Improve: Governmentality, Development, and the Practice of Politics* (Durham, NC: Duke University Press, 2007). Social analysis limited to a technical register is part of this governance apparatus.

4. Two exceptions are David M. Lapola et al., "Pervasive Transition of the Brazilian Land-Use System," *Nature Climate Change* 4, no. 1 (2013): 27–35, and articles by Brenda Baletti: "Ordenamento Territorial: Neo-Developmentalism and the Struggle for Territory in the Lower Brazilian Amazon," *Journal of Peasant Studies* 39, no. 2 (2012): 573–98, and "Saving the Amazon? Sustainable Soy and the New Extractivism," *Environment and Planning A* 46, no. 1 (2014): 5–25. My writing and collaborations on Brazilian forest policy also center this critical political economy approach; see Thaler, "The Land Sparing Complex," and Gregory M. Thaler, Cecilia Viana, and Fabiano Toni, "From Frontier Governance to Gover-

nance Frontier: The Political Geography of Brazil's Amazon Transition," *World Development* 114 (2019): 59–72.

5. Susanna Hecht, "From Eco-Catastrophe to Zero Deforestation? Interdisciplinarities, Politics, Environmentalisms and Reduced Clearing in Amazonia," *Environmental Conservation* 39, no. 1 (2011): 7.

6. "Avaliação do Plano de Ação Para Prevenção e Controle do Desmatamento na Amazônia Legal: PPCDAm 2007–2010," Instituto de Pesquisa Econômica Aplicada, Comissão Econômica para a América Latina e Caribe, and GIZ, December 2011, https://repositorio.ipea.gov.br/bitstream/11058/884/1/IPEA_GIZ_Cepal_2011_Avaliacao%20PPCDAm%202007-2011_web.pdf.

7. Marina Campos and Daniel Nepstad, "Smallholders, the Amazon's New Conservationists," *Conservation Biology* 20, no. 5 (2006): 1553–56; Stephan Schwartzman et al., "Social Movements and Large-Scale Tropical Forest Protection on the Amazon Frontier: Conservation from Chaos," *Journal of Environment and Development* 19 (2010): 274–99.

8. Christoph Nolte et al., "Governance Regime and Location Influence Avoided Deforestation Success of Protected Areas in the Brazilian Amazon," *Proceedings of the National Academy of Sciences* 110, no. 13 (2013): 4956–61; Soares-Filho et al., "Role of Brazilian Amazon Protected Areas in Climate Change Mitigation."

9. "Avaliação do Plano de Ação Para Prevenção e Controle do Desmatamento na Amazônia Legal"; Jeremy Campbell, "The Land Question in Amazonia: Cadastral Knowledge and Ignorance in Brazil's Tenure Regularization Program," *PoLAR: Political and Legal Anthropology Review* 38, no. 1 (2015): 147–67.

10. "Avaliação do Plano de Ação Para Prevenção e Controle do Desmatamento na Amazônia Legal"; "Terra Legal—Amazônia Legal," Ministério do Desenvolvimento Agrário, 2015, http://www.mda.gov.br/sitemda/pagina/acompanhe-ações-do-mda-e-incra.

11. Campbell, "The Land Question in Amazonia."

12. Benedict Probst et al., "Impacts of a Large-Scale Titling Initiative on Deforestation in the Brazilian Amazon," *Nature Sustainability* 3 (2020): 1019–26.

13. Britaldo Soares-Filho et al., "Cracking Brazil's Forest Code," *Science* 344 (2014): 363–64.

14. Lisa Rausch, "Environmental Governance as a Development Strategy: The Case of Lucas Do Rio Verde Legal" (PhD diss., University of Kansas, 2013), 263–64.

15. The other requirements were a municipal deforestation rate of less than or equal to forty square kilometers per year and a two-year average annual deforestation rate less than or equal to 60 percent of the average of the previous two-year period.

16. Andréa Azevedo et al., "Limits of Brazil's Forest Code as a Means to End Illegal Deforestation," *Proceedings of the National Academy of Sciences* 114, no. 29 (2017): 7653–58.

17. Arima et al., "Public Policies Can Reduce Tropical Deforestation."

18. "Sistema do Observatório ABC," Observatório ABC, 2014, http://observatorioabc.com.br/index.php/page/150-Sistema-do-observat%25C3%25B3rio-ABC.

19. Ben Phalan et al., "Minimising the Harm to Biodiversity of Producing More Food Globally," *Food Policy* 36, no. Suppl. 1 (2011): S69.

20. Rafael Curado Fleury and Pedro A. Arraes Pereira, "Crédito Intensifica Pecuária," *Agroanalysis* 33, no. 11 (November 2013), http://www.agroanalysis.com.br/especiais_detalhe.php?idEspecial=140&ordem=3.

21. Thaler, Viana, and Toni, "From Frontier Governance to Governance Frontier"; Thaler, "Ethnography of Environmental Governance."

22. Hecht, "From Eco-Catastrophe to Zero Deforestation?" 4; Daniel Nepstad et al., "The End of Deforestation in the Brazilian Amazon," *Science* 326 (2009): 1350–51.

23. TNC07 140402.

Chapter 6. Greening the Soy Complex in Nova Ubiratã

1. On "agrarian extractivism" and "soy complexes," see Ben M. McKay, "Agrarian Extractivism in Bolivia," *World Development* 97 (2017): 199–211. The definition of "extractivism" in the scholarly literature on Latin American commodity exports differs from the more fundamental distinction I draw between extraction and production in the capitalist world system. There is a world of developmental difference between the extractive logging and cattle towns of the deforestation frontier and the booming agro-industrial hubs of contemporary Mato Grosso, and the transition from the former to the latter has depended on processes of institutional change, fixed capital accumulation, and land-use regulation. The soy complex in the eastern Amazon is socially inequitable and environmentally damaging (like all capitalist development), but it is clearly an engine of productivist, articulated economic activity.

2. Rausch, "Environmental Governance as a Development Strategy," 160–61 (quotation).

3. "Produção Agrícola Municipal," IBGE, http://www.sidra.ibge.gov.br/bda/pesquisas/pam/default.asp?o=29&i=P; "Pesquisa Pecuária Municipal," IBGE, https://sidra.ibge.gov.br/pesquisa/ppm/quadros/brasil/2016.

4. Andréa Azevedo, "Legitimação da Insustentabilidade? Análise do Sistema de Licenciamento Ambiental de Propriedades Rurais—SLAPR (Mato Grosso)" (PhD diss., Universidade de Brasília, 2009); Raoni Rajão, Andrea Azevedo, and Marcelo Stabile, "Institutional Subversion and Deforestation: Learning Lessons from the System for the Environmental

Licencing of Rural Properties in Mato Grosso," *Public Administration and Development* 32 (2012): 229–44.

5. Rausch, "Environmental Governance as a Development Strategy," 165.

6. André Lima, "Mato Grosso, Amazônia (i)Legal" (Brasília: Instituto Socioambiental, 2005); Azevedo, "Legitimação da Insustentabilidade?"

7. NU01 140506.

8. Rausch, "Environmental Governance as a Development Strategy," 166.

9. "'Soya King' Wins Golden Chainsaw Award," Greenpeace, June 19, 2005, https://wayback.archive-it.org/9650/20200404073502/http://p3-raw.green peace.org/international/en/news/features/soya-king-wins-chainsaw/.

10. Nicole Perlroth, "Blairo Maggi's About Face," *Forbes*, December 2009, 38, https://www.forbes.com/forbes/2009/1214/thought-leaders-blairo-maggi -jungle-tree-hugger.html.

11. Rausch, "Environmental Governance as a Development Strategy."

12. Claudia Stickler and Oriana Almeida, "Harnessing International Finance to Manage the Amazon Agro-Industrial Explosion? The Case of International Finance Corporation Loans to Grupo Maggi," *Journal of Sustainable Forestry* 27, nos. 1–2 (2008): 76.

13. Alexei Barrionuevo, "Brazil Rainforest Analysis Sets Off Political Debate," *New York Times*, May 25, 2008, http://www.nytimes.com/2008/05/ 25/world/americas/25amazon.html.

14. Rausch, "Environmental Governance as a Development Strategy," 263–64.

15. José Lacerda, "MT: No Caminho Certo da Política Ambiental (Parte II)— REDD," Governo de Mato Grosso, March 15, 2012, http://www.mt.gov .br/conteudo.php?sid=151&cid=73756&; José Lacerda, "Lei de REDD+: Benefício Ambiental e Social," Governo de Mato Grosso, 2013, http:// www.controladoria.mt.gov.br/noticias?p_p_id=101&p_p_lifecycle=0&p _p_state=maximized&p_p_mode=view&_101_struts_action=%252Fasset _publisher%252Fview_content&_101_returnToFullPageURL=http %253A%252F%252Fwww.controladoria.mt.gov.br%252Fnoticias %253Fp_auth%253DL7u8gsDf%25.

16. Ivo Beuter, *Nova Ubiratã, Município—Berço do Início da Colonização do Norte do Estado de Mato Grosso: História da Colonização e Constituição do Município de Nova Ubiratã e do Novo Município de Boa Esperança do Norte e do Provável Futuro Município de Água Limpa* (Cuiabá, Brazil: Gráfica e Editora Futura, 2000), 97.

17. Alceu Sperança, Regina Sperança, and Selene Carvalho, *Ubiratã: História e Memória* (Ubiratã, Brazil: Self-published, 2008).

18. Information in this paragraph on the colonization of Nova Ubiratã is based primarily on Ivo Beuter's history of the municipality: *Nova Ubiratã, Município*.

19. "Banco de Dados de Informações Ambientais," IBGE, https://bdiaweb .ibge.gov.br/.

20. "Censo Demográfico 2000," IBGE, https://sidra.ibge.gov.br/pesquisa/censo-demografico/demografico-2000/inicial.

21. "Contagem da População 2007," IBGE, https://sidra.ibge.gov.br/pesquisa/censo-demografico/contagem-2007/tabelas.

22. NU02 140506; NU08 140513.

23. NU07 140512; NU04 140507.

24. NU02 140506; NU06 140512; NU09 140515.

25. NU09 140515.

26. NU03 140506; NU06 140512.

27. NU09 140515.

28. "Audiência Marca Início da Regularização Fundiária em Nova Ubiratã," ExpressoMT, November 8, 2012, http://www.expressomt.com.br/matogrosso/audiencia-marca-inicio-da-regularizacao-fundiaria-em-nova-ubirata-38356.html.

29. NU09 140515.

30. NU03 140506.

31. NU04 140507.

32. NU07 140512.

33. Sérgio Édison, "Nova Ubiratã Consegue no Ibama o Primeiro Desembargo Ambiental Após a Operação Arco de Fogo," ExpressoMT, April 13, 2012, http://www.expressomt.com.br/matogrosso/nova-ubirata-consegue-no-ibama-o-primeiro-desembargo-ambiental-apos-a-9472.html.

34. NU09 140515.

35. NU08 140513.

36. Ericksen Vital, "Nova Ubiratã Não Conseguirá Sair da Lista dos Desmatadores, Diz Prefeito," G1, May 27, 2011, http://g1.globo.com/mato-grosso/noticia/2011/05/nova-ubirata-nao-conseguira-sair-da-lista-dos-desmatadores-diz-prefeito.html.

37. "Decisão Impede Desmatamento em Área de Mata em Nova Ubiratã," *O Documento*, March 6, 2012, http://www.odocumento.com.br/materia.php?id=386728.

38. Vital, "Nova Ubiratã Não Conseguirá Sair Dos Desmatadores, Diz Prefeito"; Cleide Carvalho, "Nova Ubiratã, em Mato Grosso, Vive Crise Após Intervenção do Ibama e Tenta Se Reinventar," *O Globo*, May 28, 2011, http://oglobo.globo.com/politica/nova-ubirata-em-mato-grosso-vive-crise-apos-intervencao-do-ibama-tenta-se-reinventar-2764078.

39. NU09 140515.

40. NU02 140506.

41. While Badalotti and other speculators might rent illegally cleared lands for productivist land uses such as industrial soy production, the windfall profits from forest destruction are not reinvested in the productivist municipal economy but rather extracted—in Badalotti's case, to the developed southern Brazilian "core" in Paraná.

42. TNC19 140502; TNC21 140516; TNC20 140428.

43. "Virada Verde," Fundo Amazônia, 2014, http://www.fundoamazonia.gov
.br/pt/projeto/Virada-Verde/.

44. "Sistema Nacional de Cadastro Ambiental Rural," Serviço Florestal Bra-
sileiro/Ministério do Meio Ambiente, 2017, http://www.car.gov.br/.

45. TNC21 140516.

46. NU04 140507; TNC20 140427.

47. TNC19 140502.

48. NU09 140515.

49. NU03 140506; NU09 140515. The story of biome boundaries is a fas-
cinating study of the relationships between ecology, science, agricultural
production, and environmental governance. Landholders may petition
SEMA to change the designation of their property from Amazon to Cerrado by contracting a study that conducts a full inventory of the property's
vegetation (including tree species, trunk sizes, and so forth). While the
official biome line is not altered, SEMA may agree to catalog a property
as Cerrado for purposes of licensing (NU04 140507). If the property is reclassified, the landholder gains a great deal of productive area. Of course,
this process is complicated and costly enough only to be accessible to
more capitalized farmers and ranchers.

50. NU01 140506.

51. Esther Boserup, *The Conditions of Agricultural Growth* (New Brunswick,
NJ: AldineTransaction, 1965).

52. NU05 140509.

53. NU06 140512.

54. Interview material in this paragraph is from NU12 180703.

55. "Portaria No 362, de 08 de Setembro de 2017," MMA, 2017, https://lex
.com.br/legis_27508568_PORTARIA_N_362_DE_8_DE_SETEMBRO
_DE_2017.aspx.

56. NU10 180702.

57. NU07 180702.

58. NU10 180702.

59. NU10 180702. In 2020, over 60 percent of Brazil's electricity came from
hydropower. "Fontes de Energia Renováveis Representam 83% da Ma-
triz Elétrica Brasileira," Government of Brazil, 2020, https://www.gov
.br/pt-br/noticias/energia-minerais-e-combustiveis/2020/01/fontes
-de-energia-renovaveis-representam-83-da-matriz-eletrica-brasileira.
On Brazilian dam-building and controversies, see, e.g., Alexander C. Lees
et al., "Hydropower and the Future of Amazonian Biodiversity," *Biodiversity and Conservation* 25, no. 3 (2016): 451–66, and Antonio Aledo Tur et
al., "Discourse Analysis of the Debate on Hydroelectric Dam Building in
Brazil," *Water Alternatives* 11, no. 111 (2018): 125–41.

60. Argemiro T. Leite-Filho, Marcos H. Costa, and Rong Fu, "The Southern
Amazon Rainy Season: The Role of Deforestation and Its Interactions

with Large-Scale Mechanisms," *International Journal of Climatology* 40, no. 4 (2020): 2328–41; Marcos H. Costa et al., "Climate Risks to Amazon Agriculture Suggest a Rationale to Conserve Local Ecosystems," *Frontiers in Ecology and the Environment* 17, no. 10 (2019): 584–90.

61. NU12 180703.
62. NU11 180703.
63. Azevedo et al., "Limits of Brazil's Forest Code as a Means to End Illegal Deforestation."
64. Vinícius Silgueiro et al., "Mapeamento da Ilegalidade na Exploração Madeireira em Mato Grosso Entre Agosto de 2013 e Julho de 2016," Transparência Florestal no. 9, Instituto Centro de Vida, 2018.
65. NU10 180702.
66. "Operação Desarticula Quadrilha de Desmatadores Que Movimentou R$1,9 Bi no Pará," IBAMA, 2016, http://www.ibama.gov.br/publicadas/operacao-desarticula-quadrilha-de-desmatadores-que-movimentou-r-19-bi-no-para; "Tribunal Regional Federal da 1a Região TRF-1—HABEAS CORPUS (HC): HC 0037229-67.2016.4.01.0000—Decisão Monocrática," 2016, https://www.jusbrasil.com.br/jurisprudencia/trf-1/895645112.

Chapter 7. Development and Dispossession in São Félix do Xingu

1. The Portuguese name for brazil nuts, *castanha-do-pará*, translates literally as "Pará chestnuts."
2. Desirée Luíse, "Corrupção é Algo Crônico em Secretarias de Meio Ambiente na Amazônia, Diz Ex-Secretário," *Carta Capital*, March 17, 2011, http://www.cartacapital.com.br/sustentabilidade/corrupcao-e-algo-cronico-em-secretarias-de-meio-ambiente-na-amazonia-diz-ex-secretario.
3. Simmons et al., "The Amazon Land War in the South of Pará," 567.
4. Luíse, "Corrupção é Algo Crônico em Secretarias de Meio Ambiente na Amazônia, Diz Ex-Secretário"; TNC09 140217.
5. Jayne Guimarães et al., *Municípios Verdes: Caminhos Para a Sustentabilidade* (Belém, Brazil: Imazon, 2011).
6. Gibbs et al., "Did Ranchers and Slaughterhouses Respond to Zero-Deforestation Agreements in the Brazilian Amazon?"
7. Schmink and Wood, *Contested Frontiers in Amazonia*.
8. "Censo Demográfico," IBGE, 2016, https://sidra.ibge.gov.br/pesquisa/censo-demografico/demografico-2010/inicial; "Pesquisa Pecuária Municipal," IBGE.
9. "Campeão na redução de passivos ambientais" translates literally as "champion in the reduction of environmental liabilities." "Lançamento do Fundo Terra Verde" (Brasília: The Nature Conservancy, 2014).
10. Campos and Nepstad, "Smallholders, the Amazon's New Conservationists."

11. Romain Taravella and Xavier Arnauld de Sartre, "The Symbolic and Political Appropriation of Scales: A Critical Analysis of the Amazonian Ranchers' Narrative," *Geoforum* 43, no. 3 (2012): 645–56.

12. By May 2017, São Félix had over 3,800,000 hectares registered in CAR, exceeding the legally available agricultural area by over 500,000 hectares. Over 150,000 hectares had been registered in Indigenous territories and nearly 120,000 hectares had been registered in conservation areas, reflecting continued contestation over tenure and protected areas in the municipality. "Sistema Nacional de Cadastro Ambiental Rural," SFB/MMA.

13. "Terra Legal—Amazônia Legal," Ministério do Desenvolvimento Agrário.

14. SFX08 140206. Paulo is a pseudonym.

15. SFX01 140129.

16. SFX04 140204; EMATER01 140130.

17. Group interview SFX22 180613.

18. "Village Dataset of the Global Comparative Study on REDD+ (GCS REDD+) Module 2," CIFOR, 2020, https://doi.org/10.17528/CIFOR/DATA.00199.

19. Group interview SFX22 180613.

20. SFX09 180613.

21. TNC10 180611.

22. SFX08 180608.

23. SFX19 180608. Mariana is a pseudonym.

24. Group interview SFX22 180613.

25. See, e.g., "A Pathway to Zero Deforestation in the Amazon," Zero Deforestation Working Group, 2017, http://ipam.org.br/wp-content/uploads/2017/11/A-Pathway-to-Zero-Deforestation-in-the-Brazilian-Amazon-full-report.pdf.

26. TNC02 180529.

27. TNC03 180530.

28. See also Thaler, "Equifinality in the Smallholder Slot."

29. Cf. Rachael D. Garrett, Eric F. Lambin, and Rosamond L. Naylor, "Land Institutions and Supply Chain Configurations as Determinants of Soybean Planted Area and Yields in Brazil," *Land Use Policy* 31 (2013): 385–96. On the origins of Brazil's soy complex, see Philip Fearnside, "Soybean Cultivation as a Threat to the Environment in Brazil," *Environmental Conservation* 28, no. 1 (2002): 23–38.

Reflection: A Day of Fire

1. In June 2021, Salles resigned his post while under investigation for his role as minister in an illegal timber laundering scheme.

2. Denis Abessa, Ana Famá, and Lucas Buruaem, "The Systematic Dismantling of Brazilian Environmental Laws Risks Losses on All Fronts," *Nature Ecology and Evolution* 3, no. 4 (2019): 510–11.

3. "Defending Tomorrow," Global Witness, 2020, https://www.globalwitness
.org/en/campaigns/environmental-activists/defending-tomorrow/.

4. "MP Eleitoral Pede ao TSE Cassação do Governador do Pará por Abuso
de Meios de Comunicação e Uso de Fake News," Ministério Público
Federal no Pará, January 27, 2021, http://www.mpf.mp.br/pa/sala-de
-imprensa/noticias-pa/mp-eleitoral-pede-ao-tse-cassacao-do-governador
-do-para-por-abuso-de-meios-de-comunicacao-e-uso-de-fake-news; Fabiano Maisonnave, "Campeão de Desmatamento, PA Retira Apoio da
PM em Ações do Ibama," *Folha de São Paulo*, August 12, 2019, https://
www1.folha.uol.com.br/ambiente/2019/08/campeao-de-desmatamento
-pa-retira-apoio-da-pm-em-acoes-do-ibama.shtml.

5. Rancher quoted in Adécio Piran, "Dia do Fogo—Produtores Planejam
Data Para Queimada na Região," *Jornal Folha Do Progresso*, August 5, 2019,
http://www.folhadoprogresso.com.br/dia-do-fogo-produtores-planejam
-data-para-queimada-na-regiao/.

6. Leandro Machado, "O Que Se Sabe Sobre o 'Dia do Fogo,' Momento-
Chave das Queimadas na Amazônia," BBC News Brasil, August 27, 2019,
https://www.bbc.com/portuguese/brasil-49453037.

7. Jenny Gonzales, "Misinformation and Blame Spread Concerning Sources
of Amazon Fires," *Mongabay*, August 28, 2019, https://news.mongabay
.com/2019/08/misinformation-and-blame-spread-concerning-sources-of
-amazon-fires/; "Brazil's Bolsonaro Says DiCaprio Gave Cash 'to Set Amazon on Fire,'" BBC News, November 30, 2019, https://www.bbc.com/
news/world-latin-america-50613054; Mauricio Savarese, "AP Finds Brazil's Plan to Protect Amazon Has Opposite Effect," Associated Press, August 28, 2020, https://apnews.com/oed3562a94f5b20b561adbbd11b20731;
Terrence McCoy and Heloísa Traiano, "Bolsonaro Sent Soldiers to the
Amazon to Curb Deforestation. Here's How the Effort Failed.," *Washington Post*, January 4, 2021, https://www.washingtonpost.com/world/the
_americas/brazil-bolsonaro-military-amazon-deforestation/2021/01/03/
cde4d342-3fc9-11eb-9453-fc36ba051781_story.html.

8. Luís Indriunas, "Acusados de Grilagem, Desmatamento e Outros Crimes
São Eleitos Para Prefeituras no Sul do Pará," *De Olho Nos Ruralistas*,
November 17, 2020, https://deolhonosruralistas.com.br/2020/11/17/
acusados-de-grilagem-desmatamento-e-outros-crimes-sao-eleitos-para
-prefeituras-no-sul-do-para/.

9. Maurício Simionato, "Matadores Espalham Medo em Cidade do PA,"
Folha de Sao Paulo, September 21, 2003, http://www1.folha.uol.com.br/
folha/brasil/ult96u53627.shtml.

10. TNC02 180529; TNC03 180530.

11. "Operação do MP e Polícia Desmonta Esquema de Corrupção e Prende
Ex-Prefeito de São Félix do Xingu," *O Impacto*, April 11, 2018, https://
oimpacto.com.br/2018/04/11/operacao-do-mp-e-policia-desmonta
-esquema-de-corrupcao-e-prende-ex-prefeito-de-sao-felix-do-xingu/.

12. "Justiça de São Félix do Xingu Afasta Diretor de Secretaria de Meio Ambiente," Tribunal de Justiça do Estado do Pará, September 13, 2019, https://www.tjpa.jus.br/PortalExterno/imprensa/noticias/Informes/993130-justica-de-sao-felix-do-xingu-afasta-diretor-de-secretaria-de-meio-ambiente.xhtml.

13. Lucy Tompkins, "Hundreds of Companies Promised to Help Save Forests. Did They?" *New York Times*, December 2, 2021, https://www.nytimes.com/2021/12/02/climate/companies-net-zero-deforestation.html. This question of "permanence" speaks to one of the three main criteria for the evaluation of forest conservation in REDD projects. For reductions in deforestation to be valid for REDD, they must have permanence, so that forest spared one year is not cut down the next; they must not be offset by displacement or "leakage" of deforestation to other regions; and they must be "additional" in that they would not have happened absent the project intervention. Land-sparing policies in Brazil resulted in "additional" reductions in Amazonian deforestation, but those reductions have proven to be of fleeting permanence, and they were offset by displacement.

14. On soy agglomeration economies and supply-chain configurations, see Rachael D. Garrett, Eric F. Lambin, and Rosamond L. Naylor, "The New Economic Geography of Land Use Change: Supply Chain Configurations and Land Use in the Brazilian Amazon," *Land Use Policy* 34 (2013): 265–75, and Garrett, Lambin, and Naylor, "Land Institutions and Supply Chain Configurations as Determinants of Soybean Planted Area and Yields in Brazil."

15. On "greening" the soy complex, and the foreclosure of alternatives to agro-industrial development, see also Baletti, "Saving the Amazon?"

16. On the "governance frontier," see Thaler, Viana, and Toni, "From Frontier Governance to Governance Frontier."

17. Nikolas Kuschnig et al., "Spatial Spillover Effects from Agriculture Drive Deforestation in Mato Grosso, Brazil," *Scientific Reports* 11, no. 21804 (2021), https://doi.org/10.1038/s41598-021-00861-y.

18. Richards, Walker, and Arima, "Spatially Complex Land Change."

19. Cf. Robert Walker, "The Scale of Forest Transition: Amazonia and the Atlantic Forests of Brazil," *Applied Geography* 32, no. 1 (2012): 12–20.

20. Similarly, productivist economies depend always on appropriation of unpaid labor both through trade relations, where profits from labor appropriation in extractive economies are imported, and through appropriation internal to the productivist economy itself. To paraphrase Karl Marx, capitalism always robs both the worker and the soil; the question for "green" and "inclusive" capitalist development is the degree to which soil and workers are being robbed at home versus abroad.

21. Ernesto Londoño, Manuela Andreoni, and Letícia Casado, "As Amazon Fires Become Global Crisis, Brazil's President Reverses Course," *New York Times*, August 23, 2019, https://www.nytimes.com/2019/08/23/world/americas/brazil-military-amazon-fire.html; Ernesto Londoño

and Letícia Casado, "With Amazon on Fire, Environmental Officials in Open Revolt Against Bolsonaro," *New York Times*, August 28, 2019, https://www.nytimes.com/2019/08/28/world/americas/amazon-fires -brazil.html.

22. Stephanie Spera, Jonathan Winter, and Trevor Partridge, "Brazilian Maize Yields Negatively Affected by Climate after Land Clearing," *Nature Sustainability* 3 (2020): 845–52; Costa et al., "Climate Risks to Amazon Agriculture Suggest a Rationale to Conserve Local Ecosystems"; Shanna Hanbury, "Amazon Tipping Point Puts Brazil's Agribusiness, Energy Sector at Risk: Top Scientists," *Mongabay*, February 24, 2020, https://news.mongabay.com/2020/02/amazon-tipping-point-puts-brazils -agribusiness-energy-sector-at-risk-top-scientists/.

23. Michael Pooler, "High Inflation Returns to Brazil: 'Each Week There Are Different Prices,'" *Financial Times*, November 16, 2021, https://www.ft .com/content/98ffc950-8192-4a87-b82f-ba0bd8023d66.

Overview: The Vortex of Development

1. Richard K. Reed, *Prophets of Agroforestry: Guaraní Communities and Commercial Gathering* (Austin: University of Texas Press, 1995), 148, 163.

2. Avery S. Cohn et al., "Cattle Ranching Intensification in Brazil Can Reduce Global Greenhouse Gas Emissions by Sparing Land from Deforestation," *Proceedings of the National Academy of Sciences* 111, no. 20 (2014): 7236–41; A. E. Latawiec et al., "Intensification of Cattle Ranching Production Systems: Socioeconomic and Environmental Synergies and Risks in Brazil," *Animal* 8, no. 8 (2014): 1255–63; Meghan Bogaerts et al., "Climate Change Mitigation Through Intensified Pasture Management: Estimating Greenhouse Gas Emissions on Cattle Farms in the Brazilian Amazon," *Journal of Cleaner Production* 162 (2017): 1539–50.

3. SIV09 180711.

4. "La ABT Inició Estricto Control en Carreteras Para Evitar el Contrabando de Madera," *PubliAgro*, May 13, 2021, https://publiagro.com.bo/ 2021/05/abt-control-contrabando/.

5. Moore, "The Capitalocene, Part I," 614.

6. Heilmayr et al., "Brazil's Amazon Soy Moratorium Reduced Deforestation," 808.

7. Ingalls et al., "The Transboundary Displacement of Deforestation Under REDD+," 263.

8. "Informe Final: El Cambio de Uso del Suelo y Sus Efectos Actuales y Futuros en el Municipio de San Ignacio de Velasco" (Santa Cruz de la Sierra, Bolivia: FAN-Bolivia, 2019).

9. Ben M. McKay, "Control Grabbing and Value-Chain Agriculture: BRICS, MICs and Bolivia's Soy Complex," *Globalizations* 15, no. 1 (2018): 87–88. See also McKay, "Agrarian Extractivism in Bolivia."

10. Fernando Rojas M., "La 'Capital del Cebú' Duplica Su Hato Pecuario con Inversión Extranjera," *El Deber* (Santa Cruz), April 7, 2019, 12.

Chapter 8. "The Country Jumps the Fence"

1. Frederic Vallvé, "The Impact of the Rubber Boom on the Indigenous Peoples of the Bolivian Lowlands (1850–1920)" (PhD diss., Georgetown University, 2010).

2. Ben Nobbs-Thiessen, *Landscape of Migration: Mobility and Environmental Change on Bolivia's Tropical Frontier, 1952 to the Present* (Chapel Hill: University of North Carolina Press, 2020); Ben McKay and Gonzalo Colque, "Bolivia's Soy Complex: The Development of 'Productive Exclusion,'" *Journal of Peasant Studies* 43, no. 2 (2016): 583–610.

3. McKay and Colque, "Bolivia's Soy Complex," 589–90.

4. Steven M. Helfand and Gervásio Castro De Rezende, "The Impact of Sector-Specific and Economy-Wide Policy Reforms on the Agricultural Sector in Brazil: 1980–98," *Contemporary Economic Policy* 22, no. 2 (2004): 194–212; Lee Mackey, "Legitimating Foreignization in Bolivia: Brazilian Agriculture and the Relations of Conflict and Consent in Santa Cruz, Bolivia," *International Conference on Global Land Grabbing* (Sussex, U.K.: Land Deal Politics Initiative, 2011), https://www.future-agricultures.org/wp-content/uploads/pdf-archive/Lee%20Mackey.pdf.

5. Jaime Klintowitz, "O País Pula a Cerca," *Veja*, July 19, 1995, 62, 64.

6. "Eastern Lowlands: Natural Resource Management and Agricultural Production Project: Implementation Completion Report," World Bank, 1998, 4, https://documents1.worldbank.org/curated/en/801411468227710688/pdf/multi-page.pdf.

7. Quoted in Heloisa Marques Gimenez, "O Desenvolvimento da Cadeia Produtiva da Soja na Bolívia e a Presença Brasileira: Uma História Comum" (MA thesis, Universidade de São Paulo, 2010), 93.

8. Marques Gimenez, "O Desenvolvimento da Cadeia Produtiva da Soja na Bolívia e a Presença Brasileira"; McKay, "Agrarian Extractivism in Bolivia."

9. For extensive information on the Brazilian role in the Bolivian fossil-fuel sector and the greenwashing of the Santa Cruz–Cuiabá pipeline, see Derrick Hindery, *From Enron to Evo: Pipeline Politics, Global Environmentalism, and Indigenous Rights in Bolivia* (Tucson: University of Arizona Press, 2013).

10. Carin Zissis, "Bolivia's Nationalization of Oil and Gas," Council on Foreign Relations, 2006, https://www.cfr.org/backgrounder/bolivias-nationalization-oil-and-gas.

11. Felipe Bächtold, José Marques, and Paula Bianchi, "OAS Afirma que Assumiu Obra Deficitária na Bolívia por Exigência de Lula," *Folha de São Paulo*, September 16, 2019, https://www1.folha.uol.com.br/poder/2019/

09/oas-afirma-que-assumiu-obra-deficitaria-na-bolivia-por-exigencia -de-lula.shtml; Fabio Murakawa, "Lula Viaja à Bolívia Para Interceder Junto a Evo," *Valor Econômico*, August 29, 2011, https://valor.globo.com/ mundo/noticia/2011/08/29/lula-viaja-a-bolivia-para-interceder-junto-a -evo.ghtml.

12. Fabio Murakawa, "Brasil Evita Desgaste com a Bolívia por Conta da OAS," *Valor Econômico*, April 27, 2012, https://www2.senado.leg.br/bdsf/ bitstream/handle/id/470974/noticia.htm?sequence=1.

13. Urioste, "Concentration and 'Foreignisation' of Land in Bolivia," 448.

14. SCZ01 180716. The book they reference is Miguel Urioste, *Concentración y Extranjerización de La Tierra En Bolivia* (La Paz, Bolivia: Fundación TIERRA, 2011).

15. The characterization of San Ignacio as a "pole" for ranching is from SIV10 190606.

Chapter 9. San Ignacio de Velasco

1. "Noel Kempff Mercado Climate Action Project: A Case Study in Reducing Emissions from Deforestation and Degradation," TNC, 2009, https:// www.nature.org/ourinitiatives/urgentissues/global-warming-climate -change/how-we-work/noel-kempff-case-study-final.pdf.

2. SCZ06 190617.

3. SCZ11 190626.

4. Jonathan Hoekstra, "The Noel Kempff Climate Action Project: The Conservancy Responds to a Greenpeace Report," TNC, 2009, http:// blog.nature.org/2009/10/noel-kempff-climate-forest-greenpeace-nature -conservancy/. For the Greenpeace report, see Ariana Densham et al., "Carbon Scam: Noel Kempff Climate Action Project and the Push for Sub-National Forest Offsets" (Amsterdam: Greenpeace, 2009), http:// www.greenpeace.org/international/Global/international/planet-2/ report/2009/10/carbon-scam-noel-kempff-carbo.pdf.

5. SCZ02 190716.

6. Silvana Vincenti, "Áreas Protegidas, Están en la Mira de la Deforestación," *El Deber*, May 16, 2021, https://eldeber.com.bo/edicion-impresa/areas -protegidas-estan-en-la-mira-de-la-deforestacion_231876.

7. Silvana Vincenti, "Tráfico de Tierras: Chiquitania, un Botín Político y Económico," *El Deber*, March 18, 2021, https://eldeber.com.bo/especiales/ trafico-de-tierras-chiquitania-un-botin-politico-y-economico_224775.

8. Vincenti, "Tráfico de Tierras"; Silvana Vincenti, "Originarios Denuncian Amedrentamiento por Exigir Respeto a Su Territorio," *El Deber*, April 12, 2021, https://eldeber.com.bo/santa-cruz/originarios-denuncian -amedrentamiento-por-exigir-respeto-a-su-territorio_227691.

9. Nelfi Reyes, "Cívicos e Indígenas de San Miguel, San Rafael y San Ignacio Se Unen Para Denunciar Nuevo Desmonte en el Área Protegida Bajo Paraguá," *El Deber*, June 16, 2021, https://eldeber.com.bo/santa

-cruz/civicos-e-indigenas-de-san-miguel-san-rafael-y-san-ignacio-se
-unen-para-denunciar-nuevo-desmonte-en-_235644; Iván Tamayo, "Indigenous Groups Call for Gov't Intervention as Land Grabbers Invade
Bolivian Protected Area," *Mongabay*, November 12, 2021, https://news
.mongabay.com/2021/11/indigenous-groups-call-for-govt-intervention
-as-land-grabbers-invade-bolivian-protected-area/.

10. Silvana Vincenti, "Surgen Nuevas Denuncias de Comunidades Fantasma y Desmontes Grandes en La Chiquitania," *El Deber*, June 28,
2021, https://eldeber.com.bo/edicion-impresa/surgen-nuevas-denuncias
-de-comunidades-fantasma-y-desmontes-grandes-en-la-chiquitania
_236939.

11. SCZ11 190626.

12. SIV15 190612.

13. SIV08 180710.

14. "Causas, Consecuencias y Alternativas Para Combatir la Crisis del Sec-
tor Forestal en Bolivia," Proyecto de Gestión Integral de Bosques para la
Reducción de la Deforestación (PROBOSQUE) (Santa Cruz de la Sierra,
Bolivia: GIZ, 2018).

15. SIV05 180709.

16. Josué Hinojosa, "Tajibo, Morado y Almendrillo Son las Especies de Madera Más Exportadas," *Los Tiempos*, July 21, 2018, https://www.lostiempos
.com/actualidad/economia/20180721/tajibo-morado-almendrillo-son
-especies-madera-mas-exportadas; "Brasil Representa el 61% de la Im-
portación de Madera en Bolivia," *Forestal Maderero*, October 10, 2017,
https://www.forestalmaderero.com/articulos/item/brasil-representa-61
-la-importacion-madera-bolivia.html; "Bolivia: Importaciones de Mue-
bles," Boletín Electrónico Bisemanal, Instituto Boliviano de Comercio Ex-
terior (IBCE), 2018, https://ibce.org.bo//images/ibcecifras_documentos/
Cifras-694-Bolivia-Importaciones-de-Muebles.pdf.

17. SIV07 180710.

18. Polain de Waroux et al., "Land-Use Policies and Corporate Investments
in Agriculture in the Gran Chaco and Chiquitano," 4024.

19. "Factores que Llevan a la Expansión de la Ganadería en Detrimento del
Bosque," PROBOSQUE (Santa Cruz de la Sierra, Bolivia: GIZ, 2018);
field notes from event "Factores claves que llevan a la expansión ganadera
sobre el bosque," July 10, 2018, San Ignacio de Velasco, Gobierno Municipal de San Ignacio de Velasco and GIZ.

20. Jonas Wolff, "The Political Economy of Bolivia's Post-Neoliberalism: Politics, Elites and the MAS Government," *European Review of Latin American
and Caribbean Studies* 108 (2019): 109–29; Linda Farthing, "An Opportunity Squandered? Elites, Social Movements, and the Government of Evo
Morales," *Latin American Perspectives* 46, no. 1 (2019): 212–29.

21. Nathalie Iriarte and Rolando Aparicio, "INRA, la Institución que Se
Creyó Encima de la Ley," *Connectas*, 2020, https://www.connectas.org/
especiales/los-piratas-de-la-tierra/es/.

22. Raúl Domínguez, "El Gran Negocio de la Deforestación," *Revista Nómadas*, June 16, 2021, https://www.revistanomadas.com/el-gran-negocio-de-la -deforestacion/; Vincenti, "Tráfico de Tierras."

23. SIV12 190610.

24. Domínguez, "El Gran Negocio de la Deforestación"; field notes from event "Factores claves que llevan a la expansión ganadera sobre el bosque."

25. Field notes from event "Factores claves que llevan a la expansión ganadera sobre el bosque."

26. SIV11 190610.

27. "Actores Ilegales que Amenazan los Bosques y las Tierras," Autoridad de Fiscalización y Control Social de Bosques y Tierra (ABT), 2011, http://www.cfb.org.bo/downloads/reincidencias_en_el_sector_forestal_y _agropecuario.pdf.

28. "Hacienda Nelorí Cumple 30 Años Haciendo Mejoramiento Genético en Razas Cebuinas," *Noti Bolivia Rural*, September 19, 2015, http:// notiboliviarural.net/index.php?option=com_content&view=article& id=13342:hacienda-nelori-cumple-30-anos-haciendo-mejoramiento -genetico-en-razas-cebuinas&catid=302:pecuaria&Itemid=547.

29. SIV01 190605.

30. SIV10 190606.

31. SCZ08 190619; SIV08 180710; Vincenti, "Surgen Nuevas Denuncias de Comunidades Fantasma y Desmontes Grandes en La Chiquitania."

32. Cf. Kendra McSweeney et al., "Drug Policy as Conservation Policy: Narco-Deforestation," *Science* 343 (2014): 489–90; Teo Ballvé, *The Frontier Effect: State Formation and Violence in Colombia* (Ithaca, NY: Cornell University Press, 2020); Jennifer A. Devine et al., "Narco-Cattle Ranching in Political Forests," *Antipode* 52, no. 4 (2020): 1018–38.

33. E.g., SIV05 180709; SIV14 190611.

34. SCZ02 180716.

35. SIV05 180709.

36. "El Cambio de Uso del Suelo y Sus Efectos Actuales y Futuros en el Municipio de San Ignacio de Velasco," FAN-Bolivia, presentation, 2019. See also "Informe Final."

37. Rojas M., "La 'Capital del Cebú' Duplica Su Hato Pecuario con Inversión Extranjera."

38. Urioste, *Concentración y Extranjerización de La Tierra En Bolivia.*

39. See, e.g., Miguel Urioste, who writes, "The statistical information offered by ANAPO [Asociación de Productores de Oleaginosas y Trigo, a Santa Cruz soy agribusiness association] for recent years does not allow for the analysis of production characteristics by type of producer (small, medium, large) classified by nationality (Bolivian, Brazilian, other foreigners). It appears that the goal of this omission is to prevent the precise identification of the ever-increasing foreign participation in commercial soybean

cultivation, but also, in particular, their foreign properties that comprise vast expanses of land. It is also no mere coincidence that, since 2012, no official INRA data exist on the status of land adjudication and registration of large commercial units in the Department of Santa Cruz by size, type and nationality of the owner with accompanying information on cadastral and market prices. In general, data on this issue continue to be incomplete and compel the use of methods of approximation in order to venture calculated estimates." Urioste, "Concentration and 'Foreignisation' of Land in Bolivia," 447.

40. Anne Cristina de la Vega-Leinert and Christoph Huber, "The Down Side of Cross-Border Integration: The Case of Deforestation in the Brazilian Mato Grosso and Bolivian Santa Cruz Lowlands," *Environment: Science and Policy for Sustainable Development* 61, no. 2 (2019): 42.

41. Müller, Pacheco, and Montero, "The Context of Deforestation and Forest Degradation in Bolivia," 18–19.

42. SIV14 190611.

43. SCZ01 180716.

44. SIV02 190605.

45. SIV12 190610.

46. SIV07 180710.

47. SIV09 180711.

48. SIV14 190611.

49. SIV11 190610.

50. Müller, Pacheco, and Montero, "The Context of Deforestation and Forest Degradation in Bolivia," 19.

51. SCZ08 190619.

52. SIV05 180709.

53. Nicoli Dichoff, "Embrapa Leva Tecnologias à Bolívia," Embrapa, December 7, 2017, https://www.embrapa.br/busca-de-noticias/-/noticia/30435630/embrapa-leva-tecnologias-a-bolivia; "Buenas Prácticas Ganaderas en el Pantanal Despiertan Interés de Bolivianos y Brasileños," WWF, May 15, 2010, https://www.wwf.org.co/?193264/Buenas-practicas-ganaderas-en-el-Pantanal-despiertan-interes-de-bolivianos-y-brasilenos.

54. SIV07 180710.

55. SIV10 190606.

56. "El Gobierno Compra Reses de Brasil Para Repoblar Municipios," *Bolivia Rural*, March 2, 2016, http://boliviarural.org/noticias/noticias-2016/5020-el-gobierno-compra-reses-de-brasil-para-repoblar-municipios. See also Anne Cristina de la Vega-Leinert, "Too Small to Count? Making Land Use Transformations in Chiquitano Communities of San Ignacio de Velasco, East Bolivia, Visible," *Journal of Land Use Science* 15, nos. 2–3 (2020): 172–202.

57. "'Me Considero Emprendedor Hasta la Médula,'" *Negocios Press*, May 5, 2015, http://www.negociospress.com.bo/me-considero-emprendedor-hasta-la-medula/.

58. "Brasil Investe no Mercado Boliviano Para Aumentar Exportação de Genética," *Diário de Cuiabá*, October 4, 2003, https://www.diariodecuiaba .com.br/economia/brasil-investe-no-mercado-boliviano-para-aumentar -exportacao-de-genetica/156133.

59. "Hacienda Nelorí Cumple 30 Años Haciendo Mejoramiento Genético en Razas Cebuinas."

60. "Acordo Entre Brasil e Bolívia Permite Comércio de Material Genético Animal," Ministério da Agricultura Pecuária e Abastecimento, September 26, 2016, https://www.gov.br/agricultura/pt-br/assuntos/noticias/acordo -entre-brasil-e-bolivia-permite-comercio-de-material-genetico-animal.

61. Fernando Rojas Moreno, "Bolivia Exporta Genética Bovina Nelore al Mercado Brasileño," *El Deber*, January 16, 2017, http://www.eldeber .com.bo/economia/Bolivia-exporta-genetica-bovina-nelore-a-Brasil -20170116–0029.html.

62. "INDEX ASBIA 2021," Associação Brasileira de Inseminação Artificial, 2021, https://asbia.org.br/wp-content/uploads/2022/02/Index-Asbia-2021 -Midia-3.pdf.

63. "Exportar Embriones Cebuinos, el Nuevo Reto Pecuario," *El Deber*, September 25, 2019, https://eldeber.com.bo/economia/exportar-embriones -cebuinosel-nuevo-reto-pecuario_148844.

64. "Actores Ilegales que Amenazan los Bosques y las Tierras."

65. "Chiquitania for Export," *Información Independiente*, February 23, 2012, http://www.in.com.bo/2012/02/chiquitania-for-export/.

66. "Estudio de Mercado de la Carne de Res en Bolivia," Autoridad de Fiscalización de Empresas, 2016, https://www.autoridadempresas.gob.bo/ descargas?download=418:estudio-de-mercado-de-la-carne-de-res-en -bolivia.

67. SIV05 180709; author field notes, July 10, 2018.

68. "Edicto Contra de Elvis Antonio Klauk, Osias Wagner Greve, Mario Alejandro Kempff Gonzales," Edictos Legales La Estrella del Oriente, 2015, https://www.edictos.bo/edicto-contra-de-elvis-antonio-klauk-osias -wagner-greve-mario-alejandro-kempff-gonzales-2/.

69. *Conflitos No Campo—Brasil 2003* (Goiânia: CPT Nacional–Brasil, 2003).

70. Arthur Santos, "Riva Era Sócio de Frigorífico na Bolívia," *Folhamax*, September 8, 2015, https://www.folhamax.com/politica/riva-era-socio-de -frigorifico-na-bolivia/58623.

71. "Edicto Contra de Elvis Antonio Klauk, Osias Wagner Greve, Mario Alejandro Kempff Gonzales."

72. Santos, "Riva Era Sócio de Frigorífico na Bolívia"; "Testimonio Instrumento No. 1334/2016," Edictos Legales La Estrella del Oriente, 2016, https://www.edictos.bo/testimonio-instrumento-un-mil-trescientos -treinta-y-cuatro-dos-mil-diecisiete-no-1334-2016/.

73. C. Quinquivi and F. Rojas, "Frigorífico Guaraní BFC Irrumpe en San Ignacio e Invierte $ Us 3 Millones," *El Deber*, June 22, 2018,

https://eldeber.com.bo/economia/frigorifico-guarani-bfc-irrumpe-en
-san-ignacio-e-invierte-us-3-millones_121619; SCZ08 190619.

74. "Frigorífico Concepción S.A. Luxembourg Listing Prospectus," Oppen-
heimer & Co., 2020, 4, 17, https://sec.report/lux/doc/102006545/.

75. E.g., Alvaro Rosales Melgar, "BFC Pone Su Carne 'En el Asador' y Apunta
al Extranjero," *El Deber*, November 21, 2018, https://www.eldeber.com
.bo/economia/BFC-pone-su-carne-en-el-asador-y-apunta-al-extranjero
-20181121-8194.html; Quinquivi and Rojas, "Frigorífico Guaraní BFC
Irrumpe en San Ignacio e Invierte $ Us 3 Millones."

76. SIV13 190610.

77. Hudson Corrêa, "Justiça Manda Sequestrar Bens de Frigorífico Suspeito
de Sonegação," *Folha de São Paulo*, May 21, 2004, https://www1.folha.uol
.com.br/folha/dinheiro/ult91u84612.shtml.

78. Alceu Luís Castilho, "Amigo de Horacio Cartes, Dono de Frigorífico
Teve Fazenda na TI Arroyo Korá, no MS," *De Olho Nos Ruralistas*, August
23, 2018, https://deolhonosruralistas.com.br/deolhonoparaguai/2018/
08/23/amigo-de-horacio-cartes-dono-de-frigorifico-teve-fazenda-na-ti
-arroyo-kora-no-ms/; "Control del Frigorífico Concepción Se Disputa
Ante la Justicia Entre Dos Socios Propietarios Brasileños," *El Nordestino*,
November 27, 2013, https://www.elnordestino.com/id-2991-cat-1-url
-control-del-frigor-fico-concepci-n-se-disputa-ante-la-justicia-entre-dos
-socios-propietarios-brasile-os.html; "Trepan un 125,5% las Ganancias
de Frigorífico Concepción," *Revista PLUS*, September 2, 2020, https://
www.revistaplus.com.py/2020/09/02/trepan-un-1265-las-ganancias-de
-frigorifico-concepcion/.

79. "Frigorífico Concepción S.A. Luxembourg Listing Prospectus."

80. "Fiscalía Acusa a Dueño de Frigorífico Junto a 13 Personas Más y Pide
Juicio Oral," *Última Hora*, November 16, 2018, https://www.ultimahora
.com/fiscalia-acusa-dueno-frigorifico-junto-13-personas-mas-y-pide
-juicio-oral-n2779778.html; Castilho, "Amigo de Horacio Cartes, Dono
de Frigorífico Teve Fazenda na TI Arroyo Korá, no MS."

81. "Frigorífico Concepción S.A. Luxembourg Listing Prospectus," 70.

82. "Fitch Rates Frigorifico Concepcion 'B+'; Outlook Stable," Fitch Ratings,
July 7, 2021, https://www.fitchratings.com/research/corporate-finance/
fitch-rates-frigorifico-concepcion-b-outlook-stable-07-07-2021; "PPO
Advised Frigorífico Concepción and Frigorífico BFC on Debt Issuance
Abroad," PPO Legal, May 20, 2021, https://www.ppolegal.com/en/2021/
05/20/ppo-advises-frigorifico-concepcion-and-frigorifico-bfc-on-debt
-issuance-abroad/; "Frigorífico Concepción S.A. Luxembourg Listing
Prospectus"; "Frigorífico Concepción Repurchases Bonds Maturing in
2025," *Lawyer Monthly*, October 1, 2021, https://www.lawyer-monthly
.com/2021/10/frigorifico-concepcion-repurchases-bonds-maturing-in
-2025/.

Reflection: Feedbacks and False Solutions

1. "Cold Front and Wild Fires Cause São Paulo to Go Dark During the Day," *Folha de São Paulo*, August 20, 2019, https://www1.folha.uol.com.br/internacional/en/scienceandhealth/2019/08/cold-front-and-wild-fires-cause-sao-paulo-to-go-dark-during-the-day.shtml.

2. Anatoly Kurmanaev and Monica Machicao, "As Amazon Burns, Fires in Next-Door Bolivia Also Wreak Havoc," *New York Times*, August 25, 2019, https://www.nytimes.com/2019/08/25/world/americas/bolivia-fires-amazon.html.

3. "Incendios Forestales en Bolivia 2019–2020" (Santa Cruz de la Sierra, Bolivia: FAN, 2020), https://incendios.fan-bo.org/Satrifo/incendios-forestales-en-bolivia-2019-2020/; Santiago Limachi and David Mercado, "'Todo Está Quemado': Nativos Bolivianos Caminan por Región Devastada Para Presionar a Morales," *Reuters*, September 29, 2019, https://www.reuters.com/article/bolivia-incendios-marcha-idLTAKBN1WE0H4. Fire season statistics are from January to October of each year.

4. Tahia Devisscher et al., "Increased Wildfire Risk Driven by Climate and Development Interactions in the Bolivian Chiquitania, Southern Amazonia," *PLoS ONE* 11, no. 9 (2016): 1–29.

5. "Informe Final," 13–14, 34.

6. Kurmanaev and Machicao, "As Amazon Burns, Fires in Next-Door Bolivia Also Wreak Havoc."

7. SIV08 180710.

8. "Eastern Lowlands," World Bank; McKay and Colque, "Bolivia's Soy Complex."

9. Hiroko Tabuchi, Claire Rigby, and Jeremy White, "Amazon Deforestation, Once Tamed, Comes Roaring Back," *New York Times*, February 24, 2017, https://www.nytimes.com/2017/02/24/business/energy-environment/deforestation-brazil-bolivia-south-america.html.

10. "Opciones Para Reducir el Impacto Ambiental de la Expansión Ganadera," PROBOSQUE (Santa Cruz de la Sierra, Bolivia: GIZ, 2018); author field notes, July 10, 2018.

11. Dichoff, "Embrapa Leva Tecnologias à Bolívia"; "Buenas Prácticas Ganaderas."

12. Quoted in Dichoff, "Embrapa Leva Tecnologias à Bolívia."

13. "WWF Bolivia Recibe Reconocimiento por Su Contribución a Lograr una Ganadería Más Sostenible," WWF, September 25, 2021, https://www.wwf.org.ec/?370110/WWF-Bolivia-recibe-reconocimiento-por-su-contribucion-a-lograr-una-ganaderia-mas-sostenible.

14. Eduardo Gudynas, "Buen Vivir: Today's Tomorrow," *Development* 54, no. 4 (2011): 441–47.

15. Cf. Dauvergne, *Shadows in the Forest*.

16. Wallerstein, *The Capitalist World-Economy*, 29.

17. Luis Galeano, "Paraguay and the Expansion of Brazilian and Argentinian Agribusiness Frontiers," *Canadian Journal of Development Studies / Revue Canadienne d'Études du Développement* 33, no. 4 (2012): 458–70; Marcellus Caldas et al., "Land-Cover Change in the Paraguayan Chaco: 2000–2011," *Journal of Land Use Science* 10, no. 1 (2015): 1–18; Praveen Noojipady et al., "Forest Carbon Emissions from Cropland Expansion in the Brazilian Cerrado Biome," *Environmental Research Letters* 12, no. 2 (2017), https://doi.org/10.1088/1748-9326/aa5986.

Epilogue

1. Warren Dean, *With Broadax and Firebrand: The Destruction of the Brazilian Atlantic Forest* (Berkeley: University of California Press, 1995).
2. Olive Patricia Dickason, "The Brazilian Connection: A Look at the Origin of French Techniques for Trading with Amerindians," *Revue Française d'Histoire d'Outre-Mer* 71, no. 264 (1984): 129–46.
3. Dean, *With Broadax and Firebrand*, 46–47.
4. Dickason, "The Brazilian Connection"; Cameron J. G. Dodge, "A Forgotten Century of Brazilwood: The Brazilwood Trade from the Mid-Sixteenth to Mid-Seventeenth Century," *E-Journal of Portuguese History* 16, no. 1 (2018): 1–27, https://doi.org/10.7301/Z0VH5MBT.
5. Willams Oliveira et al., "Reduced Reproductive Success of the Endangered Tree Brazilwood (*Paubrasilia Echinata*, Leguminosae) in Urban Ecosystem Compared to Atlantic Forest Remnant: Lessons for Tropical Urban Ecology," *Urban Forestry and Urban Greening* 41 (2019): 303–12.
6. Walker, "The Scale of Forest Transition"; Alexander Pfaff and Robert Walker, "Regional Interdependence and Forest 'Transitions': Substitute Deforestation Limits the Relevance of Local Reversals," *Land Use Policy* 27, no. 2 (2010): 119–29.
7. Dean, *With Broadax and Firebrand*, 50.
8. Green et al., "Farming and the Fate of Wild Nature"; Loconto et al., "The Land Sparing–Land Sharing Controversy."
9. Paul Trawick and Alf Hornborg, "Revisiting the Image of Limited Good: On Sustainability, Thermodynamics, and the Illusion of Creating Wealth," *Current Anthropology* 56, no. 1 (2015): 7.
10. Moore, "The Capitalocene, Part I," 614; Richard Walker and Jason W. Moore, "Value, Nature, and the Vortex of Accumulation," in *Urban Political Ecology in the Anthropo-Obscene: Interruptions and Possibilities*, ed. Henrik Ernstson and Erik Swyngedouw (New York: Routledge, 2018), 48–68.
11. Schandl et al., "Global Material Flows and Resource Productivity."
12. Cf. Becky Mansfield, Darla K. Munroe, and Kendra McSweeney, "Does Economic Growth Cause Environmental Recovery? Geographical Explanations of Forest Regrowth," *Geography Compass* 4, no. 5 (2010): 416–27.
13. Walker and Moore, "Value, Nature, and the Vortex of Accumulation," 65; cf. Appadurai, *Modernity at Large*, 46.

14. Cf. Trauger and Fluri, "Zones of Accumulation Make Spaces of Dispossession."

15. Cf. Andreas Malm, "China as Chimney of the World: The Fossil Capital Hypothesis," *Organization and Environment* 25, no. 2 (2012): 146–77.

16. Giorgos Kallis, "Is There a Growth Imperative in Capitalism? A Commentary on John Bellamy Foster (Part I)," Entitle (blog), October 27, 2015, http://entitleblog.org/2015/10/27/is-there-a-growth-imperative -in-capitalism-a-response-to-john-bellamy-foster-part-i/.

17. Wallerstein, *The Capitalist World-Economy*, 23.

18. I am grateful to Paolo Bocci for helping me see this point.

19. Philip McMichael, "Global Development and the Corporate Food Regime," in *New Directions in the Sociology of Global Development*, ed. Frederick Buttel and Philip McMichael (Bingley, U.K.: Emerald Group, 2005), 265–99; Anthony J. Weis, *The Global Food Economy: The Battle for the Future of Farming* (New York: Zed Books, 2007); Benjamin Caballero, "The Global Epidemic of Obesity: An Overview," *Epidemiologic Reviews* 29 (2007): 1–5.

20. Andrew Jacobs and Matt Richtel, "How Big Business Got Brazil Hooked on Junk Food," *New York Times*, September 16, 2017, https://www.nytimes .com/interactive/2017/09/16/health/brazil-obesity-nestle.html.

21. Sandra R. Baptista and Thomas K. Rudel, "A Re-Emerging Atlantic Forest? Urbanization, Industrialization and the Forest Transition in Santa Catarina, Southern Brazil," *Environmental Conservation* 33, no. 3 (2006): 195–202.

22. In 2021, the independent expert panel convened by the Stop Ecocide Foundation proposed a legal definition of ecocide as "unlawful or wanton acts committed with knowledge that there is a substantial likelihood of severe and either widespread or long-term damage to the environment being caused by those acts." See "Legal Definition of Ecocide," Stop Ecocide International, 2021, https://www.stopecocide.earth/legal -definition.

23. Paul Farmer, "An Anthropology of Structural Violence," *Current Anthropology* 45, no. 3 (2004): 305–25.

24. Flavia Milhorance, "Jair Bolsonaro Could Face Charges in The Hague over Amazon Rainforest," *The Guardian*, January 23, 2021, https://www .theguardian.com/world/2021/jan/23/jair-bolsonaro-could-face-charges -in-the-hague-over-amazon-rainforest.

25. Kenneth Iain MacDonald, "Grabbing 'Green': Cynical Reason, Instrumental Ethics and the Production of 'the Green Economy,'" *Human Geography* 6 (2013): 46–63.

26. Peter Kareiva, Michelle Marvier, and Robert Lalasz, "Conservation in the Anthropocene: Beyond Solitude and Fragility," *Breakthrough Journal* 2 (Winter 2012), https://thebreakthrough.org/journal/issue-2/conservation -in-the-anthropocene.

27. For additional discussion of the logics of different actors involved in neoliberal conservation, see Thaler, "Ethnography of Environmental Governance."

28. Cf. Neil Brenner, "Between Fixity and Motion: Accumulation, Territorial Organization and the Historical Geography of Spatial Scales," *Environment and Planning D: Society and Space* 16 (1998): 459–81.

29. Elise Moreno, "A Case for Bioregionalism in Place-Based Research," *Melbourne Journal of Politics* 37 (2015): 43–60.

30. Raymond Dasmann, "Life-Styles and Nature Conservation," *Oryx* 13, no. 3 (1976): 283.

31. Dasmann, "Life-Styles and Nature Conservation," 283.

32. Robin Wall Kimmerer, "Skywoman Falling," in *Braiding Sweetgrass: Indigenous Wisdom, Scientific Knowledge, and the Teachings of Plants* (Minneapolis: Milkweed, 2013), 9.

Appendix

1. Liz Goldman and Mikaela Weisse, "Technical Blog: Comparing GFW's 2017 Tree Cover Loss Data to Official Estimates in Brazil," Global Forest Watch, June 27, 2018, https://www.globalforestwatch.org/blog/data-and-research/technical-blog-comparing-gfws-2017-tree-cover-loss-data-to-official-estimates-in-brazil/.

2. "Assessing Trends in Tree Cover Loss over 20 Years of Data," Global Forest Watch, April 28, 2021, https://www.globalforestwatch.org/blog/data-and-research/tree-cover-loss-satellite-data-trend-analysis/.

Index